Classic French Cooking

LIFE WORLD LIBRARY
LIFE NATURE LIBRARY
TIME READING PROGRAM
THE LIFE HISTORY OF THE UNITED STATES
LIFE SCIENCE LIBRARY
GREAT AGES OF MAN
TIME-LIFE LIBRARY OF ART
TIME-LIFE LIBRARY OF AMERICA
FOODS OF THE WORLD
THIS FABULOUS CENTURY
LIFE LIBRARY OF PHOTOGRAPHY

Foods of the World

Classic French Cooking

by

Craig Claiborne, Pierre Franey

and the Editors of

TIME-LIFE BOOKS

photographed by

Mark Kauffman

TIME-LIFE BOOKS, NEW YORK

THE AUTHOR: Craig Claiborne *(far left),* a native of Sunflower, Mississippi, has been food editor of *The New York Times* since 1957. In addition to writing his regular food columns for *The Times,* he is author of *The New York Times Cookbook* and *Craig Claiborne's Kitchen Primer.*

THE CO-AUTHOR: Pierre S. Franey *(left)* was born in France and worked in a number of fine Paris restaurants before coming to the United States in 1939. Formerly executive chef of the Pavillon Restaurant in New York, he is now executive chef and vice president of Howard Johnson's. Mr. Franey provided most of the recipes for this book and supervised their testing.

THE PHOTOGRAPHER: Mark Kauffman *(far left)* is a former LIFE staff photographer. His other books in the FOODS OF THE WORLD LIBRARY include *The Cooking of Provincial France* and *American Cooking.*

THE CONSULTING EDITOR: Michael Field *(left),* one of America's foremost food experts, supervised the adapting and writing of recipes for this book. His books include *Michael Field's Cooking School, Michael Field's Culinary Classics and Improvisations* and *All Manner of Food.*

THE CONSULTANTS: James A. Beard *(far left)* is a leading authority on the culinary arts. George E. Lang *(center)* is vice president of Restaurant Associates Industries. Jacques Pépin *(left),* who cooked most of the recipes for this book, is a former chef to General Charles de Gaulle. He served as an assistant to Mr. Franey at the Pavillon and is now employed by Howard Johnson's as director of research and development. Sally Darr of the FOODS OF THE WORLD test kitchen assisted in the testing of the recipes.

Valuable assistance also was rendered by Hubert De Marcy of Hamilton, Bermuda, a gastronome of distinction.

THE COVER: *Poularde à la Néva,* a showpiece of classic French cooking, stands ready for serving *(Recipe Booklet).* The medallions of chicken meat on the bird and around it are coated with *chaud-froid* sauce and decorated with truffle cutouts and leek tops.

TIME-LIFE BOOKS

EDITOR: Jerry Korn
Executive Editor: A. B. C. Whipple
Text Director: Martin Mann
Art Director: Sheldon Cotler
Chief of Research: Beatrice T. Dobie
Picture Editor: Robert G. Mason
Assistant Text Directors: Ogden Tanner, Diana Hirsh
Assistant Art Director: Arnold C. Holeywell
Assistant Chief of Research: Martha T. Goolrick
Assistant Picture Editor: Melvin L. Scott

PUBLISHER: Walter C. Rohrer
General Manager: John D. McSweeney
Business Manager: John Steven Maxwell

Sales Director: Joan D. Manley
Promotion Director: Beatrice K. Tolleris
Public Relations Director: Nicholas Benton

FOODS OF THE WORLD

SERIES EDITOR: Richard L. Williams
EDITORIAL STAFF FOR CLASSIC FRENCH COOKING:
Associate Editor: William K. Goolrick
Picture Editor: Grace Brynolson
Designers: Albert Sherman, William Rose
Assistant to Designers: Elise Hilpert
Staff Writer: Gerry Schremp
Chief Researcher: Sarah B. Brash
Researchers: Wendy Rieder, Brenda Huff, Julia K. Johnson, Patricia Mohs
Test Kitchen Chef: John W. Clancy
Test Kitchen Staff: Fifi Bergman, Sally Darr, Leola Spencer

EDITORIAL PRODUCTION
Production Editor: Douglas B. Graham
Color Director: Robert L. Young
Assistant: James J. Cox
Copy Staff: Rosalind Stubenberg, Grace Hawthorne, Florence Keith
Picture Department: Dolores A. Littles, Joan Lynch
Traffic: Arthur A. Goldberger
Studio: Gloria duBouchet

Text for this book was written by Craig Claiborne, Pierre Franey and the editors; recipe instructions by Michael Field and Gerry Schremp, other material by the staff. Aid was given by these individuals and departments of Time Inc.: Editorial Production, Robert W. Boyd Jr., Margaret T. Fischer; Editorial Reference, Peter Draz; Picture Collection, Doris O'Neil; Photographic Laboratory, George Karas; TIME-LIFE News Service, Murray J. Gart; Correspondents Maria Vincenza Aloisi (Paris), Martha Green (San Francisco), Margot Hapgood (London), Ann Natanson (Rome).

Contents

The Recipe Booklet that accompanies this volume has been designed for use in the kitchen. It contains all of the 50 recipes printed in this book plus 52 more. It also has a wipe-clean cover and a spiral binding so that it can either stand up or lie flat when open.

The True Joy of Cooking
as Seen by a Professional Chef

Whether you are a trained chef or an enthusiastic amateur, cooking can be one of the great pleasures of your life. I feel this strongly, because I have been cooking almost all of my life.

When I was a child I lived in Saint Vinnemer, a small town near Chablis in central France where some of the finest white Burgundy grapes grow. From the time I was a boy, I wanted to be a chef. I remember going hunting with my father and stopping at the country restaurants in the area and being impressed by the food. We would have *civet de lièvre* —rabbit marinated in red wine and cooked with herbs. One time we had wild boar and I loved it, but I remember after the meal someone told me it was wild hog and I was sick.

My uncle was a wine grower, and he used to deliver his wine to restaurants in Paris. With his help I obtained my first job there as an apprentice at Restaurant Thénin near the Place de la République. I was only 14 then, and I worked on the cleaning detail, washing dishes and pots and pans. I stayed six months and then moved on to the Drouant, which is one of the better restaurants in Paris. My first six months there were spent at the *entremettier* station, learning how to cut up vegetables, straining and puréeing soups and preparing omelets.

There were 10 people at the station, and the first time the chef asked me to prepare an omelet, it was all wrinkled when I turned it over in the pan. When the chef saw it, he slapped me in the face. "I wanted an *omelette fines herbes,* not an *omelette grand'mère,*" he said.

I learned all the stations of the kitchen at the Drouant. Later I worked at a string of restaurants in Paris that was owned by Jean Drouant: the Café de Paris, Fouquet's, Pré Catalan, Pavillon Royal and the restaurant at the race track at Auteuil. When the New York World's Fair opened in 1939, the French government inaugurated a restaurant at its pavilion there. Drouant was the manager, and Henri Soulé was the maître d'hôtel. The staff was selected from the best restaurants in France and the French Line. I was the *premier commis poissonnier* (first assistant fish chef), but the war came on and the restaurant closed after six months. I went home and was drafted into the French Army. Then the fair reopened and I was sent back to New York, to serve as *premier commis saucier* (first assistant sauce chef) at the pavilion restaurant until the fair finally closed for good in 1940. Soulé decided then to stay on and open a restaurant in New York, called Le Pavillon, and most of the staff stayed with him.

There never was another restaurant like the Pavillon. Soulé was a perfectionist and his ambition was to run the best restaurant in the world.

He was the first to import food fresh from France—truffles, fish, fresh langoustes. I remember that we did not often have potatoes on the menu; Soulé thought they were too filling and heavy.

I started out as *chef poissonnier* (fish chef) at the Pavillon, and became executive chef. There were 30 people on the kitchen staff, and we usually served 150 guests at lunch every day. We had two shifts, and I worked from 9:00 in the morning until 3:00 in the afternoon, then took a break for two or three hours and came back and stayed until the restaurant closed around midnight.

The menu at the Pavillon changed every day. I worked out 30 lunch and 30 dinner menus, and we varied these menus throughout the month. Essentially we had the same major ingredients every day—sole, turbot, *escalope* of veal—but the garnishes and sauces changed. Only the finest ingredients were used. Every day we gave our orders for vegetables and other foods to suppliers and once a week I would go to the meat market with Soulé and mark with a rubber stamp the pieces he wanted.

I left the Pavillon in 1960, and Soulé died in 1966, but cooking is still one of the principal joys of my life. Often I cook on weekends with Craig Claiborne, with whom I collaborated on this book. I like to improvise when I cook. Of course you learn the principles and techniques from books and from experience, but you take off from there.

When I go to the market, I do not go there with the intention of buying veal chops or a rack of veal. I buy the best things I can find there and make something of them. The great talent of French chefs is their ability to improvise. Chicken Marengo, for example, is a famous dish that was created on the spot after the battle of Marengo by Napoleon's chef. He used what he had. There was not enough chicken to make a chicken dish, so he also put in crayfish tails, fried eggs, mushrooms and truffles. He combined these things and came up with something marvelous.

At the Pavillon, when I discovered the wonderful shad roe that is available on the East Coast of the United States, I made *alose farcie*—baked stuffed shad. I boned the shad and filleted it. Then I spread the shad with a mousse of sole, with bread crumbs, hard-cooked eggs, shallots, salt, pepper, parsley and cream. I put the roe over one fillet, covered it with the other fillet, topped it with sliced mushrooms, then tied it and baked it with shallots, thyme and bay leaf. I served the shad with a sauce made of the fish juices, white wine, cream and *beurre manié*. This was improvising with the best available ingredients, but the principles—the seasoning and the sauce—were classic French. That is the heart of French cooking—applying certain well-learned principles and techniques, but at the same time improvising with the best ingredients that can be found.

Since I first came to the United States in 1939, American tastes have changed. They have grown more sophisticated. People travel a lot. They are exposed to different types of food; they read cookbooks and go to cooking schools. In the next ten years people are going to have more leisure than ever, and I expect they will spend more time cooking—in the home. It is here—in the home—that the future of classic cooking lies.

—*Pierre L. Franey*

I

A Singular Art with Dual Appeal

The twin sensuous appeals
of the classic cuisine—to
the palate and eye—are
exemplified by the fillet of
beef Richelieu *(opposite)*.
Garnished with braised
lettuce, château potatoes,
baked tomatoes and stuffed
mushroom caps, the fillet
is served in a rich sauce
with Madeira and truffles.

Above and beyond the realm of everyday cooking lies the classic French cuisine, a world of truffles and foie gras, of subtle sauces and gloriously decorated dishes, of jewellike aspics, high-rise soufflés, puffed pastries and gossamer spun-sugar desserts. Defined literally, this exalted cookery embraces the supreme French dishes, those elegant, inspired creations of the great chefs that have stood the test of time. But there is much more to it than that. For classic French cooking is a fine art, as surely as painting and sculpture are. Its great works, such as *poularde à la Néva (cover)* and *filet de boeuf Richelieu (opposite),* are masterpieces designed to enchant both the palate and the eye. And the classic French cuisine implies as well the careful planning of a menu to insure a felicitous blend of textures, colors and flavors; it means sparkling crystal, gleaming silver, and immaculate napery. When all these come together, it is one of the glories of the civilized world. As M. F. K. Fisher noted in the first volume of this series *(The Cooking of Provincial France),* it "may be one of modern man's nearest approaches to pure bliss."

Perfection is the goal of classic French cooking, and this cuisine is more demanding and more precise than any other. It has its own logic, its own elaborate structure, its own techniques, procedures and caveats. Sauces are a hallmark of this cuisine, and they must be subtle. They complement the flavor of a dish, never smother it. Sweet and sour flavors are never mixed (the way they are in Chinese cooking), and a sweet sauce is never served with fish. Nothing is overcooked or undercooked; everything must be exactly to the point. If a dish is intended to be served

hot, it must be served hot, at once, and at exactly the required hotness. If it is supposed to be served cold, it must be served cold, not cool, and certainly not lukewarm. Except for salads (which are only a minor part of the classic cuisine) raw food is rarely served.

Menus must be meticulously planned. For example, if a fish course features a fine-textured fish like sole, with a creamy white-wine sauce, the meat course that follows should consist of a meat with a more pronounced texture, such as beef, veal, lamb or game, and its sauce should be a contrasting red-wine sauce—a savory *sauce madère* or *bordelaise*. The textures and flavors of these dishes and their sauces will harmonize well, and the meal will be suitably and interestingly varied.

The proper selection of wines is an integral part of the classic cuisine. In Bordeaux and Burgundy, France produces the finest wines on earth. Nothing so perfectly enhances a fine meal, and if classic cooking is to be properly appreciated, scrupulous care must be taken in the selection of the types and vintages of wines to be served with the food.

The service of the food itself is every bit as important as its preparation. It must never be piled on the plate; the classic style dictates that the food must be served in small portions, with more available as the appetite desires. Every dish must be impeccably served—not for snobbish reasons, but to do justice to the food.

Caviar is an excellent example. Although Russian in origin, this great delicacy has been enjoyed in France for more than 400 years. The great classic chef, Auguste Escoffier, described it as, "undoubtedly the richest and most delicate of hors d'oeuvres." Yet if caviar is to be fully appreciated, it must be served properly and without regard to cost. It should be spooned onto a chilled plate, with care taken not to break the grains, which may make it oily; for esthetic reasons, a silver spoon should be used (some people insist on mother-of-pearl) and the plate should be of fine crystal. The caviar, to which may be added a few discreet drops of lemon juice squeezed from a seed-free wedge of freshly cut lemon, should be eaten with a silver fork. In my judgment, vodka is its ideal companion (although some purists insist that champagne is the only beverage to be taken before a classic meal). Only the finest Russian or Polish vodka should be served, and it should be just a degree or two this side of freezing. It should be sipped from a small glass that is kept constantly filled, and with every bite of caviar and between sips of vodka, you should munch on perfectly made, generously buttered fresh toast, hot from the oven. It is perfectly proper, if you wish, to accompany the caviar with chopped egg, onion and sour cream, but the strict constructionists say this is like making tutti-frutti, and that any of these additions detracts from the pure, gurulike contemplation that fine caviar deserves.

All this fuss about caviar? Indeed so; that is what the classic repertory is all about. Classic cooking embraces thousands of dishes that are brought to perfection by just such loving treatment and attention to detail. The indispensable French chefs' handbook, *Le Répertoire de la cuisine*, lists more than 300 designations for sole and fillet of sole alone. By contrast, the repertory of typically British and American foods seems impoverished; they probably do not encompass more than 300 or 400 readily identifiable items—from Pennsylvania pepperpot and red flannel hash to toad-in-the-hole and Yorkshire pudding.

So precise is the language of the classic cuisine that a master chef can call any dish by its proper name and another master chef will know exactly what is meant. This applies to the printed menu as well; if fillet of sole Adrienne appears, the true gastronome will recognize it as sole fillets folded, poached, coated with Polignac sauce and garnished with tartlets filled with chopped crayfish tails in Nantua sauce and puffed pastry crescents. If the menu lists fillet of sole Yvette, it will be a fillet served with chopped herbs and a garnish of small tomatoes filled with a fish stuffing.

Nothing that is "vulgar" or earthy has a place in the classic repertory. Many excellent dishes fail to qualify as classics because they lack the necessary elegance. Among them are dishes that are redolent of garlic, such as that delectable creation from the south of France, frogs' legs *provençale,* or its counterpart from Burgundy, *escargots à la bourguignonne.* The mere fact that these dishes contain garlic does not disqualify them; they fail because they are loaded with it, and in classic cooking only the subtlest hint of garlic is permitted.

There are many other outstanding regional dishes that do not make the grade as classics. Among them are such solid fare as *cassoulet toulousaine* with its beans and sausage, the Alsatian speciality *choucroute garnie*—sauerkraut garnished with sausages and other pork products—and *confit d'oie,* preserved goose which is sautéed in its own fat and served without embellishment. The proscribed list also includes most dishes made with cabbage. But there is a notable exception: *chartreuse de perdreaux (Recipe Index).* This happy combination of roast partridge and the lowly cabbage is, when perfectly molded with hundreds of carefully shaped vegetable pieces, an artistic and a gastronomic masterpiece.

Elegance of presentation is such an essential quality of this cuisine that it can elevate an ordinary dish to the level of a classic. *Poularde en demideuil* (chicken in "half mourning") is simply a glorified poached chicken. But before the fowl is cooked, slices of truffle are inserted under its skin, and when it is done, it is served with a white *suprême* sauce with truffles. With these luxurious touches it passes the test of elegance. Another simple dish that has achieved the status of a classic is *homard à la parisienne (Recipe Index).* Essentially this is cold poached lobster, but the lobster meat is carefully removed from the shell and the shell is filled with *salade russe*—finely cut vegetables in mayonnaise. It is decorated with medallions of the lobster meat, which are topped with truffle cutouts, and glazed with aspic. The platter is then garnished with artichoke bottoms, tomatoes, hard-cooked eggs and truffles. *Selle de veau Orloff (Recipe Index)* starts with a saddle of veal. It is sliced and reassembled with a *sauce soubise* (onion sauce), truffle slices and sometimes chopped mushrooms. The garnished veal is masked with a Mornay sauce, then gratinéed and served with still another sauce, made with the reduced veal juices and a *glace de viande* (a meat stock reduced to jelly).

The classic cuisine often combines separate elements that are finished dishes in themselves. For example, the dish called *bar au champagne,* bass served in champagne sauce, is garnished with *quenelles* of pike

A spoonful of grey Beluga caviar —the best—and a glass of iced vodka at the start of a meal provide a welcome boon to the most exacting taste. Although Russian in origin, this happy combination is a completely naturalized element of the classic French cuisine.

11

and steamed shrimp, both of which are delicacies in their own right.

Some of the more elaborate dishes that will be described in this book are not for the home; they are encountered only in expensive restaurants or hotels or establishments of the size and scope of the first-class dining room of the S.S. *France (Chapter 7)*. But every one of the recipes in the book was selected and tested with the reader in mind. Some are quite difficult, some less so, but with time, patience, care, proper equipment—and, not least, the will to succeed—you can do them. Others, such as the *poulet reine sauté Archiduc (Recipe Index)*, are quite simple. All you have to do to fulfill this recipe is lightly sauté a chicken and prepare a creamy Madeira-flavored sauce to go with it.

Recipes such as the *poularde à la Néva* are much more complicated. This is not the kind of thing you whip up in the kitchen on an ordinary evening, for it involves a series of dexterous culinary maneuvers. You must first poach a chicken in stock, then clarify the stock, make an aspic, prepare a white *chaud-froid* sauce and slice the chicken breasts carefully. Then you make a chicken mousse, and after that you assemble the whole dish in an intricate manner and decorate it with truffle cutouts and strips of leek tops. But the prospect need not stagger you. Start a day ahead on a weekend or a holiday when you plan to have guests, and *poularde à la Néva* will be worth all the time and trouble it takes. For the result will be something to remember, to list among the more joyous eating experiences of a lifetime.

Before undertaking *any* of the recipes in this book, you should read them carefully to ascertain how much time and effort, what equipment and what ingredients are required. You may want to prepare a whole classic dinner, or if you prefer to try just one elaborate dish and round it out with a salad and a dessert, the meal will still be memorable.

The stately *homard à la parisienne* shows what an imaginative chef can do with cold poached lobsters. When the lobsters have been cooked, the meat is removed and the shells are filled with finely cut vegetables in mayonnaise. The lobsters then provide their own decorations as medallions of the meat are arranged over the filling. The garnish around the lobsters includes artichoke bottoms, tomatoes, eggs and truffles.

As you cook from this book, you will notice that certain techniques and procedures occur over and over again. This is because the traditions of classic cooking are stricter than those of other cuisines. Stocks, sauces and garnitures are required in most classic recipes. The professional chef learns, while still an apprentice, how to make stocks, sauces and aspics, how to cut out truffles, flute mushrooms and sculpt vegetables. As a result, the recipes that he uses need not be too detailed; they employ a kind of culinary shorthand—"serve with a Madeira sauce," or "stuff with a chicken mousse," or "garnish with puff pastry crescents," or "coat the fish with aspic." In the renowned Auguste Escoffier's cookbook, the recipe for *poularde à la Néva* requires only eight lines. It says in part: "coat the pieces [of chicken] with white *chaud-froid* sauce," and "border the dish with neatly cut croutons of pale aspic-jelly." The professional chef can execute these shorthand instructions in his sleep—almost. In this book the procedures have been spelled out in detail.

The classic cuisine blossomed in the palaces and châteaux of pre-Revolutionary France, and it came to full flower in the days of the great French chefs Marie-Antoine Carême (1784-1833) and Escoffier (1846-1935). At times it has been called haute cuisine or grande cuisine, but neither of these labels is wholly satisfactory. Haute cuisine is applied to other cuisines besides the French (one frequently hears of Chinese haute cuisine), and the French themselves do not use this term (although they say haute couture for high fashion). Grande cuisine in the main refers to an extremely grand and lavish style of classic cooking that existed in a more expansive gastronomic era, chiefly in the reign of Carême. Today the term classic French cooking is altogether more apt.

Nowadays, classic French cooking is found mostly in expensive restaurants in France. But there are many homes where one can enjoy *Continued on page 20*

Classic Culinary Pleasures Preserved at Château La Dame Blanche

Drowsing in the vine-covered countryside near Bordeaux in southwestern France, Château La Dame Blanche recalls a gracious life style that has all but disappeared in most parts of the world. Built in the late 18th Century on the site of an earlier castle and fortress, and named for a legendary Moorish princess, the château today is the home of prosperous wine merchant Jean Cruse and his wife. It is also a busy winery, producing each year 30,000 bottles of red wine (Château Taillan) and the same quantity of white (Château La Dame Blanche) from roughly 50 acres of vineyards. The wine cellars are believed to date back to the 16th Century reign of Henri IV. Inside, the château is handsomely and stylishly decorated, and one of its most attractive features is the Cruse kitchen and the fine dishes it produces.

Sheep roam the meadows at La
Dame Blanche, cropping the grass
and occasionally providing a tender
spring lamb for the table. The
balustrades of the stately château are
adorned with tall classical statues
and ornamental vases overflowing
with carved fruits and vegetables.
The stone vase at left stands at the
center in the picture above, just
beyond the grazing sheep.

The quality of the culinary establishment at La Dame Blanche rests on many advantages—fresh vegetables, herbs and meat from the château's own gardens and flocks, fine wines from its cellars, fish from the Marché aux Grands Hommes in Bordeaux, the variety of fine copper pots and utensils and the open fireplace in the kitchen. But the prize advantage of all is Marie Berniard, the cook who has been with the Cruses for 20 years. At right, in the midst of preparing the elegant dinner described in this chapter (some ingredients for which are shown above), she winds up the old-fashioned weight-and-pulley mechanism that keeps a whole lamb revolving slowly on its spit for the two and a half hours needed to roast it properly.

Each course served by Louis Castang, the Cruses' major-domo, has been carefully arranged in the kitchen by Marie. Above, as the dinner party finishes the soup course (*potage crème cressonière,* cream of watercress), Louis refills Mme Cruse's glass with La Dame Blanche 1966, a dry white wine. At a later stage in the meal, he carries the main course into the dining room (*left*). It is *baron d'agneau Armenonville,* roast baron of lamb, surrounded by vegetables that have been basted with browned butter.

Between the time the Cruses' guests are first seated at the candlelit table and the completion of the final course, two hours pass and dusk turns to darkness outside the long French windows. At right Louis brings the dessert, a soaring meringue filled with *crème Chantilly*. It is garnished with *fraises des bois*—tiny wild strawberries, the earliest of the season. According to an old French custom, the guests are expected to make a wish on the strawberries. Then when dinner is finished, they retire to the dark paneled salon *(below)*, where they bring the evening to a close as they sip coffee and brandy, gaze into the fire and enjoy pleasant conversation.

superlative examples of it. When I was in France last spring with Pierre Franey, my good friend and co-author of this book, we were invited to dinner by M. Jean Cruse and his wife, who live near Bordeaux. The Cruses own an 18th Century château that produces a variety of excellent wines, and that also contains one of the finest private kitchens in the land. Legend holds that the Cruse estate is an enchanted place. Centuries ago, long before the present château was built, a Moorish princess is supposed to have fallen in love with an owner of the estate, and her ghost still wanders, it is said, through the forests and vineyards. In deference to this appealing apparition the château is called La Dame Blanche (the white lady), and the evening fog that drifts across the meadows is known as "the skirts of La Dame Blanche." Moreover, the good lady's ghost is supposed to bring prosperity and happiness to the estate.

The Cruse château is set in rolling green countryside about half an hour's drive from Bordeaux. Turning off the main road, we drove through a tall, wrought-iron gate and a small park of linden trees up to a stately, 18th Century stone mansion with a pale yellow façade and white shutters. A liveried butler met us at the door and showed us into a Louis XVI sitting room where Mme Cruse welcomed us. She offered us a glass of cognac and then showed us through the splendidly appointed rooms on the first floor: the walnut-paneled salon with its tapestried furniture, large fireplace and splashes of fresh peonies, Easter lilies and hydrangeas; the "blue room" (where ladies gather) with its pale blue and yellow brocaded chairs and draperies; and the dining room with its fireplace, painted panels of flowers, fruits, vegetables and wild game, and an enormous armoire with busts of Louis XVI and Marie Antoinette.

For all this elegance, it was the kitchen that intrigued me. In this large rectangular room with its red-tiled floor, the cream-colored walls were lined with shelves of heavy, lovingly polished copper pots and pans. There were pans for sautéeing, *bassines* for cooking confitures and other sugar dishes, a *rondin* for poaching and braising foods, a *poissonnière* for poaching fish, charlotte molds and crown-shaped molds. Perhaps the most imposing utensil was a tall, heavy, tin-lined copper vessel, a *pot à vendage,* which is used at harvest time for cooking a thick meat-and-vegetable soup that is carried to grape pickers in the vineyards.

There was a gas range in the kitchen and an old-fashioned wood stove in a small room beyond. Between them they serve almost every cooking need. The gas range with its hot, finely controlled flame is used for, among other things, blanching vegetables and preparing stocks, for which large quantities of liquids must be brought to high temperatures. The steady, even heat of the wood-burning stove is preferred for cooking the subtle sauces and keeping finished dishes warm until they are served.

Another cooking device was in impressive evidence at the far end of the kitchen—a tall, deeply recessed stone fireplace. A smiling, affable woman was standing beside it as we entered—the chief cook, Marie Berniard, who has been with the Cruse family for more than 20 of her 69 years. She was turning an iron handle that rotated a whole lamb on a spit over a wood fire. The lamb had been seasoned with fresh laurel, onions and thyme from the garden, and as it slowly turned, Marie salted it carefully. Every now and then she leaned down with a long-handled spoon, scooped up the juice dripping into a pan below and basted the meat.

Later in the afternoon M. Cruse arrived home and escorted us on a tour of the family wine cellar, located in a low-lying building a few hundred feet from the château. As we entered a shadowy room filled with wine casks in ordered rows, a tall marble statue of Dionysus the god of wine loomed ahead. The cellar smelled of must and earth and aging wine. M. Cruse told us it had once been a part of a monastery; against a wall stood a tall, softly illuminated wooden crucifix. We walked past some enormous, ceiling-high wine casks and a few steps farther along M. Cruse pointed out a secret door. He turned the lock with a hand-hammered, wrought-iron key; we stooped low and came into a series of four small connecting rooms. This, M. Cruse told us, was where the family kept its private stock of wine for birthdays, weddings and other special occasions. We asked how many bottles were here, and he answered with a wan smile, "Precious few, though I have never counted them." Then he pointed to an especially old bottle and added, "The last time we sampled a wine of that vintage was 10 years ago to celebrate a wedding. Wines, you know, are like women. You could tell that in this one's youth a long time ago, she had been a very grand lady. The perfume was still there."

M. Cruse explained that during the German occupation of France in World War II the family had hidden its valuables here, including the château's most treasured wines. "The Germans came here twice a day," he said, "and walked right past the hidden door and never discovered it."

That evening, outside the château as the dinner guests arrived, the setting sun illuminated the ladies' silken gowns and sparkling jewels, and turned the façade of the house to gold. Louis, the butler, ushered us through great paneled doors into the entrance hall, where Mme Cruse, in a pale blue full-length dress, descended a long winding staircase to greet us, and our host, M. Cruse, poured champagne.

Dinner was announced, and we followed Mme Cruse into the dining room, taking our places around the large oval table. The table was impeccably set with lustrous white linens, brilliant crystal and polished silver. The centerpiece was a silver *surtout,* with a brightly polished mirror base and a container of fresh primulas, a favorite flower in France.

The meal began with a clear *consommé Célestine (Recipe Index)* with julienne strips of crêpe, flavored with parsley, tarragon and chervil. Then Louis brought in a platter of fresh whole salmon whose silver skin had been stripped away along the sides to reveal the delicate pink flesh underneath. A *mousseline* sauce was served with it—pale yellow and thick, but so gentle in texture and flavor that it did not overpower the fish. The salmon itself, with its delicate nutty flavor, was tender and moist. A perfect companion was the white wine we drank with it, a 1966 Cruse vintage appropriately called La Dame Blanche.

After the salmon Louis returned with a platter bearing the lamb that had been cooking on the spit in the kitchen fireplace that afternoon. It was a *baron d'agneau Armenonville,* the two hind legs and the saddle of the lamb with a special garnish. Before the meat was done it had been coated with a mixture of shallots and a suggestion of garlic, bread crumbs,

Overleaf: The saddle of lamb *Armenonville* provides an impressive alternative to the baron of lamb served at the Cruse château and described in this chapter. Garnished with artichoke bottoms, green beans, tomatoes and *cocotte* potatoes, the lamb is coated with bread crumbs, parsley, shallots, garlic and melted butter. The savory sauce served with it is made by reducing the meat juices and brown stock to concentrate their flavors.

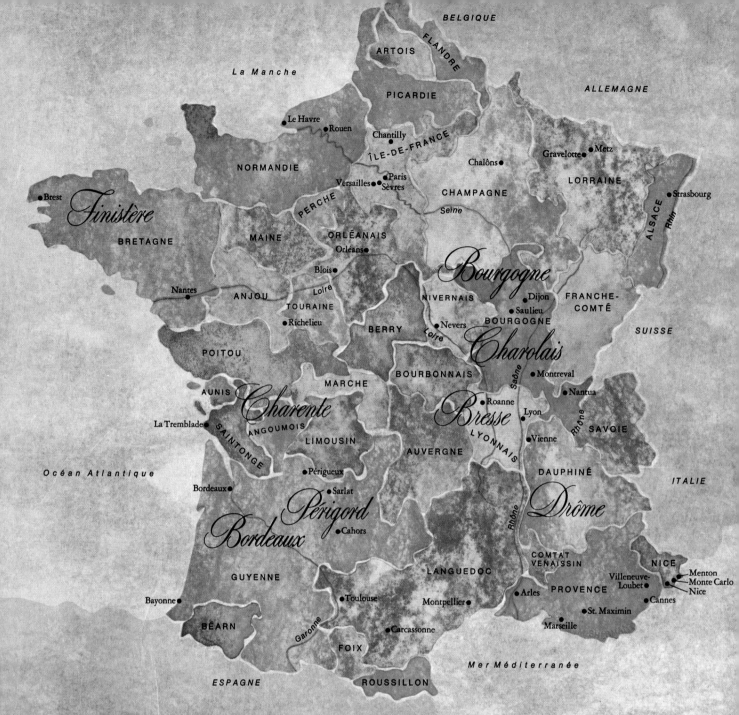

The Gastronomic Grandeur of France

France is where all good gastronomes go before they die—to really live. The regions indicated on this map produce some of the world's best food. From Bordeaux and Bourgogne (Burgundy) come the finest wines; Bresse is known for its chickens; Drôme for its sheep; Périgord for its truffles and foie gras; Brittany for its seafood; Normandy for its dairy products. In preparing this book the co-authors (who already knew France well) journeyed from the Cruse château near Bordeaux to the Escoffier museum at Villeneuve-Loubet, near Nice. Later, they dined at the Pyramide in Vienne, then drove to Paris, where they visited many of the city's finest restaurants. From there they went by rail to Le Havre, to board the S.S. *France* for home.

24

parsley and melted butter served with a sauce made from its own juices and a brown stock. Around the lamb lay a garnish of artichoke bottoms filled with tomato fondue, green beans, butter beans, braised lettuce, baby carrots and tiny green peas—all basted with *beurre noisette,* butter heated until it turns nutty brown. The lamb was perfection itself—pink inside, juicy and tender. With it we drank another Cruse wine, a Château Pontet-Canet 1949 that was full-bodied, but light enough for the meat.

After the lamb came a salad of leafy lettuce, served with a sauce vinaigrette that was lightly flavored with lemon juice. Then came a tray of assorted cheeses: a creamy Valençay goat cheese, a soft Brie, a mild Pont l' Évêque, and a smooth, lemon-colored Cantal. For them Louis poured a Château Lafite-Rothschild 1949, a truly great Bordeaux. And then to climax the meal, he brought in a towering meringue filled with wild strawberries, and with it a *crème Chantilly* (lightly sweetened whipped cream). As the meal ended everyone was willing to concede that Château La Dame Blanche was indeed enchanted.

Few of us can duplicate the elegant setting of the Cruse dinner, but everything that was served there could have been prepared in an American kitchen. Neither the soup nor the fish is beyond the skill of the careful cook. A saddle of lamb *(pages 22-23)* or leg of lamb could readily be used in place of the baron, cooked on a rotisserie or in an oven. As for the dessert, wild strawberries or ordinary strawberries could be used.

At this point it is reasonable to ask: Why did the world's greatest cuisine develop in France? Why not somewhere else? The answer, I believe, lies partly in the country and partly in its people.

France starts with many natural advantages. This immensely beautiful and diverse land can claim more fertile soil in temperate regions than any other European country. It produces a remarkable variety of the choicest foods and beverages, including the world's finest wines. It boasts superb butter, cream, poultry, lamb, veal, fruits and vegetables. The sea is another important factor; France's shores are washed by the Mediterranean, the Atlantic, the English Channel and the North Sea, and these waters provide an abundance of excellent seafood.

Moreover, the distribution of foodstuffs is so well organized that these foods can be enjoyed all over France while they are still fresh. The French trucking and rail industries give the highest priority to perishable foods. Everything is gathered, shipped and sold as quickly as possible. Furthermore, the French have the good sense to eat things at the peak of their season. They eat wild strawberries in June and July, asparagus in the spring. Americans may insist on eating corn on the cob all year round, even when it is tasteless and hard, but in France when a vegetable or fruit goes out of season, the family cook turns to something else. The French not only insist on fresh foods, they cultivate them for their flavor. They choose their tomatoes for their taste rather than their resistance to insects and drought, and they let them ripen on the vine to acquire the maximum goodness. On the other hand, they pick their string beans before they reach full size—*"en aiguilles"* (needle thin) the French call them—because their flavor is at the peak at this point.

We were particularly impressed with the superiority of France's fresh produce when we visited the canvas-covered Marché des Grands Hommes, the retail food market in the center of Bordeaux. Inside the market we saw long neatly arranged rows of beautiful artichokes, green and firm; long bunches of white leeks, gleaming white onions and those small, tender pink or pale yellow new potatoes that never seem to taste the same outside France. There were those incomparable young French beans, ripe tomatoes, tiny peas, crisp green heads of lettuce, and fruits of every sort —purple and green grapes, apricots, melons, oranges, lemons and peaches —juicier, sweeter and more beautiful than anything we have seen in a long time. The fish stands displayed fine small gray or pink shrimp, speckled sea bass, oysters, delicate crayfish, spiny lobsters, glistening salmon; all seemed to have been lifted from the sea the instant before. The same quality and variety were evident in the meats and poultry, and the whole effect was to make me wonder how one could avoid wanting to cook, or fail to cook well, with such ingredients to inspire him.

French chefs, maîtres d'hôtel and restaurateurs keenly appreciate the importance of fine ingredients. The late Fernand Point, the owner of the world-famous Pyramide Restaurant in Vienne, used to say, "You can't think of money or you are licked from the start. You have to go out yourself, and get the best, the freshest ingredients—and from the best places." Paul Bocuse, who runs a fine restaurant near Lyons *(map page 24)*, gets his beef from Charolais, his lamb from the Drôme district in southern France, his butter from Normandy in the far north, and his cream, veg-

A herd of Charolais cattle relaxes in a soft meadow by the river Allier in the Nivernais province of central France. A native breed, these sleek cattle produce some of the world's best beef. In the background stands the Château d'Apremont, which was built in the Middle Ages.

etables, fruit and crayfish from his own sources in the area around Lyons.

France's good fortune has not been limited to the ingredients she produces. It has also included an abundance of great chefs—men such as Carême, Escoffier, Prosper Montagné and hundreds of others. Why one country should have produced so many excellent chefs no one can say precisely, but these uniquely gifted men have produced an endless array of inspired dishes, from *chartreuse de perdreaux,* to *pêche Melba* and *selle de veau Orloff (Recipe Index).*

Through the ages France has given inspiration to her chefs. In the palaces and châteaux of the high-living pre-Revolutionary era, the chef was encouraged to produce each day something more dazzling and more extravagant than yesterday's creation. Traditionally, he has been honored and appreciated in France as in no other land. "The old nobility knew how to appreciate a chef and a good dinner," said Carême; "far from blushing when they spoke of cooking, they always talked about it with pleasure. They bestowed their esteem on their chefs, in the same way our contemporary lords do." Frenchmen have continued to bestow their esteem on chefs. Escoffier was made a Chevalier of the Legion of Honor in 1919 and elevated to the rank of Officer nine years later. Alexandre Dumaine, the now-retired chef of the Hôtel de la Côte-d'Or in Saulieu, Burgundy, received in his day almost as many medals and decorations as General Douglas MacArthur.

There is another even more important reason why France is the home of such an outstanding cuisine. While great cooking requires superior ingredients and talented cooks for its fulfillment, it also requires an appreciative audience. Nowhere do these three elements exist in happier combination than in France. The French simply care more about their food than other people do. The average Frenchman grows up well versed in his region's notable foods—the rich cream of Normandy, the seafood of Brittany, the chickens of Bresse. He comes to know the quality of the fresh vegetables and fruits in his local markets and he hears food discussed and passionately debated throughout his life. He takes his food seriously and expects it to be good.

To see this philosophy in action you need only visit a restaurant in France and observe the intense care with which a Frenchman orders a meal. On another level, you need only consider the many gourmet and wine organizations in France devoted to the propagation of fine food and superior wines. The Académie Culinaire, for example, is an elite group of chefs and restaurant owners who meet regularly to pass judgment on new recipes, to determine whether they are in harmony with French taste and based on tested French cooking techniques. (An Académie negative consigns a recipe to instant oblivion.) The nation's most prestigious gourmet society is the Club des Cents, a group of 100 food-lovers who meet every Thursday for lunch in Paris—usually at Maxim's. Several times a year the club hires a private railroad car and journeys into the provinces to dine at a top-quality restaurant. The menu is planned by members of the club in lengthy consultations with the restaurant's master chef, and exactly two hours are allotted to eating the meal, in line with Escoffier's dictum that this was the proper time span. On one occasion club members

At low tide on the Biscay coast, near La Tremblade, breeders gather *marennes* oysters, a gourmet delicacy in France.

traveled to the Hôtel de la Côte-d'Or in Saulieu while the celebrated Alexandre Dumaine was presiding there. Dumaine prepared for them a pâté of snipe, warbler, quail, partridge, chicken livers, and brandy—baked in a fine pie crust and served hot. The pâté took four days to make and, predictably, it was pronounced a triumph.

More recently, the Club des Cents visited Paul Bocuse's restaurant near Lyons, where Bocuse regaled them with a *lièvre à la royale*—a boned, stuffed, stewed hare from an ancient Poitou recipe. The hare was so tender club members were warned that "to use a knife for this heavenly hare stew would be sacrilegious. Only the spoon is permissible."

With this kind of blue-ribbon grand jury looking over their shoulders, French chefs, cooks, restaurateurs and maîtres d'hôtel have long taken their jobs with great—sometimes even deadly—seriousness. In the reign of Louis XIV, for example, a man named Vatel was employed by the King's cousin, Le Grand Condé, Louis II de Bourbon, who lived outside Paris at Chantilly. Vatel's status has never been fully clarified; he has sometimes been described as a chef, but nowadays experts tend to classify him as a maître d'hôtel. Whatever his title, he was in charge of all culinary arrangements at Le Grand Condé's estate.

In April 1671 Le Grand Condé planned a round of festivities in honor of the King's impending visit. When the monarch arrived on a moonlit evening, supper tables were spread for the most important nobles and guests. But as they were being served, Vatel discovered that there were not enough roasts for all of the tables. He was panic stricken. "I have lost my honor," he said. "I cannot stand such an affront."

Vatel went to his room, disconsolate. Meanwhile, orders had been dispatched to various fishing ports to procure fish for the next day. At 4 o'clock in the morning he came out of his room, wandered about the estate and met a fishmonger with two consignments of fish.

"Is that all?" he asked in desperation.

"Yes," the fishmonger replied, unaware that other orders of fish were already en route. Vatel went back to his room, placed his sword against the door and ran upon it three times, falling dead at the third try.

For all of Vatel's finely honed sense of honor, French chefs have such pride of accomplishment that they were still trying to disclaim him two centuries after his death. Writing in *Larousse gastronomique*, Philéas Gilbert, colleague and friend of Escoffier, noted that Vatel "did not have the character of a cook, because he did not know how to make the best of a bad job. He could not rise above difficult circumstances."

When Vatel committed hara-kiri, the do-or-die spirit did not expire with him. The case of the Relais de Porquerolles restaurant on the Left Bank in Paris proves the point. In the early 1960s the restaurant was rated two stars by the *Guide Michelin*. (The eminently reliable *Guide* awards one star to "a good restaurant in its class," two stars to one that is "worth a detour," and three stars to one that is "worth a journey.") The founder of the Relais de Porquerolles retired, and subsequently the Michelin people took away both of the restaurant's stars and completely dropped it from the *Guide*. When the chef heard the news, he was so upset that he shot himself. Vatel would have understood.

STOCKS: Fine French cooking owes much of its distinction to the stocks used in its preparation. These stocks are called "fonds de cuisine"—foundations of cooking—and no classic French cook would be without them. Stocks are easily made from various kinds of meats, fowl or fish trimmings, vegetables, herbs and water—simmered slowly together to concentrate their flavors.

Though their cooking often takes many hours, the process requires little supervision. The completed stocks may be refrigerated for days or frozen for weeks or even months. (For freezing, divide a stock into small quantities that can be thawed or melted quickly.) With the exception of chicken stock, canned broths cannot be considered an acceptable substitute for the homemade varieties.

The recipes below and on the following pages describe the most frequently used chicken, beef, veal and fish stocks as well as the techniques for clarifying them, making aspic and reducing meat stock to the essence known as "glace de viande."

Fond blanc de volaille
WHITE CHICKEN STOCK

To make about 5 quarts

Combine the fowl or the chicken and chicken parts with 5 quarts of the water in a 10- to 12-quart stock pot or casserole. If the water does not cover the chicken by at least 2 inches, add up to 1 quart more.

Bring the liquid to a simmer slowly over moderate heat, skimming off and discarding the foam and scum with a large spoon as they rise to the surface. Reduce the heat and simmer undisturbed and uncovered for 30 to 45 minutes. (Do not let the liquid come to a boil at any point, or the finished stock will be cloudy.)

Then add the carrots, leeks, celery, onion, parsley, garlic, bay leaf, thyme, salt and black peppercorns. Partially cover the pot and continue to simmer over low heat for 2½ hours longer, or until the stock has acquired an intense and definite flavor.

Turn off the heat. With tongs or a slotted spoon, pick out and discard the chicken or fowl, and the vegetables. Strain the stock into a large deep bowl through a fine sieve lined with a double thickness of dampened cheesecloth. Do not add salt or season the stock further. Set the bowl aside uncovered and, stirring the stock from time to time, let it cool to room temperature.

Refrigerate the stock uncovered until it is thoroughly chilled and the surface is covered with a layer of solidified fat.

Sealed with its fat, the stock may be safely kept in the refrigerator for 3 or 4 days. Before using it, carefully lift off and discard the fat. If you prefer to freeze the stock (it can be kept frozen for several months), remove the layer of fat as soon as it has solidified and cover the bowl or other container tightly with foil or plastic wrap.

A 6-pound stewing fowl, cut into 6 or 8 pieces, plus 2 pounds of chicken wings, necks and backs, or a 3-pound chicken, cut into quarters, plus 5 pounds of chicken wings, necks and backs

5 to 6 quarts cold water

3 medium-sized carrots, scraped and coarsely chopped

2 medium-sized leeks, including 2 inches of the green tops, trimmed, cut lengthwise into quarters and washed thoroughly to remove any hidden pockets of sand

2 celery stalks with the leaves

1 medium-sized onion, peeled and pierced with 1 whole clove

⅓ cup coarsely chopped parsley

1 medium-sized unpeeled garlic clove, crushed with the side of a cleaver or heavy knife

1 medium-sized bay leaf

2 fresh thyme sprigs or ½ teaspoon crumbled dried thyme

1 teaspoon salt

10 whole black peppercorns

The classic *petite marmite* is a rich beef consommé, with cubes of chicken and beef, and finely cut turnips, carrots and celery.

To make about 2 quarts

3 pounds fish trimmings: the heads, tails and bones of any firm white fish, preferably flounder, whiting or halibut
2 quarts cold water
1 cup coarsely chopped onions
¾ cup coarsely chopped celery with the leaves
⅓ cup coarsely chopped leek tops, thoroughly washed
1 medium-sized bay leaf
2 fresh thyme sprigs or ½ teaspoon crumbled dried thyme
1 teaspoon salt
5 whole black peppercorns

To make about 2 quarts

3 pounds beef shin bones, sawed into 2-inch lengths
3 pounds beef marrow bones, sawed into 2-inch lengths
2 pounds beef short ribs, sawed into 2-inch lengths
2 pounds veal shank, sawed into 2-inch lengths
1 pound chicken parts: wings, necks and backs
5 to 6 quarts cold water
2 medium-sized onions, peeled
2 medium-sized leeks, including the green tops, trimmed and thoroughly washed to rid them of sand
2 medium-sized carrots, scraped and cut into 1-inch lengths
5 fresh parsley sprigs
2 fresh thyme sprigs or ½ teaspoon crumbled dried thyme
1 unpeeled garlic clove, crushed with the side of a cleaver or heavy knife
1 medium-sized bay leaf
½ teaspoon whole black peppercorns
1 teaspoon salt

ADDITIONAL INGREDIENT FOR FOND BRUN DE BOEUF

2 tablespoons clarified butter *(page 34)*

Fumet de poisson
FISH STOCK

Wash the fish trimmings in a deep bowl set under cold running water. Drain, then mash the pieces of fish with the back of a large spoon.

Place the mashed fish in a 6- to 8-quart enameled or stainless-steel saucepan or casserole, and pour in the water. Bring slowly to a simmer over moderate heat and cook uncovered for 5 minutes, skimming off the foam and scum as they rise to the surface. Add the onions, celery tops, leek tops, bay leaf, thyme, salt and peppercorns, and reduce the heat to low. Partially cover the pan and simmer for 30 minutes, skimming the surface of the stock every 10 minutes or so.

Remove the pan from the heat and, with a slotted spoon, lift out and discard the fish and vegetables. Strain the stock into a deep bowl through a fine sieve lined with a double thickness of dampened cheesecloth. The stock will keep refrigerated for 2 or 3 days or it can be cooled to room temperature, covered tightly and frozen.

Fond blanc de boeuf et fond brun de boeuf
WHITE AND BROWN BEEF STOCK

FOND BLANC DE BOEUF (WHITE BEEF STOCK): Combine the shin and marrow bones, short ribs, veal, chicken and 5 quarts of water in a 12-quart stock pot. The water should cover the meat and bones by at least 2 inches; if necessary add up to 1 quart more. Bring to a simmer slowly over moderate heat, skimming off and discarding the foam and scum as they rise to the surface. Then reduce the heat and simmer undisturbed and uncovered for about 30 minutes. (Do not let the liquid come to a boil at any point, or the finished stock will be cloudy.)

Add the onions, leeks, carrots, parsley, thyme, garlic, bay leaf, peppercorns and salt. Stir, partially cover and simmer for 7 to 8 hours.

With a slotted spoon, pick out and discard the meat, bones and chicken. Strain the stock into a large bowl through a fine sieve lined with a double thickness of dampened cheesecloth. Discard the vegetables.

Let the stock cool to room temperature; then refrigerate uncovered until it is thoroughly chilled and the surface is covered with a layer of solidified fat. Sealed with its fat, the stock may be kept safely in the refrigerator for 3 or 4 days. Before using it, carefully lift off and discard the fat. If you prefer to freeze the stock (it can be kept frozen for several months), remove the layer of fat as soon as it has solidified and cover the bowl or other container tightly with foil or plastic wrap.

FOND BRUN DE BOEUF (BROWN BEEF STOCK): In a heavy 12-inch skillet, preferably a sauté pan, heat 2 tablespoons of clarified butter over moderate heat for 10 seconds. Brown the shin and marrow bones, short ribs, veal and chicken in separate batches, taking care not to crowd the pan. Turn the pieces frequently with tongs so that they color richly and evenly, and regulate the heat to prevent the meat or bones from burning. As they brown, transfer the pieces to a 12-quart stock pot.

Add the onions and carrots to the fat remaining in the skillet and, stirring from time to time, brown them lightly on all sides. With a slotted spoon transfer the onions and carrots to the stock pot. Pour 1 quart of the water into the skillet and bring to a boil over high heat, stirring constantly and scraping in the brown particles that cling to the bottom and sides of the pan. Pour the entire contents of the skillet into the stock pot and add the remaining 4 to 5 quarts of cold water (or as much as you need to cover the meat and bones). Following the recipe above, bring to a simmer slowly over moderate heat, skimming off and discarding the foam and scum as they rise to the surface. Then simmer the brown stock for 7 to 8 hours and follow the straining, cooling and storing procedures described above for the white stock.

Fond blanc de veau et fond brun de veau
WHITE AND BROWN VEAL STOCK

FOND BLANC DE VEAU (WHITE VEAL STOCK): Combine the shank, shin, marrow bones, chicken and 5 quarts of water in a 12-quart stock pot. The water should cover the meat and bones by at least 2 inches; if necessary add up to 1 quart more. Bring to a simmer slowly over moderate heat, skimming off the foam and scum as they rise to the surface. Reduce the heat and simmer undisturbed and uncovered for 30 minutes. (Do not let the liquid boil at any point, or the stock will be cloudy.)

Add the onions, carrots, celery, leeks, garlic, parsley, thyme, bay leaf, peppercorns and salt. Stir, partially cover and simmer for 7 to 8 hours.

With a slotted spoon, pick out and discard the meat, bones and chicken. Strain the stock into a large bowl through a fine sieve lined with a double thickness of dampened cheesecloth. Discard the vegetables.

Let the stock cool to room temperature, stirring it from time to time; then refrigerate uncovered until it is thoroughly chilled and the surface is covered with a layer of solidified fat. Sealed with its fat, the stock may be kept safely in the refrigerator for 3 or 4 days. Before using it, carefully lift off and discard the fat. If you prefer to freeze the stock (it can be kept frozen for several months), remove the layer of fat as soon as it has solidified and cover the container tightly with foil or plastic wrap.

FOND BRUN DE VEAU (BROWN VEAL STOCK): In a heavy 12-inch skillet, preferably a sauté pan, heat 2 tablespoons of clarified butter over moderate heat for about 10 seconds. Brown the veal shank, shin, marrow bones and chicken in batches, taking care not to crowd the pan. Turn the pieces frequently with tongs so that they color richly and evenly, and regulate the heat to prevent the meat or bones from burning. As they brown, transfer the pieces to a 12-quart stock pot.

Add the onions and carrots to the skillet and, stirring from time to time, brown them lightly on all sides. With a slotted spoon, transfer the onions and carrots to the stock pot. Pour 1 quart of the water into the skillet and bring to a boil over high heat, scraping in the brown particles that cling to the bottom and sides of the pan. Pour the contents of the skillet into the stock pot and add the remaining 4 to 5 quarts of cold water (or as much as you need to cover the meat and bones). Following the recipe above, bring to a simmer slowly over moderate heat, skimming off and discarding the foam and scum. Add the tomatoes and tomato purée. Then simmer the brown stock for about 7 hours and follow the straining, cooling and storing procedures described above for the white stock.

To make about 2 quarts

5 pounds meaty veal shank, sawed into 2-inch lengths
2 pounds meaty veal shin bones, sawed into 2-inch lengths
1 pound veal marrow bones
2 pounds chicken parts: wings, necks and backs
5 to 6 quarts cold water
2 medium-sized onions, peeled and cut into quarters
2 medium-sized carrots, scraped and cut into 1-inch-thick rounds
2 medium-sized celery stalks, including the green leaves, cut into 1-inch lengths
2 medium-sized leeks, including 2 inches of the green tops, trimmed, cut lengthwise into quarters and washed thoroughly to remove any hidden pockets of sand
1 large unpeeled garlic clove, crushed with the side of a cleaver or heavy knife
10 fresh parsley sprigs
2 fresh thyme sprigs or ½ teaspoon crumbled dried thyme
1 large bay leaf
½ teaspoon whole black peppercorns
1 teaspoon salt

ADDITIONAL INGREDIENTS FOR FOND BRUN DE VEAU
2 tablespoons clarified butter (page 34)
2 medium-sized firm ripe tomatoes, quartered
½ cup canned unflavored tomato purée

To make 10 or 12 tablespoons

½ pound unsalted butter, cut into
¼-inch bits

Beurre clarifié
CLARIFIED BUTTER

In a small, heavy saucepan, heat the butter over low heat, turning it about to melt it slowly and completely without letting it brown. Remove the pan from the heat and let the butter rest for a minute or so. Then skim off the foam and discard it. Tipping the pan slightly, spoon the clear butter into a bowl. Discard the milky solids that will settle at the bottom of the pan. If you are not using the butter immediately, refrigerate it in a tightly covered container. Clarified butter can safely be kept for a month.

To make about ½ cup

2 quarts *fond brun de veau (page 33)*, strained and thoroughly degreased

Glace de viande
MEAT GLAZE

Pour the *fond brun de veau* into a heavy 12-inch enameled-iron or copper skillet and bring it to a simmer over moderate heat. Reduce the heat to low and let the stock cook until it has reduced to 2 cups.

Transfer the stock to a small, heavy copper or enameled-iron pan and cook over the lowest possible heat, stirring occasionally, until it is reduced to ½ cup of thick syrupy glaze.

Strain the glaze into a small bowl or jar through a fine sieve lined with dampened cheesecloth. The glaze, tightly covered, can safely be kept in the refrigerator for several months. If any mold should form on the top, simply scrape it off with a spoon.

To make about 7 cups

CONSOMMÉ
½ cup coarsely chopped fresh
    celery leaves
½ cup coarsely chopped green leek
    tops
½ cup coarsely chopped scraped
    carrots
¼ cup coarsely chopped fresh
    parsley leaves and stems
2 medium-sized firm ripe tomatoes,
    coarsely chopped
½ cup egg whites
3 or 4 egg shells, finely crushed
2 quarts of any of the stocks
    described, cold or cooled to room
    temperature

CONSOMMÉ DOUBLE
1 pound lean ground beef or 1
    pound cut-up chicken wings and
    backs

GELÉE
6 envelopes unflavored gelatin

Consommé; consommé double; et gelée
CONSOMMÉ; DOUBLE CONSOMMÉ; AND ASPIC

CONSOMMÉ: Drop the celery leaves, leek tops, carrots, parsley, tomatoes, egg whites and egg shells in a heavy 4- to 5-quart copper or enameled-iron saucepan, mix well and pour in the stock. Set the pan over high heat and, stirring constantly, bring to a boil.

Reduce the heat to low and simmer the stock undisturbed and uncovered for about 20 minutes. Then pour the contents of the pan slowly into a large sieve lined with a double thickness of dampened cheesecloth and set over a deep bowl. Allow the liquid to drain through without disturbing it. The consommé may be used at once as it is, or garnished *(Recipe Index)*, or cooled to room temperature, covered tightly and stored in the refrigerator for 3 or 4 days or in the freezer for several months.

CONSOMMÉ DOUBLE (DOUBLE CONSOMMÉ): To make a richer "double" consommé, mix 1 pound of raw meat with the basic vegetable ingredients. Use lean ground beef with beef stock; and chicken wings and backs with chicken stock. Pour in the stock and bring the mixture to a boil over high heat, stirring constantly. Cook undisturbed and uncovered for 45 minutes, then strain it following the directions above.

GELÉE (ASPIC): Pour 2 cups of the cool stock into a heavy 4- to 5-quart copper or enameled-iron saucepan and sprinkle the gelatin evenly over it. When the gelatin has softened for several minutes, add the vegetables, egg whites and egg shells and mix well. Pour in the remaining 6 cups of stock, set the pan over high heat and, stirring constantly, bring to a boil. Then proceed as described in the basic consommé recipe.

SAUCES: Sauces are the hallmark and the glory of classic French cooking. At first glance, they seem to be innumerable. In fact, however, there are about a dozen basic formulations and the myriads of recipes in a "saucier's" repertory are usually made by simply amplifying them with other ingredients. Thus "sauce velouté" with cream added to it becomes "sauce suprême"; "sauce béchamel" with grated cheese and sometimes with egg yolks, is "sauce Mornay." Most sauces are best prepared shortly before serving, but the three basic sauces which follow—"fond lié," "béchamel," and "velouté"—may be prepared at your leisure and stored in the refrigerator for days, or in the freezer for months. (For freezing, divide a sauce into small quantities that can be thawed or melted quickly.) These sauces should not be reheated more than once or twice; after that they may thin out and separate. "Fond lié," which is a sauce of brown stock thickened with arrowroot, has taken the place of the more complicated "sauce espagnole" in most contemporary French kitchens. For traditionalists, there is a recipe for "sauce espagnole" in the Recipe Booklet.

Fond lié
BROWN SAUCE WITH ARROWROOT

To make about 1 quart

In a heavy 2-quart saucepan, bring the *fond brun de veau,* mushrooms and parsley to a simmer over moderate heat. Reduce the heat to low and cook uncovered for about 15 minutes. Combine the arrowroot and water in a bowl and stir until the arrowroot has dissolved. Stirring with a wire whisk, gradually pour the mixture into the stock. Add the caramel a few drops at a time until the sauce is a rich brown color, ¼ teaspoon will probably be enough. Simmer the sauce for 8 to 10 minutes, stirring occasionally. The sauce is ready when it thickens lightly. Pour the contents of the pan through a fine sieve set over a bowl, pressing down gently on the mushrooms with the back of a spoon.

1 quart *fond brun de veau (page 33)*
½ cup coarsely chopped fresh mushrooms
3 sprigs fresh parsley
5 tablespoons arrowroot
⅓ cup cold water
Caramel *(Recipe Booklet)*

If you are not using the *fond lié* at once but plan to set it aside, dot the top with 1 tablespoon unsalted butter cut into ¼-inch bits. Tip the pan from side to side until the butter melts and coats the entire surface of the sauce. When cooled to room temperature the sauce may be covered and refrigerated up to a week, or kept in the freezer up to three months.

Sauce béchamel
BÉCHAMEL SAUCE

To make about 2 cups

Combine the milk, onions, nutmeg, thyme and pepper in a small saucepan and bring to a boil over moderate heat. Immediately remove the pan from the heat, cover tightly and set aside for about 10 minutes.

In a heavy 1- to 2-quart enameled-iron or copper saucepan, melt the butter over low heat. Remove the pan from the heat and stir in the flour with a wire whisk to make a smooth roux. Then return to low heat and, stirring constantly, cook for about 2 minutes, or until the roux foams.

Pour in the milk mixture and beat vigorously with a whisk until the roux and liquid are thoroughly blended. Scrape the sides of the pan to ensure that all of the roux is incorporated into the sauce. Increase the heat to moderate and, still stirring constantly, cook until the béchamel sauce

2 cups milk
1 tablespoon finely chopped onions
⅛ teaspoon ground nutmeg, preferably freshly grated
1 sprig fresh thyme or ⅛ teaspoon crumbled dried thyme
⅛ teaspoon ground white pepper
4 tablespoons unsalted butter, preferably clarified butter *(opposite)*
6 tablespoons flour

35

comes to a boil and thickens enough to coat the wires of the whisk heavily.

Reduce the heat to the lowest possible point and, stirring occasionally, simmer the sauce gently for about 15 minutes to remove any taste of raw flour. Then strain the sauce through a fine sieve set over a bowl, pressing down gently on the onions with the back of a spoon to extract all their moisture before throwing them away. If you do not plan to use the sauce immediately, cool it to room temperature, stirring occasionally. Tightly covered, the béchamel may safely be kept in the refrigerator for 10 days, or in the freezer up to three months.

To make about 2 cups

2 cups white stock: *fond blanc de volaille, fond blanc de veau* or *fumet de poisson (pages 31,32 and 33)*
4 tablespoons unsalted butter, preferably clarified butter *(page 34)*
6 tablespoons flour

Sauce velouté

Bring the stock to a simmer over moderate heat. Meanwhile, in a heavy 1½- to 2-quart saucepan, melt the butter over low heat. Remove the pan from the heat and stir in the flour with a wire whisk. Then return to low heat and, stirring constantly, cook for about 2 minutes, or until the roux foams. The roux should be very pale yellow color.

Pour in the heated stock and beat vigorously with a whisk until the roux and liquid are thoroughly blended. Scrape the sides of the pan to ensure that all of the roux is incorporated into the sauce. Increase the heat to moderate and, still stirring, cook until the sauce comes to a boil and thickens enough to coat the wires of the whisk heavily.

Reduce the heat to the lowest possible point and simmer the sauce gently for 15 minutes, whisking it every few minutes to prevent the bottom from scorching. Then strain the sauce through a fine sieve set over a bowl. If you do not plan to use the sauce immediately, cool it to room temperature, stirring occasionally. Tightly covered, the velouté may safely be kept in the refrigerator for 10 days, or in the freezer up to three months.

To serve 4 to 6

4 cups fresh shelled green peas (about 4 pounds unshelled), or substitute 4 cups defrosted frozen peas (about three 10-ounce packages)
2 cups *sauce béchamel (page 35)*
2 cups *fond blanc de volaille (page 31)* or 2 cups canned chicken stock, chilled, then degreased
½ cup heavy cream
2 sprigs fresh chervil or ½ teaspoon crumbled dried chervil leaves
2 tablespoons unsweetened butter, chilled and broken into ½-inch bits

Potage crème de petits pois
CREAM OF FRESH PEA SOUP

Drop the fresh peas into enough lightly salted boiling water to cover them. When the water returns to a boil, reduce the heat to moderate and cook uncovered for 5 to 10 minutes, or until the peas are almost tender but still slightly resistant to the bite. Drain the peas in a sieve or colander and plunge them into a pot of cold water to set their color. Drain and set aside. (Frozen peas need only to be thoroughly defrosted and drained.)

Combine the béchamel and chicken stock in a heavy 2- to 3-quart saucepan and, stirring constantly, bring to a simmer over moderate heat. Add the peas and cook for 5 to 10 minutes longer, stirring from time to time. When the peas are soft enough to be easily mashed with a spoon, purée the contents of the saucepan 2 or 3 cups at a time in the jar of an electric blender or through the finest blade of a food mill set over a bowl.

Return the purée to the saucepan and, over low heat, pour in the cream in a slow stream, whisking constantly. Simmer only long enough to heat the soup through, but don't let it boil. Add the chervil and taste for seasoning. Remove the pan from the heat, swirl in the butter bits and serve at once from a heated tureen or individual soup plates.

Petite marmite
BEEF CONSOMMÉ WITH FINELY CUT CHICKEN, BEEF AND VEGETABLES

Trim off and discard any discolored or badly bruised outer leaves of the cabbage and wash it under cold running water. Place it in enough boiling water to cover it completely and cook briskly for about 5 minutes. Lift it out of the pot but keep the water at a boil. Carefully peel off as many of the outside leaves as you can without tearing them. When the leaves become difficult to separate, return the cabbage to the pot and boil it for a few minutes longer. Repeat until you have peeled off 6 perfect leaves.

Spread the 6 leaves on a flat surface and one by one, with a small, sharp knife, trim off the tough rib end at the base of each. Cut each leaf into quarters and return to the boiling water for 5 minutes. Drain and pat the pieces dry with paper towels. Roll each piece into a ball and set it in the middle of a 10-inch square of doubled cheesecloth. Bring the corners of the cheesecloth together and twist them until you form a tight ball of cabbage in the center. Each cabbage ball with be about 1 inch in diameter. Set the cabbage balls in a pan just large enough to hold them, and pour in enough water to barely cover them. Add ½ teaspoon of the salt and bring to a boil over high heat. Reduce the heat to low and poach uncovered for 20 minutes. Set the cabbage balls aside at room temperature in the poaching liquid.

To prepare the beef marrow, refrigerate it in a bowl of cold water for about 15 to 20 minutes to remove all traces of blood. Pat the marrow dry with paper towels and cut it into ¼-inch-thick rounds with a sharp knife that has been dipped into hot water. Set aside.

In a heavy 8-inch skillet warm 4 tablespoons of the butter over moderate heat for 10 seconds. Add the bread triangles 5 or 6 at a time and, turning them frequently with a slotted spatula, fry until they are crisp and golden brown on both sides, adding more butter to the pan if necessary. Arrange the croutons side by side on paper towels and let them drain while you are preparing the other ingredients.

In a 2- to 3-quart saucepan, bring 1 quart of water to a boil over moderate heat. To blanch the chicken pieces, drop them into the water, return the water to a boil, reduce the heat and simmer the chicken for about 1 minute. Drain the chicken in a sieve or colander and, tossing the pieces about with a spoon, run cold water over them to remove all traces of foam or scum. Drain once more and set the blanched chicken aside. Wash the saucepan and in it bring another quart of water to a simmer over moderate heat. Drop in the beef, return the water to a boil, reduce the heat and simmer for 2 minutes. Drain the beef in a sieve or colander, rinse it under cold water, then drain it again.

Combine the blanched beef, the beef consommé and the remaining ½ teaspoon of salt in a heavy 4- to 5-quart *marmite* or casserole. Bring to a simmer slowly over moderate heat, reduce the heat to low and cook partially covered for 15 minutes. Add the carrots and simmer 10 minutes; then add the blanched chicken and the turnips and cook 10 minutes more. Drop in the leek and celery strips and continue cooking for about 5 minutes, or until the meat and vegetables are tender. Taste for seasoning.

Meanwhile, bring 2 cups of lightly salted water to a simmer over moderate heat and drop in the reserved marrow. Immediately remove the pan

A 2-pound white cabbage

1 teaspoon salt

6 ounces fresh beef marrow, in the largest pieces possible

4 to 6 tablespoons clarified butter (*page 34*)

3 slices homemade-type white bread, each about ½-inch thick, squared and trimmed of all crusts, and cut diagonally into 4 triangles

A 6- to 8-ounce chicken breast, skinned, boned and cut into ½-inch cubes

2 chicken thighs, skinned, boned and cut into ½-inch cubes

1 pound lean boneless beef, preferably top round, trimmed of excess fat and cut into ½-inch cubes

2 quarts consommé (*page 34*) made with *fond blanc de boeuf*

3 medium-sized carrots, scraped and cut into 12 olivelike shapes each about 1 inch long

3 medium-sized white turnips, peeled and cut into 12 olivelike shapes each about 1 inch long

1 large leek, white part only, trimmed, cut lengthwise into quarters, washed thoroughly to remove any hidden pockets of sand, and cut lengthwise into strips ⅛ inch wide and 1 to 1½ inches long

1 celery heart, all ribs removed and the base cut into strips about ⅛ inch wide and 1 inch long

1 cup freshly grated imported Parmesan cheese

from the heat and let the marrow poach for 3 or 4 minutes. With a slotted spoon transfer the rounds to a small serving dish.

Serve the consommé directly from the *marmite* or ladle it into a heated tureen or individual bowls. Present the cabbage balls, croutons, and grated cheese along with the marrow, in separate serving dishes. Just before serving, pour about ½ cup of the hot consommé over the marrow.

Paupiettes de sole Dugléré
ROLLED FILLETS OF SOLE IN CREAMY VELOUTÉ SAUCE WITH TOMATO

To serve 6

4 large firm ripe tomatoes
4 tablespoons cold butter, plus 4
    tablespoons softened butter
¼ cup finely chopped shallots
¼ cup finely chopped onions
Salt
Freshly ground white pepper
Six 6-ounce sole fillets, cut
    lengthwise into halves and lightly
    pounded with the side of a
    cleaver to a uniform thickness of
    about ¼ inch
3 tablespoons finely chopped fresh
    parsley
½ cup dry white wine
½ cup *fumet de poisson (page
    32)*
⅔ cup *sauce velouté (page 36)*
    made with *fumet de poisson*
¼ cup heavy cream

OPTIONAL GARNISH
tomato balls made
    from six small ripe
    tomatoes *(see selle d'agneau
    Armenonville, page 40)*
1 teaspoon finely chopped fresh
    parsley
12 *fleurons (Recipe Booklet)*

Drop the tomatoes into a pan of boiling water and remove them after about 10 seconds. Run them under cold water, and peel the tomatoes with a small, sharp knife. Cut out the stems and slice the tomatoes in half crosswise. Squeeze the halves gently to remove the seeds and juice and chop the tomatoes coarsely. In a small enameled or stainless-steel saucepan, melt 2 tablespoons of the cold butter over moderate heat. When the foam begins to subside, drop in the tomatoes. Stirring frequently, cook briskly until most of the liquid in the pan evaporates and the tomatoes are reduced to a thick purée. Set aside off the heat.

Preheat the oven to 350°. With a pastry brush, spread the 4 tablespoons of softened butter evenly over the bottom and sides of a 12-by-7-inch enameled or glass baking dish. Scatter the shallots and onions over the bottom of the dish and sprinkle them with a little salt and white pepper. Spoon about half the tomato purée into the dish, smoothing it to the edges with the back of the spoon.

To make each *paupiette,* roll a strip of sole lengthwise into a tight cylinder and fasten the ends securely with a plain wooden toothpick. Stand the *paupiettes* upright side by side in the dish, then spread the remaining tomato purée on top and sprinkle with the parsley. Pour the white wine and *fumet de poisson* down the sides of the dish. Cover the fish with a sheet of buttered wax paper cut to fit snugly inside the dish. Bring to a simmer over moderate heat, then place the dish in the middle of the oven. Poach the *paupiettes* for 10 to 12 minutes, or until they are tender enough to flake easily when prodded gently with a fork.

With a slotted spoon or spatula, carefully lift the *paupiettes* from the dish and arrange them attractively on a heated platter. Remove and discard the toothpicks, then drape foil loosely over the fish to keep it warm while you prepare the sauce.

Transfer the entire contents of the dish to a small, heavy saucepan. Bring to a boil over high heat and, stirring occasionally with a wire whisk, cook briskly until the liquid is reduced to about 1 cup. Whisk in the velouté and ¼ cup of heavy cream and simmer slowly, stirring for about 5 minutes, until the sauce is smooth and heated through. Taste for seasoning. Remove the pan from the heat and swirl in the remaining 2 tablespoons of cold butter.

With a bulb baster, remove any trace of liquid that has accumulated around the *paupiettes* and stir it into the sauce. Pour the sauce evenly over them and serve at once. If you like, you may garnish the top of each *paupiette* with a tomato ball and sprinkle parsley over it. Arrange the *fleurons,* if you wish to serve them, in a ring around the edge of the platter.

Paupiettes of sole Dugléré are crowned with tiny tomato balls and are encircled with little puff pastry crescents.

Potage crème cressonière
WATERCRESS SOUP

Separate the bunches of watercress and wash under cold running water. Pat dry with paper towels, then cut off about ½ cup of the most perfect leaves with scissors and set them aside. Chop the remaining leaves and all the stems coarsely with a sharp knife.

In a heavy 3- to 4-quart casserole, heat the 4 tablespoons of clarified butter over moderate heat for about 10 seconds. Drop in the onion and leeks and, stirring frequently, cook for about 5 minutes until they are soft but not brown. Add the potatoes and turn them with a spoon until they glisten with butter. Then pour in 2 cups of the stock and cook partially covered over moderate heat until the potatoes are tender and show no resistance when pierced with the point of a small, sharp knife.

Pour in the remaining 4 cups of stock and the milk, and add the chopped watercress, salt and pepper. Stirring occasionally, bring to a simmer over moderate heat and cook uncovered for 15 minutes. Purée the contents of the saucepan through the medium disc of a food mill set over

To serve 8

2 bunches fresh watercress (about 6 ounces each)
4 tablespoons clarified butter *(page 34)*, plus 1 tablespoon unsalted butter, chilled
1 medium-sized onion, peeled and thinly sliced
2 medium-sized leeks, including 2 inches of the green tops, trimmed, cut into quarters lengthwise and thoroughly washed to remove any hidden pockets of sand
3 large boiling potatoes (about 1 pound), peeled and thinly sliced

Continued on next page

6 cups *fond blanc de volaille (page 31)*, or substitute 6 cups canned chicken stock, chilled, then degreased
1 cup milk
½ teaspoon salt
Freshly ground black pepper
2 egg yolks
½ cup heavy cream

To serve 6

SELLE D'AGNEAU
A 4- to 6-pound saddle of lamb (a short double loin), with kidney and inner fat removed and all but ⅛ inch of fat removed from the surface of the meat
1 teaspoon salt
¼ teaspoon freshly ground black pepper
¼ cup soft fresh crumbs made from homemade-type white bread, trimmed of crusts and pulverized in a blender or finely shredded with a fork
2 tablespoons finely chopped fresh parsley
1½ tablespoons finely chopped shallots
½ teaspoon finely chopped garlic
¼ cup butter
1½ cups *fond brun de veau* or *fond brun de boeuf (pages 32 and 33)*
1 tablespoon unsalted butter, cooked over low heat until it is delicately browned

a deep bowl, or rub through a medium-meshed sieve with the back of a spoon. Return the purée to the saucepan and bring it to a simmer over low heat. Combine the egg yolks and cream in a small bowl and beat them lightly with a wire whisk. Then, whisking the soup constantly, pour in the egg yolks and cream in a slow stream. Stir over low heat for 2 or 3 minutes to heat the soup through. Do not let the soup come near the boil or it will curdle.

Remove the pan from the heat and swirl in the tablespoon of butter. Taste for seasoning. Stir the reserved watercress leaves into the soup and serve at once from a heated tureen or individual soup plates.

Selle d'agneau Armenonville
ROAST SADDLE OF LAMB WITH GREEN BEANS, COCOTTE POTATOES AND ARTICHOKE BOTTOMS FILLED WITH TOMATO

SELLE D'AGNEAU (SADDLE OF LAMB): Ask the butcher to prepare the lamb for roasting, or do it yourself in the following fashion: With a mallet or the flat of a cleaver, pound flat the flaps of lamb that hang from the sides, then trim off the rough edges of the flaps and tuck them under the saddle. Score the fat on top of the saddle with crisscrossing diagonal slashes 1 inch apart, cutting almost completely through to the meat beneath. With white cord, tie the saddle crosswise in at least 3 places to hold it in shape.

Preheat the oven to 425°. Rub the salt and pepper over the top of the saddle and insert a meat thermometer at least 2 inches into one end of the lamb. Do not let the tip of the thermometer touch any fat or bone. Place the lamb, fat side up, on a rack in a roasting pan.

Roast the lamb uncovered and undisturbed in the middle of the oven for 30 minutes, or until the thermometer registers 120° to 130°. Meanwhile mix the bread crumbs, parsley, shallots and garlic in a bowl. Melt the ¼ cup of butter. Remove the lamb from the oven, cut off the strings and raise the heat to 450°. Pat the bread-crumb mixture evenly on top of the saddle and dribble the butter over it. Roast the lamb for about 10 minutes longer, or until the crumb coating is golden brown (the thermometer should now register 130° to 140°). Then transfer the saddle to a large heated platter while you make the sauce.

Discard the fat remaining in the roasting pan. Pour in the *fond brun* and quickly bring it to a boil on top of the stove, stirring constantly and scraping in the brown bits that cling to the bottom and sides of the pan. When the stock has been reduced to about 1 cup, strain it through a fine sieve into a small saucepan. With a bulb baster, collect any juices that may have accumulated around the lamb and stir them into the sauce. Taste for seasoning, then stir in the tablespoon of browned butter. Pour the sauce into a sauceboat.

To serve, arrange the previously prepared garniture *(below)* of green beans, potatoes and artichoke bottoms with tomatoes in a ring around the lamb and present the platter at the dining table. Carve the saddle following the directions on page 41 and serve it at once, accompanied by the sauce.

GARNITURE: The beans may be blanched as much as 3 hours beforehand; the potatoes, artichoke bottoms and tomatoes can be shaped hours before serving, but they must be completed at the last minute.

HARICOTS VERTS (GREEN BEANS): Drop the beans, a handful at a time, into 3 quarts of lightly salted boiling water. Cook the beans briskly, uncovered, for 8 to 10 minutes, or until they are just tender. Immediately drain them in a large sieve, then plunge the sieve into a large pot of cold water for 2 or 3 minutes. Drain the beans, pat them dry with paper towels and set aside. Just before serving, heat 2 tablespoons of clarified butter over moderate heat in a heavy 10- to 12-inch skillet for about 10 seconds. Add the beans and, tossing them about with a spoon, warm them over moderate heat for 3 or 4 minutes. Taste for seasoning.

POMMES COCOTTE (COCOTTE POTATOES): With a small knife, peel the potatoes and cut them into quarters and then into elongated olivelike shapes about 2 inches long (*photograph, page 22*). As you shape them, drop the potatoes into cold water to prevent them from discoloring. Before sautéing the potatoes, pat them dry with paper towels. In a heavy 10-inch skillet, heat the clarified butter over high heat for about 10 seconds. Add the potato olives and turn them in the butter to coat them evenly. Then sauté for 8 to 10 minutes, shaking the pan and turning the potatoes from time to time until they are evenly browned and show no resistance when pierced with the point of a small, sharp knife. Sprinkle them with salt and serve at once.

FONDS D'ARTICHAUTS AUX TOMATES (ARTICHOKE BOTTOMS WITH TOMATOES): Trim the stems and leaves from the artichokes (*Recipe Booklet*). In a heavy 10-inch skillet, whisk the flour and ½ cup of the cold water together until smooth. Beat in the remaining 7½ cups of water, the lemon juice and 1 tablespoon of salt. Add the artichoke bottoms, choke side down. Bring to a boil, reduce the heat to low and simmer covered for 30 minutes, or until the artichokes are tender and show no resistance when pierced with the point of a sharp knife.

HARICOTS VERTS
1½ pounds fresh green string beans, washed and trimmed evenly to about 3½-inch lengths
Water
Salt
2 tablespoons clarified butter (*page 34*)

POMMES COCOTTE
2½ pounds medium-sized boiling potatoes
¼ cup clarified butter (*page 34*)
½ teaspoon salt

FONDS D'ARTICHAUTS AUX TOMATES
6 medium-sized artichokes, each 3 to 3½ inches in diameter
¼ cup flour
8 cups cold water
¼ cup fresh lemon juice
1 tablespoon plus 1 teaspoon salt
3 medium-sized firm, ripe tomatoes, about 2½ inches in diameter
¼ cup clarified butter (*page 34*)
½ teaspoon salt
Freshly ground white pepper

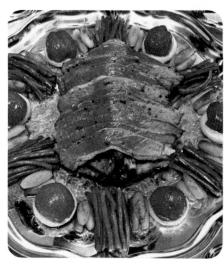

To carve the saddle of lamb, place it on a chopping board. Then—holding the knife at a diagonal—vertically and parallel to the backbone, carve the loin into long thin slices (*left*). Discard the first (outside) slice, return the remaining slices to the saddle and serve (*center*). Or slice both loins and drape all the meat across the saddle bones (*right*).

Remove the artichokes from the liquid and wash them under cold running water. With a spoon, carefully scoop out all the chokes. Return the artichoke bottoms to their poaching liquid and set aside until ready to use. (They can safely wait at room temperature for 2 or 3 hours.)

Drop the tomatoes into a pan of boiling water and boil briskly for about 10 seconds. Run cold water over them and peel them with a small, sharp knife. Cut out the stems, then slice the tomatoes in half lengthwise. Squeeze the halves gently to remove the seeds and juice. One at a time, place a tomato half on a kitchen towel. Pull the towel up tightly around the tomato. Twist the ends of the towel together close to the tomato and squeeze gently to shape the tomato into a compact ball. Melt the ¼ cup of clarified butter and brush the tomatoes with it. Set them in a baking dish and lightly salt and pepper them. Cover with foil and set aside for an hour or so before baking.

To serve, bake the tomatoes for 8 to 10 minutes in a 450° oven, or until they are tender. Meanwhile, wash the artichoke bottoms and pat them dry with paper towels. Then heat the ¼ cup of clarified butter in a heavy 12-inch skillet over moderate heat for 10 seconds. Add the artichoke bottoms, concave side down, and baste them with the hot butter. Sprinkle them with ½ teaspoon salt, reduce the heat to the lowest possible point, cover and cook for several minutes until they are heated through. Do not let the artichokes brown. Transfer the artichoke bottoms to a heated platter and place a tomato ball in each one.

Bisque de homard
LOBSTER BISQUE

With a cleaver or large, heavy chef's knife, chop off the tail section of each lobster at the point where it joins the upper body and twist off the large claws. Split the body of the lobster in half lengthwise, then remove and discard the gelatinous sac (stomach) in the head and the long intestinal vein attached to it. Scoop out and set aside the greenish brown tomalley (or liver) and the black roe (or coral) if any. Cut the tail crosswise into 2-inch-thick slices. Cut the body shells in half crosswise. Separate the claws at the joint and crack each large claw with a blow of a heavy knife.

In a heavy, deep 12-inch skillet, preferably a 12-inch sauté pan, melt 3 tablespoons of the butter over moderate heat. Add the celery, carrots, onions, thyme, bay leaf, cayenne, white pepper and salt. Stirring frequently, cook for 5 minutes, or until the vegetables are soft but not brown. Add the lobsters to the skillet. Turning them frequently, cook over high heat for 2 or 3 minutes, or until the shells are red. Warm ½ cup of the cognac in a small saucepan over low heat, ignite it with a match and slowly pour it flaming over the lobster, meanwhile sliding the pan gently back and forth until the flames die. Pour in the wine and bring to a boil over high heat. Baste the lobster with the pan juices, reduce the heat to low, and simmer tightly covered for about 10 minutes.

Lift out the pieces of lobster and place them on a plate; set the skillet aside. Remove the shell from the tail pieces, cut the meat into ½-inch dice and reserve it in a bowl. With a pick or small knife, remove all the meat from the claws and joints. Cut the meat into ¼-inch dice and add

To serve 6

3 live 1- to 1½-pound lobsters
4 tablespoons unsalted clarified butter *(page 34)*
¾ cup finely chopped celery
¼ cup finely chopped scraped carrots
¼ cup finely chopped onions
⅛ teaspoon crumbled dried thyme
½ small bay leaf, crumbled
⅛ teaspoon ground hot red pepper (cayenne)
⅛ teaspoon ground white pepper
⅛ teaspoon salt
½ cup plus 3 tablespoons cognac
1 cup dry white wine
7 cups *fond blanc de volaille (page 31)*, or substitute 7 cups canned chicken stock, chilled, then degreased
¼ cup long grain white rice, not the converted or precooked type
2 medium-sized firm ripe tomatoes, cut into quarters
1 tablespoon tomato paste
3 tablespoons unsalted butter, softened
½ cup heavy cream

them to the skillet. Stir in 1 cup of the chicken stock, and then purée the mixture in an electric blender. Pour the purée into a heavy 4-quart enameled-iron casserole and set aside.

Chop the lobster shells into small pieces with a cleaver and place them in a 3- to 4-quart saucepan. Pour in the remaining 6 cups of chicken stock and bring to a boil over high heat. Reduce the heat to low and simmer uncovered for 15 minutes. Strain the stock through a fine sieve directly into the purée and discard the shells. Bring to a boil over high heat. Add the rice, tomatoes and tomato paste. Reduce the heat to moderate and cook partially covered for 20 minutes, or until the rice is soft. Purée the soup in a food mill with a fine disc or, with a spoon, rub the contents of the pan through a fine sieve set over a bowl and return it to the pan.

Combine the reserved tomalley and coral (if any) with the softened butter and rub them through a small sieve into a bowl. In a 6- to 8-inch skillet, melt the remaining tablespoon of butter over high heat. Drop in the reserved diced lobster and toss it about in the butter for a minute or so. Then remove the pan from the heat. Warm the remaining 3 tablespoons of cognac in a small pan, ignite it with a match, and pour it over the lobster. Slide the pan back and forth until the flames die.

Just before serving the bisque, bring it to a simmer over moderate heat. Stirring constantly with a whisk, add the tomalley-and-butter mixture a tablespoon at a time, and pour in the cream in a thin stream. Add the flamed lobster meat and all its juices, then taste for seasoning. Serve at once, from a heated tureen or in individual soup plates.

Potage crème de laitue
CREAM OF LETTUCE SOUP

To serve 6

4 firm 6-inch heads Boston or Bibb lettuce (about 4 pounds)
5 tablespoons unsalted butter plus 4 tablespoons unsalted butter, chilled and cut into ½-inch bits
3 cups *sauce béchamel (page 35)*
5 cups *fond blanc de volaille (page 31)*, or substitute 5 cups canned chicken stock, chilled, then degreased
¼ teaspoon sugar
½ cup heavy cream

Remove the wilted outer leaves of the lettuce and rinse the heads in cold water, spreading the leaves gently to remove any sand. With a large, sharp knife, cut the heads into quarters and remove the cores. Slice each quarter crosswise into the finest possible chiffonade strips and set 1 cup of the chiffonade aside.

In a heavy 4-quart casserole, melt 4 tablespoons of the butter over moderate heat. Add all but the reserved cup of chiffonade and toss with a spoon to coat it evenly with butter. Reduce the heat to low, cover and cook for 3 minutes, or until the lettuce wilts.

Combine the béchamel, stock and sugar in a bowl and whisk until they are thoroughly blended. Stirring constantly, pour the mixture over the lettuce and bring to a simmer over moderate heat. Cook uncovered for about 10 minutes, whisking occasionally. Purée the soup through the finest disc of a food mill, or rub it through a fine-meshed sieve. Return the soup to the casserole and whisk in the cream. Warm the soup over moderate heat, stirring from time to time, but do not let it boil.

Meanwhile, melt 1 tablespoon of butter in a small skillet over moderate heat. Add the reserved cup of chiffonade and, stirring constantly, cook for 1 or 2 minutes. Set aside off the heat.

Remove the casserole from the stove and swirl in the butter bits. Taste for seasoning and pour the soup into a heated tureen or individual soup plates. Sprinkle the reserved chiffonade on top and serve.

II

The Bright Jewel
of the West

For centuries the galantine has provided a festive touch for classic dinners and parties. The eye-catching version shown here is a galantine of duck. Flecked with truffles, fresh pork fat, pistachio nuts and ham, this ground mixture of duck with pork and veal is garnished with a realistic tomato rose.

A great cuisine does not suddenly appear on the scene like a newly risen soufflé. It emerges through a slow process of evolution and refinement. Classic French cooking, that bright jewel of Western civilization, is the product of long development, the ultimate expression of an age-old fondness for wining and dining in style. Although it is mainly the creation of great French chefs of the 19th and 20th Centuries, it owes something to earlier eras as well: to the splendid cuisines of the châteaux of pre-Revolutionary France and the *palazzi* of Renaissance Italy, to the exotic, extravagant fare of imperial Rome, and even before then, to the elegant cooking of ancient Greece.

In the sophisticated world of the Greeks, moderation was regarded as the highest virtue in eating as in all else. The center of Greek culture was, of course, Athens. The Athenians held the civilized conviction that dinner was a time to relax and to restore the spirit as well as the body. They dined to the accompaniment of music, poetry and dancing, while reclining on couches, and they made an art of dinner conversation—a feat that centuries later was to prove particularly attractive to the French. Even when flouting the rule of moderation, the Athenians did so with grace. They took the precaution of wearing crowns of flowers around their brows to prevent hangovers just in case they should imbibe too much of the grape.

It was the Greeks who inadvertently provided a philosophical basis for good eating. The philosophy was Epicureanism, and its adherents believed that the main object of life was pleasure. By this they did not mean

BIBULOUS BIBLICAL BOTTLES

In one of the best-known feasts of all time King Belshazzar, his wives and concubines drank wine and fell to praising false gods. In retribution Belshazzar was slain that same night, but he attained gastronomic immortality (though much later) by having an oversized (416-ounce) champagne bottle named after him. Other Biblical characters —Nebuchadnezzar, Jeroboam, Rehoboam, Methuselah, Salmanazar —also had giant champagne bottles named after them. Most of these bottles proved impractical, but two of them survive, as seen below. From left to right the bottles are:

REHOBOAM (156 oz.—STANDARD BOTTLES)

JEROBOAM (104 oz.—4 BOTTLES)

MAGNUM (52 oz.—2 BOTTLES)

FIFTH (26 oz.—BOTTLE)

IMPERIAL PINT (23 oz.)

HALF BOTTLE (13 oz.)

SPLIT (6.5 oz.—QUARTER BOTTLE)

overindulgence, but a serene harmony of mind and body. As their teacher Epicurus saw it, life's principal satisfaction lay in having as few needs and desires as possible—in practicing self-restraint. Ironically, the doctrine of Epicureanism later was corrupted to mean a devotion to ease and luxury, or at least a purposeful pursuit of pleasures, and to this day the dictionary defines an epicure as "one with sensitive and discriminating tastes in food and wine."

With the advent of the Romans came dining on a grandiose scale. True, there was a distinct gap between rich and poor. Lesser folk subsisted mostly on barley or wheat porridge, cabbages, poultry, fish and ground pine nuts, while the wealthy and the aristocratic ate in frankly sumptuous fashion. They served more than 100 species of fish; their tastes in meat and fowl ran to beef, pork, veal, lamb, wild boar, venison, goat, hare, dormice, ducks, geese, ostriches, swans and peacocks; they relished dozens of different kinds of cheeses, some of them as big as tabletops. Further to stoke their appetites, they kept their private pools stocked with trout, sturgeon and carp, maintained aviaries for breeding thrushes, pheasants, cranes and other edible birds, and cultivated oysters in special beds. They not only hauled snow and ice over the Alps to refrigerate their perishable foods, but tapped the resources of their far-flung Empire for all sorts of exotic comestibles. They sometimes dispatched special emissaries to France to gather mushrooms and bring them back to Rome in baskets protectively covered with damp moss. The Second Century satirist Juvenal describes a sumptuous dinner at his patron's house which featured lobster with asparagus, and such exotic specialties

as mullet from Corsica and lamprey from Sicily—along with a fattened goose's liver, a huge capon, a boar with truffles and a peacock.

Yet while the Romans prized hard-to-get delicacies, they were not gourmets as we understand the word, for it implies an exquisiteness of palate that they lacked. Their cooking was heavy, and sauces and spices were used with enough abandon to disguise the original flavors of the food. One Roman favorite, for example, was boiled ostrich drenched with a sauce of pepper, mint, cumin, celery seed, dates, honey, vinegar, sweet wine, oil and *liquamen*—a liquid seasoning of fermented fish in brine.

Moneyed citizens were obsessed with the bizarre, and their cooks were expected to produce astounding dishes, with a surprise at every meal. Some of the Caesars carried this eccentricity to wild extremes. In their estimation, nothing succeeded like excess, as Oscar Wilde said in a later context. Caligula drank pearls dissolved in vinegar, and as he did so further amused himself by having prisoners tortured before his eyes. Maximinus reportedly ate 60 pounds of meat a day; while at a single sitting Albinus downed 300 figs, 100 peaches, 10 melons, 20 pounds of grapes, 100 garden warblers and 40 oysters. Heliogabalus once served his guests 600 ostrich brains, accompanied by peas with grains of gold, lentils with precious stones and other dishes garnished with pearls and amber.

A whimsical tyrant, Heliogabalus generously rewarded cooks who produced sauces to his liking, but those whose creations met with his disfavor were forced to eat nothing else until they came up with a dish he liked. Guests found him quite a practical joker. One of his pranks was to inflate a leather couch with air, and send its occupants sprawling on the floor by suddenly letting the air out. Guests who passed out from drinking were lugged off to bedrooms where they might awaken to see live tigers and leopards roaming the room. Some died of fright, not knowing the animals were tame.

The profligacies of the Roman cuisine and of the lavish banquets in imperial Rome were burlesqued by Petronius, Nero's *arbiter elegantiae* (arbiter of taste) in the *Satyricon*, a sardonic account of the manners and vices of his time. Petronius describes a banquet laid on by a vulgar multimillionaire, a former slave named Trimalchio, who dazzles his guests with one culinary spectacle after the other, each more stupefying than the last. A donkey of Corinthian bronze is brought in on a large tray, carrying panniers of green and black olives. Flanking the donkey are silver dishes filled with dormice dipped in honey and rolled in poppy seeds. A wooden peahen is brought in with "eggs" bedded in straw around it. The eggs are really pastry shells, and when the guests crack them open they discover finely seasoned orioles inside. After this, an enormous wild sow is carved and live thrushes fly up from the platter. A roast pig is borne in on an immense tray, and Trimalchio discovers that the pig has not been gutted. On the spot the chef cuts into the pig's belly and roast sausages and blood puddings tumble out. Wine is served, and Trimalchio decrees that those who do not drink it must have it poured over their heads.

Much of the lavishness of Roman dining carried over into the Middle Ages. Affluent inhabitants of Gaul might dine on great quarters of beef, mutton, pork or goat, and on such exotic foods as roebuck, hedgehog, boar,

CATHERINE DE' MEDICI
(1519-1589)

When she was only 14 Catherine went to France to marry the future king Henry II. She brought with her, besides refined manners, many of the delicacies that were then enjoyed in Renaissance Italy: sweetbreads, truffles, artichoke hearts, *quenelles* of poultry, ice cream and frangipane tarts.

Overleaf: Sweetbreads, a delicacy favored by Renaissance Italians and later served by Catherine de' Medici at the royal court of France, are presented here in a sumptuous classic style under the impressive title of *ris de veau à la financière au vol-au-vent* (*financière* meaning "bankers' style"—very rich). The sweetbreads are garnished with olives, fluted mushrooms, and veal *quenelles*, and served in the flaky pastry known as *vol-au-vent*.

crane, heron and peacock. They also savored a Gallic specialty—grilled snails—which they ate as a dessert along with soft cheese, honey cakes, chestnuts, figs, peaches and grapes. Their festive occasions, however, were crude affairs. Feasters would sit on bundles of straw and gobble whole joints of meat; if the meat proved too tough, they would draw knives from sheaths on their sword scabbards and saw off huge chunks. More often than not the meal would end in a fight, for the diners' own amusement at first, but inevitably tempers flared and they had to be pulled apart.

By the time of the great Frankish King Charlemagne, feasting had acquired a touch of elegance. Banquet halls were hung with ivy and decked with flowers; according to an eyewitness of one occasion, "the table itself had more roses on it than a whole field."

A typical lavish banquet of the later Middle Ages sounds as if it might have been staged by Cecil B. de Mille. Guests were summoned by the blowing of a horn and washed their hands in perfumed water. The repast itself, eaten with the fingers and gusto, included roast peacocks, swans and pheasants with gilded beaks and claws. Between courses and after the meal, jugglers, acrobats, jesters, minstrels and troubadours entertained the banqueters. On some occasions the food was served by men in armor mounted on horseback, and at other times the tables, fully laden, were lowered into the dining hall from the floor above or raised from the floor below, to be removed by the same means as soon as the feasters had devoured the contents.

The state of the culinary art in France by the 14th Century can be gauged by a contemporary cookbook called *Le Viandier,* the first French cookbook of importance. It was written by a man named Guillaume Tirel, better known as Taillevent (a name that was to be adopted in modern times by a popular restaurant in Paris). Taillevent was chef to a number of French nobles and kings, including Philip VI of Valois, Charles V and Charles VI. His book represented the first attempt to establish cooking as a science, and it provides many illuminating insights into the culinary practices of the day. Taillevent thickened his sauces with bread instead of the flour used in roux today, and he made abundant use of spices. He presented recipes for 17 sauces, the most important of which was *cameline,* a sauce that included ginger, cinnamon, clove, nutmeg, vinegar and bread. When he prepared a hare, for example, he skinned it, cleaned it, put it on the spit, cooked it and then put it in a pot with onions, croutons, beef broth, wine, vinegar, ginger, cinnamon, clove and a pinch of pepper. It was not the flavor of the hare, but the flavor of the spices that really counted at this point in the cuisine's development.

Taillevent's menus relied heavily on soups, meats and poultry. For a banquet for Charles VI he featured capons with cinnamon broth, capons in wine, stewed pigeons, venison pâtés, jellies and sugared tarts. The food was heavy, and as yet gave no hint of the variety, subtlety and contrasts of textures and flavors that were later to exalt the French cuisine.

The break with the strongly spiced dishes and repetitive menus of the Middle Ages came with the Renaissance, and here, as with the other arts, Italy led the way. The spirit of the imperial Roman cuisine was revived without its excesses; the foods were more subtle and the service more elegant than anywhere else in Europe. Renaissance Italians enjoyed truffles, artichokes and *tournedos,* those delicious slices from the heart of the fillet of beef. They began their meals with fresh fruits: raspberries, apricots, cherries, peaches, plums and melons. They no longer piled the food on their plates in the voracious manner of medieval men. Their table linen, tableware and crystal, as well as the foods themselves, were the finest that could possibly be obtained.

Evidence of this new splendor appears in a firsthand account of the wedding feast of the Duke of Mantua in May 1581. Among those present, the observer noted, were "100 ladies beautiful beyond measure and most richly garbed. Beyond, on a handsome sideboard, was visible a perspective of divers cups, carafes and goblets, and such beautiful vessels of Venetian glass as I think would defy competition. . . ."

The report went on to relate that the banquet lasted three hours. "The first table was laid with four tablecloths delicately embroidered, and upon each cloth its stamped leather cover to prevent it from being soiled. . . . The first service from the sideboard was large salads decked out with various fantasies such as animals made of citron, castles of turnips, high walls of lemons; and variegated with slices of ham, mullet roes, herrings, tunny, anchovies, capers, olives, caviar, together with candied flowers and other preserves. Then there were venison patties in the shape of gilded lions, pies in the form of upright black eagles, pastries of pheasant, which seemed alive, white peacocks adorned and re-clothed with their fanned-out tails, and decked with silken ribbons of gold and divers colors, as well as long gilded confections which hung everywhere about the peacocks which stood erect, with a perfume emanating from the kindled wad in their beaks and an amorous epigram placed between their legs."

On a table "there were three large statues in marzipan, each four hands high. One was the horse of Campidoglio to the life, the second Hercules with the lion, and the third a unicorn with its horn in the dragon's mouth. The table was filled with many other things—jellies, blancmanges in half relief, spiced hard-bake, royal wafers, Milanese biscuits, pine kernels, minced meat, cakes of pistachio nuts, sweet almond twists, flaky pastries, pasta with meat sauce *a la Romana,* salami, olives, salted tongues, Indian turkey hens stuffed and roasted on the spit, marinated pullets, fresh grapes, strawberries strewn with sugar, wild cherries, and asparagus cooked with butter in various ways. The napkins were marvelously folded in various ways with columns and arches, which presented a beautiful sight with innumerable streamers of colored cloth gilded with the arms of all the noble lords who were at the table—in all thirteen, who after washing their hands in perfumed water, took their places to the accompaniment of sweet music and songs."

In the late 15th and early 16th Centuries three successive kings of France— Charles VIII, Louis XII, and Francis I—visited Italy to claim disputed lands, fight in wars or transact business with the popes. All three were smitten with the splendors of the Renaissance. Charles VIII brought back Italian furnishings for his Château d'Amboise on the Loire River and the great Italian gardener, Pacello di Mercogliano, to landscape his gardens with balustrades, terraces and summerhouses that can be

Continued on page 56

When Man's Best Friend Is His Pig

Through the ages truffles have been particularly prized by connoisseurs of food. Aristocrats of Rome enjoyed them; Renaissance Italians savored them and today devotees of classic French cooking hold their distinctive bosky flavor in the highest esteem. Yet even though these strange wild fungi are highly valued, no one knows exactly how they grow and no one has been able to cultivate them successfully. "The most learned men have been questioned as to the nature of this tuber," wrote Alexandre Dumas, "and after two thousand years of argument and discussion their answer is the same as it was on the first day: we do not know. The truffles themselves have been interrogated, and have answered simply: eat us and praise the Lord." Even people of Périgord, the region of southwestern France where the finest truffles grow, do not know exactly where to look for them. But fortunately, their pigs know how to root them out. (Dogs are also sometimes used.) Beginning in December and continuing through March, *truffiers* like Robert Leygonie set out with their keen-nosed pigs *(left)* to scour the countryside. Trailing the scent of these elusive delicacies *(above)* often takes hours, for truffles grow in clusters among the roots of some (not all) oak trees and are found anywhere from 2 to 15 inches below the surface of the ground.

Truffle-hunting is a cooperative effort between the *truffier* and his pig, which acts as a kind of mine detector for the buried gastronomic treasure. When M. Leygonie, who owns a farm near the village of Nadaillac in the Périgord, takes his sow out on a leash, man and beast patiently wander through a grove of oaks until the pig finally scents a truffle and begins nosing into the ground for it *(above)*. A neighbor then quickly distracts the pig with a potato kept in readiness *(above, right)* while Leygonie finishes unearthing the truffle with a spike. At right he proudly displays the find, a medium-sized specimen worth perhaps 68 cents an ounce to him —and almost four dollars an ounce at a specialty grocery in New York. Truffles range from objects no bigger than a peanut to splendid giants the size of an orange, although most are walnut-sized. M. Leygonie sells them directly to gourmet friends or delivers them to a processing plant in nearby Sarlat, where they are weighed *(opposite)* and graded. Sold to distributors and fine shops, they are used to flavor other foods, are combined with foie gras—another delicacy from the Périgord—or are cut into fancy shapes as garnishes for classic dishes.

seen to this day. Francis I captured a more impressive prize, bringing back Leonardo da Vinci to design a château for the Queen Mother, Louise of Savoy; unfortunately, she died, and the château was never built.

But it remained for a slip of a girl to make the impact of Italy truly felt in France. In October 1553 Catherine de' Medici, great-granddaughter of Lorenzo the Magnificent, married the youth who was to become King Henry II of France. She was only 14 at the time, but she brought with her a retinue of Florentine cooks who knew how to prepare Italian soups, sauces, aspics and desserts. When Henry became King in 1547, his Queen ushered in a new era of manners and etiquette. Before Catherine's time, French nobles had been notorious for their gorging and guzzling. Ladies did not dine with the sovereign because they felt, as one observer put it, that "the movement of the jaws deforms the contours of their faces and detracts from the ethereal appeal of their beauty." Catherine brought the ladies to the royal table where, amid silver adornments fashioned by Benvenuto Cellini, they dined from colorfully glazed dishes and sipped wine from Venetian glass. In place of medieval slabs of meat, they savored such delicacies as sweetbreads, truffles, *tournedos,* artichoke hearts, grated Parmesan cheese, liver *crépinettes, quenelles* of poultry, macaroons, zabaglione, ice cream and frangipane tarts. Catherine threw out the jugglers and acrobats, and entertained her guests with troupes of ballet dancers. So scintillating were her banquets, balls and musical evenings that one admirer asserted: "The court of Catherine de' Medici was a veritable earthly paradise and a school for all the chivalry and flower of France. Ladies shone there like stars in the sky on a fine night."

About a century after Catherine, during the reign of the Sun King, Louis XIV, a tremendously important new cookbook appeared in France. It was called *Le Cuisinier françois* and was written by a man named François Pierre de La Varenne, who is believed to have learned to cook in the kitchens of Marie de' Medici, a cousin of Catherine, who married Henry IV of France in 1600.

La Varenne was a great chef, and his cookbook represented a giant stride toward the classic French cuisine. His recipes—the first, incidentally, to be presented in alphabetical order—reflected the profound changes that had occurred since Taillevent's day. La Varenne included the first cooking instructions for vegetables, which until then had not been widely appreciated. He discarded heavy spices, introduced truffles and mushrooms to provide subtle accents for meat dishes, and he instructed cooks to serve roasts in their natural juices. Fish were to be prepared in a fumet, or stock made with their trimmings—bones, head, tail and seasonings. The sauce thickener we use today, the roux—made of flour and butter or another animal fat—replaced coarse bread crumbs. Butter was substituted for meat fat in pastries. Food was no longer to be disguised, but appreciated for its true flavor. The object of cooking, at last, was to bring out the natural flavor of a food, not hide it, a key point of modern French cooking.

Yet La Varenne lived in a gluttonous age, and the greatest glutton of them all was Louis XIV. In his pleasure dome at Versailles, the food was prepared in kitchens some distance from the royal apartments, and no

LE DINÉ DV ROY A L'HOTEL DE VILLE DE PARIS
CALENDRIER POUR L'ANNÉE BISSEXTILE MDCLXXXVIII.

Classic canapés include a six-petaled flower *(center of picture)* made of smoked salmon, decorated with butter piped through a pastry tube. The squares at the ends of the petals are caviar on toast, adorned with butter flowers. Alternating with these are foie gras rounds on bread. At the corners stand diamond-shaped canapés with slices of Bayonne ham piped with butter.

fewer than 324 people were engaged in its preparation. At a signal from an officer of the kitchen, a solemn procession headed by two archers, and followed by the Lord Steward and other notables escorted the food to the King's quarters. A special basket laden with knives, forks, spoons, napkins, toothpicks, salt, ginger, pepper and spices was included in the order of march. As the cry "The King's meat!" proclaimed the procession's approach, members of the court lifted their hats and bowed from the waist. When the bearers finally made their way through the maze of corridors and galleries to the King's apartment, the food had to be sampled by a functionary to make sure it had not been poisoned. By the time the dishes were served to the King, they were inevitably cold.

Louis usually lunched alone, or with his Queen, Maria Theresa. But in the evenings he was served his dinner in a formal salon with the entire court standing by to watch as he wolfed his food. His sister-in-law, the Princess Palatine, reported that at a single sitting he consumed "four plates of different soups, an entire pheasant, a large plateful of salad, a partridge, mutton cut up in its juice with garlic, two good pieces of ham, a plateful of cakes, and fruits and jams." Sometimes at small suppers attended by the princesses and ladies of the court Louis would playfully toss rolls, apples and oranges at them, and they were allowed to retaliate.

For all his excesses at the table the Sun King appreciated good food and his reign produced many important culinary innovations. The general manager of the gardens at Versailles was a lawyer-agronomist named La Quintinie. He installed the famous vegetable garden at the palace and Louis loved to walk there, showing a keen interest in the cultivation and availability of fresh vegetables and fruit. He wanted to be able to enjoy them ahead of season: asparagus in December, strawberries in April, green peas in May and melons in June. By using glass covers for the plants, La Quintinie was able to gratify the King's wish.

The King's concern for culinary matters extended to the kitchen as well. He gave the title of officer to all his cooks and divided them into categories according to their duties. There were officers of food, roasting and sweets, as well as officers of the buffet, goblets and glass. The officers of food outranked all the others, and could be distinguished by the swords that they alone were entitled to wear.

A new *batterie de cuisine*—a set of kitchen utensils—made of tin plate and wrought iron appeared in Louis' day. The fork, which came from Italy, was first used in France at this time, and the manufacture of the exquisite porcelain tableware known as Sèvres was begun. Many important new dishes and sauces were created—among them béchamel sauce, a basic white sauce of the classic cuisine. The King's sweet tooth produced another major innovation: sweets, hitherto reserved for special occasions, appeared on the table every day.

Louis XIV died in 1715, suffering from gout, enlarged intestines and —at 77 years—old age. For the next eight years his nephew, the Duke of Orleans, ruled as regent. In that role he was a disaster economically, politically and in every other way, but his little suppers—*petits soupers*— gave new distinction to the French cuisine. Guests often helped with the cooking at these stylish, intimate affairs, and the Duke himself was known to lend a hand with the pastry. Recounting the *petits soupers* in his brilliant book, *The Physiology of Taste*, the celebrated Jean Anthelme Brillat-Savarin later noted that the Duke, "a witty prince and one worthy to have friends, partook with them of meals as choice as they were well-contrived . . . The distinguishing features of those meals were the highly appetizing sauces, fish *à la matelote* [fish with a velouté sauce flavored with mushrooms and cayenne] tasting as fresh as if they had only just been taken from the water, and turkeys gloriously truffled."

Another notable feature of the *petits soupers* was that champagne was served. For the first time the bubbling wine became fashionable, and one observer of these suppers reported, "It was an agreeable sight to see the wine announced all of a sudden by a popping explosion. . . . Soon you see it warm spirits up, loosen tongues, and produce gaiety, laughter and joy around the table."

The age of culinary enlightenment continued through the reign of

JEAN ANTHELME BRILLAT-SAVARIN
(1755-1826)

"The discovery of a new dish does more for the happiness of mankind than the discovery of a new star," wrote Brillat-Savarin. A celebrated gastronome and chronicler of French cooking, he is best known for *The Physiology of Taste,* a book of epigrams and gastronomic lore that he worked on for 25 years.

Louis XV (1715-1774). The aristocracy maintained elaborate establishments, with staffs of 40 to 50 servants, where meals were marked by their order, propriety and elegance. The custom arose of naming new dishes after influential people. *Bouchées à la reine* (creamed chicken in puff pastry shells) was named after Maria Leszczyńska, Louis XV's wife. *Cailles Mirepoix* (quails with a mixture of finely chopped vegetables) honored the aristocratic Mirepoix family, and *sole Pompadour* (sole with tomatoes, white wine sauce and truffles) paid homage to Madame de Pompadour, Louis XV's sparkling mistress.

The last pre-Revolutionary king of France, Louis XVI, was as much a trencherman as his ancestor the 14th Louis. Even as his throne toppled, he persisted in this penchant for stuffing himself with prodigious quantities of food. On the day he was condemned to die on the guillotine—a fate also assigned his frivolous Queen, Marie Antoinette—he returned to prison and ate six cutlets and a large piece of chicken, washed them down with two glasses of white wine and a glass of Alicante, and went to sleep, presumably all the more fortified to meet his Maker.

Despite Louis XVI's own intemperate habits, his reign saw notable advances in the culinary art. Summarizing the period in *The Physiology of Taste,* Brillat-Savarin concluded: "The ranks of every profession concerned with the sale or preparation of food, including cooks, caterers, confectioners, pastry cooks, provision merchants and the like, have multiplied in ever-increasing proportions . . . New professions have arisen; that, for example, of the petit four pastry cook—in his domain are biscuits, macaroons, fancy cakes, meringues . . . The art of preserving has also become

Oeufs en gelée (eggs in aspic), an attractive cold buffet dish or luncheon appetizer, appears in two versions in this chapter. Shown here are eggs molded individually in aspic, garnished with truffles and slivers of chicken breast. On page 62 is a more elaborate version of the dish. Recipes are on page 63.

a profession in itself, whereby we are enabled to enjoy, at all times of the year, things naturally peculiar to one or other season . . . French cookery has annexed dishes of foreign extraction such as curry and the roast beef of England; relishes such as caviar and soy; drinks such as punch, negus and others. Coffee has come into general use, as a food in the morning and after dinner as a tonic and exhilarating drink. A wide variety of vessels, utensils and accessories of every sort has been invented, so that foreigners coming to Paris find many objects on the table the very names of which they know not, nor dare to ask their use."

More important than any of these specific contributions was the new subtlety and sophistication of French cooking. Writing in 1781, Louis Sebastien Mercier, author of *Tableau de Paris,* noted: "The dishes of the present day are very light and they have a particular delicacy and perfume. The secret has been discovered of enabling us to eat better. . . . Who could enumerate all the dishes of the new cuisine? . . . I have tasted viands prepared in so many ways and fashioned with such art that I could not imagine what they were."

When these felicitous words were written the French Revolution was less than a decade away. With that cataclysmic event France and indeed the whole world were irrevocably changed politically, socially, economically—and gastronomically. Louis XVI went to the guillotine, and most of the nobility either followed him or fled the country. French cooking went into eclipse—but only for a time. In the Napoleonic era it would re-emerge in a more elegant, refined form, and an extraordinary chef, Carême, would lay the foundations of the great cuisine of today.

Oeufs en gelée
EGGS IN ASPIC

Only farm-fresh eggs will produce neat ovals when poached. If your eggs are more than a day or two old, make the "oeufs en gelée" in molds.

OEUFS EN GELÉE (EGGS IN ASPIC): Pour cold water into a 12-inch sauté pan or skillet to a depth of about 2 inches, and add the vinegar. Bring to a simmer, then reduce the heat so that the surface of the liquid barely shimmers. Break 4 eggs into individual saucers. Gently slide one egg into the water, and with a large spoon, lift the white over the yolk. Repeat once or twice more to enclose the yolk in the white. One at a time, quickly slide the 3 other eggs from the saucers into the pan, enclosing them in their whites and spacing them at least 1 inch apart.

Poach the eggs for 3 or 4 minutes until the whites are set and the yolks still feel soft when prodded gently with the tip of your finger. With a slotted spoon, transfer the eggs to a bowl of cold water and let them cool completely. Repeating the procedure, poach the 4 remaining eggs. Then lift the eggs from the water and with scissors trim each egg into a smooth oval, being careful not to pierce the yolk. Place the eggs on a wire rack set in a jelly-roll pan and refrigerate for at least 2 hours.

Meanwhile prepare the decoration for the eggs. Drop the leek or scallion leaves into boiling water and boil for 1 or 2 minutes. Drain the greens in a sieve, run cold water over them, then spread them on paper towels and pat them dry. Cut the leek or scallion leaves into bladelike leaf shapes and a dozen or more thin strips to use as stems. Slice the truffle into rounds ⅛ inch thick. With a lily-of-the-valley truffle cutter, make truffle flowers and set them aside with the leaves and stems.

With a small, sharp knife, peel the skin of the tomato in spiral fashion to make a long continuous strip about ¾ inch wide. Shape the strip into a roselike coil and set aside. Coarsely chop the tomato and set aside.

GELÉE (ASPIC): Combine the chopped tomato, chopped leek, gelatin, egg whites, egg shells and tarragon in a heavy 2- to 3-quart enameled or stainless-steel saucepan and pour in the stock. Set the pan over moderate heat and, stirring constantly, bring the stock to a simmer.

When the mixture begins to froth and rise, remove the pan from the heat and let the stock rest for 10 minutes. Then pour the entire contents of the pan into a fine sieve lined with a double thickness of dampened cheesecloth and set over another enameled or stainless-steel pan. Allow the liquid to drain through undisturbed. Season with more salt if needed.

Set the pan in a large pot half-filled with crushed ice or ice cubes and water, and stir the aspic with a metal spoon until it thickens enough to flow sluggishly. Then spoon a little aspic over one of the eggs. It should cling and cover the surface with a thin translucent glaze. Coat the other eggs with aspic and return them to the refrigerator until the aspic is firm. (Keep the remaining aspic at room temperature so that it remains liquid

To serve 8 as a first course

OEUFS POCHÉS
¼ cup tarragon vinegar
8 fresh eggs

GARNITURES POUR LES OEUFS EN GELÉE
2 or 3 large green leaves from the top of a leek or scallion
1 black truffle (*see Glossary*)
1 small firm ripe tomato

GELÉE
1 small firm ripe tomato, coarsely chopped
¼ cup coarsely chopped leeks, including 2 inches of the green tops, thoroughly washed
3 envelopes unflavored gelatin
¼ cup egg whites
2 egg shells, finely crushed
2 tablespoons finely cut fresh tarragon leaves or 1 tablespoon crumbled, dried tarragon
1 quart cold *fond blanc de volaille (page 31),* or substitute 1 quart canned chicken stock, chilled, then degreased

A glittering version of *oeufs en gelée* features poached eggs with green leeks, truffles and a tomato rose, set in a jewellike bed of aspic.

and ready to use; if it begins to set, warm briefly over low heat to soften it, then stir it over ice again until it is thick but still fluid.)

Dip the truffle flowers and green leaf blades and stems one at a time into the aspic and arrange them fancifully on top of 7 of the eggs. Dip the tomato rose in aspic, place it in the center of the remaining egg and create a swirl of stems and leaves around it. Refrigerate again until the decorations are anchored firmly. Then carefully spoon aspic over the eggs two more times, chilling them to set the glaze after each coating.

With a rubber spatula, scrape up the aspic left in the jelly-roll pan and add it to the aspic remaining in the pan. Melt it over low heat, then pour a ⅛-inch layer of aspic over the bottom of a serving platter and pour the rest into a small loaf pan. Refrigerate the platter and pan until the aspic has firmly set. Remove the pan from the refrigerator, dip it in hot water, then place an inverted plate over it. Grasping pan and plate together firmly, turn them over. The aspic should slide out easily. Cut the aspic into ¼-inch slices, and then into diamonds or other shapes. Finely dice the scraps.

Arrange the eggs decoratively on the chilled platter with the tomato-topped egg in the center. Use the aspic diamonds to ring the platter and scatter the dice between the eggs. Refrigerate until ready to serve.

GARNITURES POUR LES OEUFS EN
GELÉE EN MOULES
2 black truffles, thinly peeled *(see
Glossary)*
An 8-ounce chicken breast
¼ teaspoon salt

OEUFS EN GELÉE EN MOULES (EGGS MOLDED IN ASPIC): To prepare eggs in individual molds, select the smallest ones you can find. Pullet eggs are best if they are available. Poach and trim the eggs as described above.

Meanwhile, slice and cut the truffles in whatever shapes you wish, to decorate the top of the molded eggs, and chop the truffle scraps into ¼-inch dice and set aside. In a small heavy skillet, combine the chicken breast, ¼ teaspoon of salt and 2 cups of water. Bring to a simmer over moderate heat and poach partially covered for about 10 minutes, or until the chicken is tender. Remove the chicken from the pan and, with a small knife, pull off the skin and cut away the bones. Cut the meat into julienne strips about 1 inch long and ¼ inch wide and refrigerate covered with plastic wrap until ready to use.

Prepare the aspic as described above, cool it over ice and when it is a thick syrup, pour an ⅛-inch layer into each of 8 four-ounce egg molds. Chill until firm, then dip the truffle cutouts into the aspic and center one in each mold. Refrigerate again to anchor the truffle securely. Pour in another ⅛-inch layer of aspic and chill until it is firmly jelled.

Carefully set the eggs in the molds and pour enough aspic into each mold to reach about ¼ inch up the side of the egg. Chill, and when the jelly is firm, fill the molds with aspic to just cover the eggs. Refrigerate to set the jelly. Sprinkle the chopped truffle and the chicken into the molds, dividing the dice and julienne strips evenly among them. Now fill the molds with enough aspic to come to the rim. Refrigerate for at least 6 hours, or until very firm. (Any remaining aspic may be chilled in a loaf pan and used chopped or cut into decorative shapes to garnish the eggs.)

To unmold and serve, run a knife around the sides of each mold and dip the bottom in hot water for a few seconds. Wipe the mold dry, place an inverted plate over it and, grasping plate and mold together, turn them over. Rap the plate sharply on a table and the jelly should slide out. (If it does not, repeat the dipping and drying process once more.) Arrange the eggs on a chilled platter and refrigerate until ready to serve.

Frangipane cream, a favorite of Renaissance Italians, and poached pears are the main ingredients of *poires Bourdaloue (Recipe Index)*.

To serve 10 to 12

A 2-pound oven-ready pheasant

MARINADE

⅓ cup truffle juice *(see Glossary)*

3 tablespoons cognac

½ teaspoon Spice Parisienne *(see Glossary)*

The strips of pheasant breast

The pheasant liver, trimmed of any fat or bits of green, and cut in half

2 fresh chicken livers, trimmed of any fat or bits of green, and cut in half

4 large black truffles, thinly peeled and cut in half *(see Glossary)*

6 strips fresh pork fatback (or side pork) each about 6 inches long, ½ inch wide and ¼ inch thick

GLACE DE FAISAN

The skin and bones of the pheasant

The pheasant heart

1 medium-sized leek, including 3 inches of the green top, trimmed, coarsely chopped and washed thoroughly in a sieve set under running water

1 medium-sized onion, peeled and coarsely chopped

1 medium-sized carrot, scraped and coarsely chopped

2 medium-sized unpeeled garlic cloves, crushed with the side of a cleaver or large knife

1 medium-sized bay leaf

1 fresh thyme sprig or ⅛ teaspoon crumbled dried thyme

Pâté de faisan en croûte
PHEASANT PÂTÉ BAKED IN A PASTRY CRUST

Start the pâté at least six or seven days in advance to allow the ingredients to marinate and develop flavor.

Ask your butcher to remove each side of the pheasant breast as neatly as possible in one piece. Strip off the skin and cut the breast meat into 6 or 8 long strips of equal width. Set aside.

Cut the thighs, drumsticks and wings from the bird; skin them and remove all the meat from the bones. Then peel the skin from the pheasant carcass and remove any clinging bits of meat. Chop all the meat coarsely and reserve. (There should be about ½ cup.) With a cleaver, chop up all the bones and set them aside with the skin.

MARINADE: In a glass loaf dish or deep bowl, combine the truffle juice, 3 tablespoons of cognac and ½ teaspoon Spice Parisienne. Add the strips of pheasant breast, the pheasant and chicken livers, the truffle halves and the 6-inch strips of pork fat, turning them about gently in the marinade until they are evenly moistened. Cover tightly with foil or plastic wrap and marinate in the refrigerator for 3 days.

GLACE DE FAISAN (PHEASANT GLAZE): In a heavy 6- to 8-quart enameled cast-iron casserole, sauté the pheasant skin and bones, the pheasant heart, the leek, onion and carrot over moderate heat, stirring constantly until they are all lightly colored. Pour in enough cold water to cover the contents by at least 2 inches, and add the 2 crushed garlic cloves and the bay leaf.

Bring to a boil over moderate heat, skimming off and discarding the foam and scum as they rise to the surface. Add the sprig of fresh thyme or ⅛ teaspoon crumbled dried thyme. Then boil undisturbed and uncovered for about 1 hour. Strain the entire contents of the casserole through a fine sieve into a deep bowl, pressing down hard on the skin, bones and vegetables with the back of a large spoon to extract all their juice before discarding them.

Skim all fat from the surface of the stock. Pour the stock into a small, heavy saucepan and boil briskly, uncovered, until it is reduced to about 1 cup. Turn the heat to low and, stirring occasionally, reduce the stock to ½ cup of thick syrupy glaze, or *glace de faisan*.

FARCE (STUFFING): To prepare the *farce,* or ground-meat stuffing mixture, drop the reserved chopped pheasant meat, shallots and crushed garlic clove into a heavy 12-inch skillet.

Stirring constantly, cook for about 5 minutes over moderate heat until the meat is lightly browned. Then stir in the 1 teaspoon Spice Parisienne, the sprig of fresh thyme or ⅛ teaspoon crumbled dried thyme, white pepper and salt, and add the cognac and the white wine. Stirring all the while and scraping in the brown particles that cling to the bottom of the pan, bring to a boil over high heat.

Strain the entire contents of the skillet through a fine sieve and set the liquid aside. Put the strained meats and seasonings, the boneless pork, the fatback chunks, and the foie gras (if you are using it) through the finest blade of a food grinder.

Add the reserved liquid, the *glace de faisan* and the saltpeter. Knead vigorously with both hands, then beat with a wooden spoon until the *farce* is smooth and fluffy. (There should be about 4 cups.) Cover tightly and refrigerate for 3 days.

PÂTE FINE (FINE PASTRY): In a large chilled mixing bowl, combine the flour, butter and lard. With your fingertips rub the flour and fat together until they look like flakes of coarse meal. Add the egg yolks and mix them thoroughly into the dough.

Pour 4 tablespoons of the ice water over the mixture all at once, knead vigorously, and gather the dough into a ball. If the dough crumbles, add up to 4 more tablespoons of ice water, a spoonful at a time, until the particles adhere. Dust the dough with a little flour and wrap it in wax paper. Refrigerate for at least 1 hour before using. (The dough may be made 1 or 2 days in advance, if you prefer. In that event, let it soften at room temperature just long enough to become malleable.)

FINAL ASSEMBLY: Separate the sides and bottom of a fluted oval *pâté en croûte* mold 9¼ inches long and 4 inches deep. On a lightly floured surface, roll the dough out into a rough rectangle about ⅛ inch thick.

With a ruler and pastry wheel or sharp knife, cut two rectangles each 11 inches long and 5 inches wide. Place the sides of the mold next to one another, concave surfaces up. Then press the dough rectangles into the concave sides of the mold, leaving a ½-inch overhang on the top long edges but trimming off the rest of the excess dough.

Place the bottom of the mold on the remaining rolled dough and use it as a guide to cut out two ovals, one exactly the size of the mold and the other about ½ inch wider all around. Cover the larger oval with wax paper and set it aside; gather the scraps of dough into a ball and return it to the refrigerator.

Hinge the two sides of the lined mold and press the ends of the dough together where they meet to join them securely. Lift the sides of the mold and carefully snap them into the base. Set the smaller oval of dough into the bottom of the mold. Join it to the sides by pressing the pieces of dough firmly together and smoothing the seam with a moistened finger.

Line the bottom and sides of the mold with paper-thin slices of fatback, overlapping the slices slightly where they meet and arranging them so that no dough shows through in any area.

Pour the marinade from the meat and truffles into the *farce* and beat it. Set the meats and truffles aside on a plate. To test the *farce* for seasoning, fry 1 teaspoon of it over moderate heat for 2 or 3 minutes, taste, then add salt or pepper to the raw *farce* if necessary.

Spoon 1 cup of the *farce* into the mold and smooth the top with your hands. Place 2 strips of the marinated fatback lengthwise over the *farce* and lay 3 or 4 strips of pheasant meat end to end in rows between them.

Spoon in another cup of *farce,* smooth it to the edges of the mold, then place a thin, wide slice of fatback lengthwise down the center. Press a groove down the length of the slice with the side of your hand and set the truffle halves into it, laying them end to end. Cover the truffles with the pheasant and chicken livers. Set another thin, wide slice of fatback over the livers and place a strip of the marinated fatback along each side of the arrangement.

Add a cup of the *farce* and smooth it to the sides of the mold. Place the remaining 2 strips of fatback along the sides and arrange the rest of

FARCE

The chopped pheasant meat
½ cup shallots, peeled and thinly sliced
1 large garlic clove, peeled and crushed with the side of a cleaver or large knife
1 teaspoon Spice Parisienne *(see Glossary)*
1 fresh thyme sprig or ⅛ teaspoon crumbled dried thyme
½ teaspoon freshly ground white pepper
1 tablespoon salt
⅓ cup cognac
½ cup dry white wine
1 pound lean boneless pork, trimmed of all fat and cut into small chunks
½ pound fresh pork fatback, cut into small chunks
2 ounces foie gras, preferably *en bloc (see Glossary),* optional
⅛ teaspoon saltpeter

PÂTE FINE

4 cups all-purpose flour
8 tablespoons unsalted butter (1 quarter-pound stick), chilled and cut into ¼-inch bits
8 tablespoons lard, chilled and cut into ¼-inch bits
4 egg yolks
4 to 8 tablespoons ice water
1 egg yolk combined with 1 tablespoon water

1½ pounds fresh pork fatback, cut horizontally with the rind into thin, wide slices about ⅛ inch thick, 9 inches long and 3 inches wide, then pounded between 2 sheets of wax paper until paper-thin

gelée de fond blanc de volaille (page 34)

An Encrusted Glory of French Cooking

The pheasant *pâté en croûte (receipe page 66),* one of the most glorious creations of French cookery, takes the better part of a week to prepare. The pheasant meat, pork and pork fat are marinated for 2 or 3 days in cognac and truffle juice with seasonings. Then the mixture is baked inside a pastry crust. After cooking it is refrigerated for 2 or 3 days to heighten the flavors.

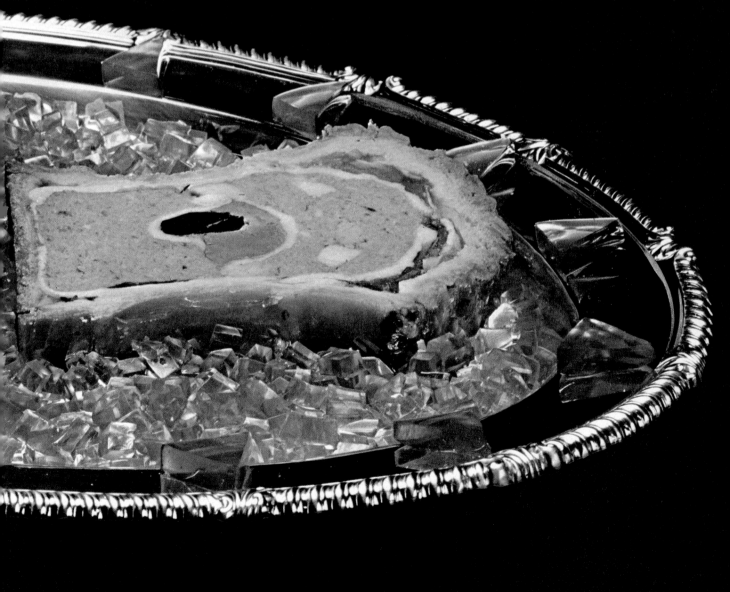

the pheasant strips between them. Now spoon in all the remaining *farce,* spreading it evenly over the entire surface and mounding it in the center. Cover the *farce* with a layer of the thin, wide slices of fatback. Trim off any excess. (Discard any leftover fat slices or save them for another use.)

Place the reserved, larger oval of dough gently on top of the filled mold, pressing it gently but snugly toward the rim. Fold the overhanging dough to meet the top evenly and trim off the excess. Then moisten the seam with water and smooth it with a knife or your fingers.

On a lightly floured surface, roll out the reserved dough to a thickness of ⅛ inch and cut off 2 strips about ½ inch wide and 12 inches long. Moisten the edges of the pastry-covered mold with water and carefully lay the strips around the edge of the oval, rounding the edges of the strips with your fingers as you proceed and pressing them gently to secure them. Cut off the excess where the strips overlap and crimp the dough attractively.

With the base of a pastry tube or a sharp knife cut a hole about 1 inch in diameter in the middle of the top. If you like you may form a little ring of pastry and anchor it around this opening, moistening the dough before setting it in place.

Using small pastry or cookie cutters, or cutting out designs with a small, sharp knife, decorate the top as fancifully as you like with flower and leaf shapes. Moisten the bottom of each decoration lightly with water before setting it in place. Then brush the entire top surface of the pastry with the egg-yolk-and-water mixture. Insert a 1-inch cylinder, made from a double thickness of heavy duty foil, into the hole in the crust.

Preheat the oven to 375°. Insert the tip of a meat thermometer at least 2 inches into the pâté through the hole in the top and set the mold on a jelly-roll pan to collect the fat that will bubble out when the pâté bakes. Bake in the middle of the oven for 10 minutes, then reduce the heat to 350° and continue baking for 2 hours longer, or until the thermometer registers 160° to 165°.

Remove the pâté from the oven and set it aside at room temperature for 15 to 20 minutes.

GELÉE (ASPIC): Meanwhile, set the pan or bowl of *gelée de fond blanc de volaille* into a pot half filled with crushed ice or ice cubes and water and stir the aspic with a large metal spoon until it thickens enough to flow sluggishly off the spoon. With a funnel, pour about 2 cups of the aspic very slowly into the hole in the pâté until the liquid reaches the top. If any aspic runs out of the bottom of the mold, seal the leaks with cold butter and then set the molded pâté on a tray or plate in the refrigerator.

(Keep the remaining aspic at room temperature so that it remains liquid and ready to use; if it begins to set, warm briefly over low heat to soften it, then stir it over ice again until it reaches the same thick but still fluid consistency as before.)

After an hour or so, add another 1 to 2 cups of aspic to the pâté to fill the pastry shell as completely as possible, pouring it slowly into the foil cylinder. Cover the pâté tightly with plastic wrap and refrigerate it in the mold for about 24 hours. Cover and chill the remaining aspic.

The next day, check the level of the aspic in the chilled pâté; it probably will have settled somewhat. If so, melt the reserved pan of aspic over low heat and cool it in a pot of ice as described above. When the aspic is syrupy, pour it slowly through the hole in the pâté to again fill the shell completely. Tightly cover and return to the refrigerator for another day or two to allow the flavors to develop further. Pour the leftover aspic into a small loaf pan, cover, and chill.

To serve, carefully lift the sides of the mold from the base and set the *pâté en croûte* on a chilled platter. Unhinge and remove the sides of the mold. Dip the loaf pan of aspic briefly into hot water, then place an inverted plate over the top. Grasping dish and plate together firmly, turn them over and the aspic should slide out easily.

Slice the aspic ¼ inch thick and cut some of the slices into triangles or other decorative shapes to ring the edge of the platter. Cut the remaining slices of aspic into strips and then into cubes. Scatter the cubes around the *pâté en croûte.*

TERRINE DE FAISAN (TERRINE OF PHEASANT): Lacking the *pâté en croûte* mold, or the time to prepare *pâté en croûte,* you may make a terrine of pheasant as described above, using the same ingredients except for the pastry and the aspic.

Line a 6-cup terrine with the thin slices of fatback and assemble the *farce* and marinated meats and truffles in the fashion outlined in the recipe. Top the final layer of fat with a large bay leaf, cover the terrine tightly with foil, and place it on a jelly-roll pan.

Insert a meat thermometer into the center of the terrine and bake on the middle shelf of a preheated 350° oven for about 2 hours, or until the thermometer reaches a temperature of 160-165°. Do not remove any liquid fat from the terrine; it will solidify when chilled and seal the terrine. Cool to room temperature, then refrigerate the *terrine de faisan* for 2 to 3 days until the flavors have developed. Serve directly from the terrine.

Endives braisées
BRAISED ENDIVE

To serve 4

8 medium-sized firm endives with tightly closed unblemished leaves
6 tablespoons water
2 tablespoons strained fresh lemon juice
2 tablespoons unsalted butter, cut into ¼-inch bits, plus 2 tablespoons clarified butter *(page 34)*
½ teaspoon sugar
½ teaspoon salt
¼ cup *fond lié (page 35),* warmed to serving temperature over low heat
2 tablespoons finely chopped fresh parsley

With a small, sharp knife trim the base of the endives and remove and discard any bruised or discolored leaves. Wash the endives thoroughly under cold running water.

Combine the water, lemon juice, 2 tablespoons of butter bits, sugar and salt in a heavy enameled or stainless-steel skillet just large enough to hold the endives in one layer, and stir well. Add the endives and cover them with a buttered piece of wax paper cut to just fit the pan.

Bring to a simmer over moderate heat, then reduce the heat to the lowest possible setting and braise the endives for about 20 minutes, or until they are tender and their bases show only the slightest resistance when pierced with the point of a small skewer or knife. With a slotted spoon transfer the endives to a plate.

Discard the cooking liquid, dry the skillet, and in it warm the clarified butter over moderate heat for 10 seconds. Add the endives and turn them over and over in the hot butter until they glisten, but do not let them brown. Arrange the endives attractively on a heated serving plate, pour the *fond lié* over them, and spoon the butter remaining in the pan on top. Sprinkle with parsley and serve at once.

III

The Architect of the Cuisine

Agleam with copper and sunlight, the vast kitchen of the Prince Regent's pleasure pavilion at Brighton, England, looks much as it did when the great Antonin Carême cooked there more than 150 years ago. Only slightly modernized and retaining many of its original fittings (roasting spits, bronze smoke canopies and 1,100 copper utensils), the kitchen is still in use for special civic occasions.

Cooking is an ephemeral art. The painter, the sculptor, the musician may create enduring works, but even the most talented chef knows that his masterpieces will quickly disappear. "A bite or two, a little gulp and a beautiful work of thought and love is no more," as the British author Sybil Ryall notes.

What does survive is the reputation, rather than the creations, of the chef. Yet, among the many thousands of men who have ruled the kitchens of France only a dozen or so have achieved lasting fame. In that select company two names stand out: Marie-Antoine Carême and Georges Auguste Escoffier. Between them, they spanned almost a century and a half. Carême was born shortly before the French Revolution; Escoffier died shortly before World War II. Each played a crucial—and very different—part in the development of the classical French cuisine.

Carême—who preferred to be called Antonin—was born in Paris in 1784, and died there 49 years later. While he lived his chief claim to glory lay in the spectacular feasts he prepared and the dazzling succession of potentates he fed. But what won him immortality was the series of books he lovingly and laboriously produced in his spare time.

Before Carême, culinary knowledge was passed from one generation to the next by word of mouth, scribbled notes, or an occasional, unsatisfactory cookbook. Carême's contribution was to document for posterity all of the best formulas and methods of French cooking. By preserving this lore in published form he provided a solid foundation on which future generations of chefs could build and expand. He was the Moses of classic cooking, and the laws that he carefully inscribed in his books served as a kind of holy writ.

Carême came along at a uniquely opportune moment. The Bastille fell when he was only five, and within a few years the rush of revolutionary events changed everything in the world around him—not only politically, socially and economically but also from a culinary point of view. The lavish living habits of the nobility passed into history, along with their concern for fine food. But the eclipse of the cuisine proved only temporary. As France emerged from the Revolution, into the rule of the Directoire and the brilliant Napoleonic era, the cuisine revived in a more elegant and orderly form. It was to be Carême's destiny to bridge the gap between the old and new regimes.

A less likely candidate for such a role would have been hard to find. The 16th child of an unprovident stonemason, Carême began life in a Paris slum. Soon, however, he escaped from that environment, in a manner to satisfy even the most maudlin novelist. Indeed the episode was recorded in after years by Alexandre Dumas père, who was not only a celebrated novelist but a gastronome of renown.

In his *Dictionary of Cuisine,* Dumas reported that when Carême was 11, the boy's father took him to a tavern near the city's outskirts. The two had supper, then the father led Carême into the street and, according to Dumas, left him with this melodramatic farewell: "Go, little one. There are good trades in this world. Let the rest of us languish in the misery in which we are doomed to die. This is a time when fortunes are made by those who have the wit, and that you have. Tonight or tomorrow, find a good house that may open its doors to you. Go with what God has given you and what I may add to that." Dumas tells us that the father then blessed his son and left him forever.

As Carême himself once recalled the experience, fate might well have led him that night to the door of a shoemaker, a carpenter or a chimney sweep. But it guided him instead to the lighted window of a modest eating house whose proprietor took him in and put him to work the next day. Carême remained there long enough to master the various tasks required in a small, undistinguished kitchen, then, after a few years, he became apprenticed to the owner of a pastry shop, the finest *pâtissier* in Paris, a Monsieur Bailly.

The years with Bailly were decisive for Carême. While acquiring the tools of his trade he also learned to read and write and draw. His skill as a draftsman was to prove indispensable in later years, for his job gave him time to explore the city, and its great buildings awakened in him a passionate interest in architecture. In the hall of prints and engravings at the Bibliothèque Royale, he came under the spell of the architectural masterpieces of ancient Egypt, Greece and Italy. So enthralled was he that only the lack of funds prevented him from becoming an architect.

By happy chance, his job provided a direct outlet for his interest. As a pastry chef, he was called upon to prepare, among other things, those wildly elaborate, highly adorned, wedding-cakelike table decorations called *pièces montées.* Such "mounted pieces" had been a traditional feature of banquets and feasts in France in the days of the old regime,

MARIE-ANTOINE CARÊME
(1784-1833)

Founder of the classic cuisine, Carême set forth the recipes, menus and kitchen techniques of great cooking in a monumental series of cookbooks. An architect at heart, he gave the classic cuisine a logical form and a matchless elegance.

and their popularity persisted in the period that followed the Revolution.

These towering replicas of temples, pavilions, rotundas, bridges and cascades were made of biscuits, glue, wax, almond paste, pastry dough and spun sugar—almost anything that could be shaped, fitted or pasted together. Set in the center of the table or placed around it at regular intervals, they were sometimes edible, either in part or in whole, and sometimes strictly decorative.

Before Carême's day, *pièces montées* had been grandiose and vulgar almost beyond belief. One of the most striking was described by that caustic chronicler of his times, Horace Walpole, in an account of a banquet celebrating the birth of the Duke of Burgundy. "The centerpiece," he reported, "was covered with wax figures moved by clockwork, which at the conclusion of the feast were set in motion, and gave a representation of the labor of the Dauphiness, and the happy birth of an heir to the monarchy." Another memorable *pièce montée* that Walpole described from a dinner in his own England consisted of a ship with guns containing real gunpowder and a castle made of pies filled with live frogs and birds; feminine guests were advised, when the guns went off, to spray perfume into the air to offset the acrid smell of gunpowder.

The *pièces montées* that Carême executed for Bailly were of a very different sort. The shop boasted some of the most fashionable and affluent clientele in Paris, including the foreign minister, Talleyrand. Carême was entrusted with the execution of *pièces montées* for Talleyrand and other patrons. Bailly encouraged his young assistant to visit the Bibliothèque Royale and study its reproductions of classical designs. Carême would go there every Tuesday and Friday, and spend long hours in meticulous copying. Then he would work through the night, laboriously building replicas of antique structures; temples were a favorite, but there were also fountains and forts and towers and even classical ruins. Carême thought of himself as an architect in his work—"architecture's main branch," he once said, "is confectionery"—and he executed his *pièces montées* with an architect's care and precision. Sometimes he spent weeks or even months on a single piece. His passion for detail was unremitting. His notes for a Corinthian column for a piece called the "Ruins of Athens" sound as specific as a blueprint for the Parthenon itself. "The height of this column has ten diameters, of which the base is one module," he wrote, "and the capital two modules and six parts; the pedestal, six modules and twelve parts; the entablature five modules with one and a half for the architrave, the same for the frieze, and two modules for the cornice; for the center of the column four modules and sixteen parts and the general height, thirty-one modules."

A proper color scheme for these creations was also essential. The plans for a Carême construction entitled "The Tower of Rhodes" noted: "This piece must be striped with white and with chocolate: these are the most suitable colors. The trelliswork of the windows and the gallery should be in orange. The bridge, marbled in white and green, the same as the roofing of the turrets."

Not the least of his problems was the need to adapt the classical designs to the scale and proportions of table displays. "I was limited in the

JULES GOUFFÉ
(1807-1877)

Carême's leading disciple, he worked under the master for seven years as a young cook and pastry chef. Later he became head chef at the fashionable Jockey Club, one of the leading restaurants of Paris. His cookbooks—especially *Le Livre de cuisine*—rank as culinary classics.

The Cook with an Architect's Eye

In his book, *Le Maître d'hôtel* (1822), Antonin Carême includes menus for every day in the year. Nestled among the menus is this drawing for a colossal, symmetrical buffet of a kind that only Carême could have conceived. Apparently the multi-tiered conception was hypothetical, and Carême never explained how he would get it all under one roof. All he said was that the buffet was set for 100 people, with eight different soups and *grosses pièces* (great pieces) of fish, fowl and game. There also were *pièces montées* that looked like classic temples, as well as fruit jellies, apple *suédoises,* Bavarian creams, soufflés, fondues and cakes with cream. But what is really fascinating about the sketch is its symmetry. A fish on one side is balanced by a fish on the other side; a fowl balances another fowl, and a temple is matched by another temple reflecting Carême's quest for order.

height and width of the objects I presented," he later recalled, "because at most my great *pièces montées* could only be 20 to 24 inches in diameter and 30 to 48 inches in elevation." Whatever the difficulties en route, the finished products were a triumph. Carême's creations were every bit as splendid as the *pièces montées* of the old era, without their blatant excesses; his genius managed to combine magnificence and restraint, to suggest that even in something so transient as a table decoration, esthetic principles of harmony and order should prevail. This rational approach was to characterize Carême's culinary efforts throughout his life.

After three years in Bailly's shop he was hired away by Talleyrand. In employing Carême as his personal pastry chef, Talleyrand was also subtly serving his country's cause. A confirmed gastronome as well as the wiliest negotiator in Europe, he looked on pleasurable dining as a useful adjunct to diplomatic maneuvering. (" Sire, I have more need of casseroles than of written instructions," he remarked to King Louis XVIII before departing for the Congress of Vienna in 1814.)

Talleyrand's house in Paris, one visitor reported, was a "model of taste, luxury and manners." The dinners he staged, usually for 10 to 12 guests, were the talk of the town. A typical meal was impeccably cooked and served and featured two soups, a fish course, four entrées, two roasts, four vegetable dishes and dessert. However busy he might be with affairs of state, Talleyrand personally went over the menu every morning. Carême found him "a most competent judge . . . his expenditure is both great and wise at the same time." Talleyrand, in turn, found his pastry chef an all too envied asset. Carême's masterly *pièces montées* and elaborate cold dishes for a series of banquets given by his employer spread his reputation among the wealthiest and most influential people in Europe, crowned heads included.

In 1815, Czar Alexander I of Russia staged a magnificent review of his troops at Châlons-sur-Marne. Carême catered a series of feasts for the Czar, and France's own royalty sampled his art that same year at a gigantic feast he catered at the Louvre. With Napoleon by now safely exiled, and the Bourbon dynasty re-established, privileged Parisians were primed for a truly monumental affair, and Carême saw to it that they had one. Places were set for 1,200 and a salvo of cannon proclaimed the arrival of Louis XVIII and the royal family. Among the delectable surprises to which the diners were introduced was the Carême invention that later came to be called *charlotte russe.* In a kitchen crisis reminiscent of the incident that drove the 17th Century maître d'hôtel Vatel to suicide, the supply of gelatine for the dessert ran short, and the charlottes sagged a bit. But fortunately for the fate of the classic French cuisine, Carême did not take the experience as hard as Vatel had.

His next assignment for royalty took him across the Channel. In 1816 England's high-living Prince Regent—later George IV—sent the comptroller of his household to Paris in search of a chef accomplished enough to add some zest to England's pallid dishes, and when two of the leading cooks of the French capital recommended Carême for the post the culinary quest was ended.

As the Regent's *chef de cuisine,* Carême was installed at the stylish seaside resort of Brighton, where the Prince had built himself a haven from official cares. Originally envisioned as a modest little refuge, it had gradually been transformed into a flamboyant white-and-gold pavilion with domes and minarets, a dizzying blend of Indian, Moorish and Chinese styles that called to mind a supercolossal *pièce montée*. What Carême, with his taste for the classical, thought of this architectural mishmash is unrecorded. The kitchen of the pavilion, in any event, was a gleaming expanse, elaborately equipped to satisfy any whims of the Regent's considerable appetite. But among the "ponderous *batterie* of polished copper . . . the troops of chuckleheaded little English aides . . . and hecatombs of constitutional English beef," as the Irish novelist and social historian Lady Morgan put it, Carême felt ill at ease. The soggy English climate depressed him, and the task of elevating and organizing the English cuisine proved more than even he could manage. As Lady Morgan explained: "He found that he had a vocabulary to invent, a grammar to compose; and he shrank from the Herculean labor imposed upon him." After only eight months he retreated to France. Within a year, acceding to Czar Alexander's pleas to take charge of the imperial Russian cuisine, Carême journeyed to St. Petersburg. He did not like it any better than Brighton, nor did he approve of the Russian style of table service. The Russians served their meals course by course, dish by dish, instead of spreading dozens of dishes on the table all at once, as the French did at that time. This meant that Carême's most elaborate cold dishes had to be carved in the kitchen instead of being brought to the table intact. The whole point of constructing a beautiful dish was lost.

Carême stuck it out in the Russian capital for a while and then went home for good. In the years that followed, his last employer made up in regal tastes what she lacked in royal blood. The Baroness Rothschild maintained one of the most luxurious households on the Continent. The ubiquitous Lady Morgan reported that the Rothschild dining room in Paris "was an elegant oblong pavilion of Greek marble, refreshed by fountains that shot in the air through scintillating streams, and the table, covered with the beautiful and picturesque dessert, emitted no odor that was not in perfect conformity with the freshness of the scene and fervor of the season." With so discerning an employer, Carême's art came to full flower. Under his direction, only the most delicate and beautifully decorated foods were served at the Rothschild table, and he was able to achieve his highest refinements of cuisine. Lady Morgan recorded that there were "no highly spiced sauces, no dark-brown gravies, no flavor of cayenne and allspice, no tincture of catsup and walnut pickle."

Working for the Rothschilds gave Carême enough leisure time to devote to composing his books of recipes, menus and culinary techniques. He was still laboring over these works in 1833 when he died, "burned out by the flame of his genius and the charcoal of his rotisseries," as Laurent Tailhade, author of the *Little Breviary of Gourmandise,* put it.

Pictures of Carême show him to have been an unusually handsome man, with dark hair and penetrating eyes. In his writings, as in his personal manner, he could be pompous and vain. He once recorded that "Lord Stewart wrote to me to go with him to Vienna, as he could find no cook who reminded him of me." Another time he noted: "It was thus at the British Regent's house that I served for the first time my *brochet à la Régence* (pike) surrounded by a garnish composed of all types of fish. The Royal host and his noble guests remarked on it and I was complimented. This flattering encouragement made me realize how right I had been in my judgment."

This lack of modesty was understandable, for Carême was indisputably a genius. The new elegance and order he brought to the French cuisine raised it to classic status. At French banquets before his time hundreds of dishes were prepared and diners were not served individually but ate as much as they wanted from whatever dishes were within reach. The menu for a banquet for 100 people, designed by a celebrated chef of the early 18th Century, Vincent la Chapelle, called for 322 different dishes, not including 66 plates of oysters, 66 salads and 30 sauces. These foods were served on enormous platters, and even though they were brought to the dining room in relays, the platters cluttered the table. Moreover, the food was not arranged in any particular order. La Chapelle tried to dispel the confusion by diagramming the table according to the sizes and shapes of the platters, but this failed to enlighten the waiters as to where a particular meat, fowl or fish should be placed. The result was an overpowering jumble of food. "I cannot keep myself from remarking to the reader how much the tables of the time of M. Vincent la Chapelle were confusedly loaded with platters," Carême wrote in *Le Maître d'hôtel français.* "It seems to me that distaste must have overcome the sensitive guests as soon as they arrived at the table."

Carême's own style was based on a particular trend of his times. After the chaos of the French Revolution, artists in every field yearned for the disciplined forms of ancient Rome and Greece. A classical revival followed naturally. In Paris mammoth new buildings such as the Pantheon and the Madeleine featured Corinthian porticoes and Roman columns; indeed, the main thrust of Napoleon's ambitious construction program for his capital, when he was Emperor of France, was to transform the city of Paris into a latter-day Rome, complete with triumphal arches and commemorative columns.

It was this same neoclassical urge that moved Carême to vow to bring order and symmetry out of the hodgepodge of the French cuisine. True, his contemporaries continued to be addicted to the old customs of serving scores of dishes and decorating tables with temples, ruins and trophies, and Carême wholly gratified them. But he insisted that every item on a table be balanced by an appropriate counterpart and that the whole arrangement be as symmetrical as possible.

"I want order and taste," he said, explaining his architectural approach. "A well displayed meal is enhanced one hundred per cent in my eyes . . . a vase must be served with an elegant basket, a lyre must be accompanied by a harp, an antique helmet with a modern one, a war trophy with a navy trophy, a hut with a rustic grotto, a Chinese pavilion with a Turkish pavilion, a cascade with a cascade."

Carême further insisted that not only the table decorations but the food itself be presented as attractively as possible. His views sound less

URBAIN DUBOIS
(1818-1901)

Dubois popularized the Russian table service in France in the 1860s. Until then, all dishes for a meal —hot and cold—were arrayed on the table at the same time. Under the Russian style, meals were served course-by-course, and dishes were brought directly from the kitchen to the individual diners.

like a set of opinions than a series of royal decrees. He declared, for example, that emerald was the perfect color for cold dishes, and that a cold dish should be "accompanied by pretty mayonnaise sauces, one white and the other a pretty pistachio with ravigote and Montpellier butter which is a tender green and with a sharp taste." He went on to say that large entrées should be "decorated with art and as simply as possible with truffles, the white meat of fowl, scarlet beef tongue; jelly cutouts that are well placed to form rich and elegant borders. . . . Once all of these elements have been achieved, one must complement these elements with very white pedestals . . . with a simple but elegant decoration, lightly colored aspics that are quite transparent, using only two colors, foie gras loaves or loaves of fowl or game smooth and fleshy and well glazed and decorated with jelly; galantines garnished with good forcemeat."

A striking example of Carême's gift for meticulous planning appears on pages 76-77, his own drawing of a buffet intended for 100 people. At first glance modern eyes may find the scheme a monstrosity. But a closer look will reveal what Carême was up to, and how his passion for architectural balance and order influenced the classic cuisine. For the essential feature of this drawing is its symmetry, the precision with which every item—every temple, ruin, fish, duck—on one side is perfectly countered by a corresponding item on the other side. This careful structuring is a key point of classic cooking.

As gargantuan as some of Carême's table displays may seem today, they should be viewed in the context of his own era and the one preceding it. By contrast with La Chapelle's menus, Carême's were modest. La Chapelle served three times as many dishes as Carême, and his use of large platters and plates further complicated matters. "Given the diameter of the plates," said Carême of La Chapelle's helter-skelter arrangements, "there were only 18 inches for each person, which must have been extremely bothersome at the table."

Carême introduced smaller platters and plates, spacing them more widely around the table to allow the guests more room. He also keyed his table arrangements to his menus. Entrées and side dishes that were to be eaten together were marked with the same numbers—for the guidance of waiters serving them; dishes that contained color were indicated so they could form a harmonious pattern on the table, and sweets were marked so they could be placed at a distance from other pastry concoctions. Henceforth waiters were able to bring dishes to the table in sequence, arrange them tastefully, and group those that were to be eaten together.

Carême not only revolutionized the old disorderly methods of displaying and serving but also explored new ways to refine the quality and appearance of the food itself. Before his time chefs had been known to serve beef, fish and poultry on the same plate. One instance of Carême's culinary breakthrough in this regard was the *brochet à la Régence* he created while working for England's Prince Regent. In preparing this dish, based on pike, he devised the unprecedented idea of garnishing the pike with other kinds of fish to produce a subtle blend of textures and flavors. To this day compatibility of textures and flavors is a cardinal principle of classic cooking and menu planning, one that holds true not only for a single dish but for the entire sequence of dishes. Everything that is served, from the start of a meal to its finish, must contribute to a harmonious whole.

Carême also made an art and a science of recipe writing, bringing both poetic feeling and precision to his instructions for the preparation of great dishes. Even now, his recipe for a *chartreuse*—that glorious partridge and cabbage dish—is a model of exactitude and at the same time a revelation of Carême's intense feeling for food.

"Among all the entrées that one might serve," he says, "the *chartreuse* is surely the queen. It is made of roots and vegetables but is only perfect in May, June, July and August, that smiling and propitious season, where everything in nature is renewed and seems to invite us to apply new care to our work. . . ."

Describing the garnish for this elaborate, carefully prepared dish, he goes on: "Sometimes asparagus tips are used to decorate the *chartreuse* as it is being molded, as are green beans and large peas; but I think this is a mistake, because no matter what we do, these vegetables will not retain their natural green, and this is easy to understand if we consider that they are cooked for an hour in a double boiler, which always makes their beautiful green spring color unrecognizable.

"I think I have avoided this inconvenience by preparing the top of my *chartreuses* separately. When they are sauced, I place on them a pretty rose or a double star made from roots and green vegetables which produces a charming effect, especially as these vegetables are placed in relief at the top of the *chartreuse*. . . . The carrots should be as thick as the asparagus and 18 lines long. Cook them as you did for the *chartreuse*. Then place in the middle a beautiful mushroom, or a turnip pared round, or a truffle. To garnish the base of the *chartreuse*, surround it with a chain of little turnips shaped like pears and glazed. . . . This type of accessory makes these beautiful entrées infinitely richer and more elegant than they normally are."

All of Carême's innovations—and much more besides—were set down in his books. In *L'Art de la cuisine au dix-neuvième siècle*, he offered hundreds of recipes, together with detailed explanations of the techniques and pitfalls of classic cooking. In *Le Pâtissier royal parisien*, he compiled an exhaustive list of classic dishes that would serve future chefs as a virtual encyclopedia of cuisine. In other works, he chronicled the history of cooking and provided menus for every day in the year, telling what foods are best at what seasons; he discussed the preparation of sauces, sweets, cold dishes and *pièces montées*, garnishes and decorations, the problems of marketing and provisioning and the organization of the kitchen. No culinary concern escaped him, including such matters as how to get rid of bugs in the kitchen and what kind of wood makes the best kitchen table (beechwood, "because of its whiteness").

For half a century after Carême died his refining influence on French cooking persisted, although the classic cuisine continued to be marked by ornateness and extravagance. Then, as life in France became more industrialized and democratic, a new culinary revolution began which gave the cuisine its modern, simplified form and brought to the forefront another great master, Escoffier.

Potage Bagration
CREAM OF VEAL SOUP WITH MACARONI AND CHEESE

Prepare the velouté, following the directions on page 36 but using a 2- to 3-quart saucepan to hold the doubled quantity of ingredients.

In a heavy 12-inch skillet, melt 3 tablespoons of butter over moderate heat. When the foam subsides add the veal and, turning it frequently, sauté for 5 minutes, or until it is lightly colored, but not brown. Remove the veal with a slotted spoon, chop coarsely and return to the pan.

Stirring constantly with a wire whisk, gradually add the velouté, the quart of *fond blanc* and salt, and bring to a simmer over moderate heat. Reduce the heat to the lowest possible point and cook uncovered for 30 minutes, whisking the soup occasionally to keep it smooth.

Strain the contents of the skillet through a fine sieve set over a heavy 3- to 4-quart saucepan, pressing down hard on the pieces of veal with the back of a spoon to extract all their juice before discarding them. Combine the egg yolks and cream in a bowl and beat them together with the whisk.

Whisking the soup constantly, pour in the egg-yolk-and-cream mixture in a slow, thin stream. Stir over low heat for 2 or 3 minutes until the soup thickens lightly, but do not let it come to a boil. Add the macaroni and continue to simmer, still stirring until the pasta is heated through. Remove the pan from the heat and swirl in the 2 tablespoons of butter bits. Taste for seasoning. Pour the soup into a heated tureen or individual soup plates. Serve the cheese separately.

NOTE: To make a *potage crème de volaille* (cream of chicken soup), substitute chicken meat and stock for veal and veal stock. Follow the recipe exactly but omit the macaroni and the cheese.

Consommé de volaille royale
CHICKEN CONSOMMÉ WITH CUSTARD GARNISH

Preheat the oven to 300°. With a pastry brush, spread the softened butter over the bottom and sides of an 8-inch-square glass baking dish.

With a whisk or a rotary or electric beater, beat the egg and egg yolks together in a deep bowl. Beat in the cream, chicken stock, nutmeg, pepper and salt and pour into the buttered dish. Place the dish in a roasting pan set in the middle of the oven. Add enough boiling water to the pan to reach about halfway up the sides of the dish. Bake for 20 minutes, or until a knife inserted in the center comes out clean. Cool to room temperature, then refrigerate until the custard (*royale*) is thoroughly chilled.

To unmold the *royale*, run a spatula around the sides of the dish and dip the bottom in hot water for a few seconds. Place an inverted plate on top of the dish and, grasping plate and dish together firmly, turn them over. Rap the plate on a table and the *royale* should slide out easily.

Bring the consommé to a simmer. With a truffle cutter or a knife, cut the *royale* into decorative shapes. Place the *royale* garnish in a heated tureen or individual soup plates and pour in a little consommé. Let the garnish heat for a minute, then add the remaining consommé and serve.

To serve 6 to 8

SAUCE VELOUTÉ

1 quart *fond blanc de veau* or *fond blanc de volaille (pages 31 and 33)*, or substitute 1 quart canned chicken stock, chilled, then degreased

8 tablespoons clarified butter *(page 34)*

¾ cup flour

SOUP

3 tablespoons unsalted butter plus 2 tablespoons unsalted butter, chilled and cut into ½-inch bits

2 pounds lean boneless veal, preferably shoulder, trimmed of fat and cut into ½-inch cubes

1 quart *fond blanc de veau* or *fond blanc de volaille (pages 31 and 33)*, or substitute 1 quart canned chicken stock, chilled, then degreased

½ teaspoon salt

3 egg yolks

½ cup heavy cream

1 cup cooked macaroni, cut into ¼-inch lengths (½ cup uncooked)

1 cup freshly grated imported Parmesan cheese

To serve 8

1 teaspoon butter, softened

1 whole egg

2 egg yolks

¼ cup heavy cream

¼ cup *fond blanc de volaille (page 31)*, or substitute ¼ cup canned chicken stock, chilled, then degreased

A pinch of ground nutmeg, preferably freshly grated

A pinch of freshly ground white pepper

⅛ teaspoon salt

Consommé de fond blanc de volaille (page 34)

The Queen of All Entrées

Antonin Carême, founder of the classic cuisine, called the *chartreuse* "the queen" of all the entrées. He sketched many beautiful designs for this elaborate dish, including the one executed here. The essential ingredients for his recipe are simple: cabbages, other vegetables and partridges, wild game or poultry. But what lends the dish its regal quality is its imaginative decoration. The *chartreuse* is crowned with sautéed onions and garnished with slices of sausage and bacon topped with more sautéed onions. (A simpler model and its recipe appear on the following pages.)

4 one-pound oven-ready young
   partridges
Salt
Freshly ground black pepper
4 to 5 tablespoons melted clarified
   butter *(page 34)*, plus 6
   tablespoons unsalted butter,
   softened, plus 2 tablespoons
   unsalted butter, chilled and cut
   into ¼-inch bits
½ cup dry white wine
½ cup fresh green peas (about ½
   pound unshelled), or substitute
   ½ cup frozen peas
½ pound fresh green string beans,
   trimmed, washed and cut into
   1½-inch lengths
2 medium-sized white turnips, each
   about 2½ inches in diameter,
   peeled and cut into strips about
   1½ inches long, ½ inch wide
   and ¼ inch thick
3 large carrots, scraped and cut into
   strips about 1½ inches long, ½
   inch wide and ¼ inch thick
4 medium-sized heads Savoy
   cabbage (about 2 pounds each)
1½ pounds lean mildly cured salt
   pork in one piece
The partridge necks, hearts,
   gizzards and livers
½ cup finely chopped onion
½ teaspoon finely chopped garlic
½ cup finely chopped carrots
½ cup finely chopped celery
2 sprigs fresh thyme or ½ teaspoon
   crumbled dry thyme
2 whole cloves
1 medium-sized bay leaf
6 whole black peppercorns
2 cups *fond blanc de volaille (page
   31)*, or substitute 2 cups canned
   chicken stock, chilled then
   degreased
1½ pounds *saucisson à l'ail,* or
   substitute 1½ pounds *cotechino*
   or *kielbasa (see Glossary)*
16 medium-sized boiling potatoes,
   trimmed as in *filet de boeuf
   Richelieu, page 138*
2 teaspoons finely chopped parsley

Chartreuse de perdreaux
PARTRIDGES MOLDED WITH CABBAGE AND DECORATED WITH VEGETABLES

The "Chartreuse de perdreaux" is named for La Grande Chartreuse Convent near Grenoble—where the entrée was invented many centuries ago by the vegetarian Carthusian monks. Originally a chartreuse was made solely of vegetables, cooked in a mold. Over the years, the term came to be applied to similarly molded compositions that included meat, game birds or poultry.

Preheat the oven to 425°. Sprinkle the partridge cavities lightly with the salt and a few grindings of pepper, and truss the birds neatly with white kitchen string *(see Recipe Booklet)*. With a pastry brush, coat the entire outside surface of each partridge evenly with 3 or 4 tablespoons of the clarified butter. Lay the birds on their backs side by side on a rack set in a shallow roasting pan. Then roast in the middle of the oven for about 15 to 20 minutes, or until they are golden brown, brushing them once or twice with the remaining clarified butter. Transfer them to a plate, cut off the trussing strings, and with a long, sharp knife slice each bird in half lengthwise. With scissors, remove the main carcass bones, leaving the legs and wings intact. Set the birds and bones aside.

Lower the oven heat to 350°. Pour off the fat remaining in the roasting pan and in its place add the white wine. Bring to a boil on the top of the stove over high heat, scraping in the brown bits clinging to the bottom and sides of the pan. Strain the sauce through a sieve into a bowl and set it aside.

Cook the fresh peas, green beans, turnip and carrot strips in the following fashion: Drop the fresh peas into 2 quarts of lightly salted boiling water, boil briskly for about 8 to 10 minutes, then scoop them out with a slotted spoon and drop them into a bowl of cold water to set their color. (Frozen peas need only be thoroughly defrosted and drained.) When cool, transfer the peas to another bowl and set aside. Add the green beans to the same saucepan of boiling water and cook for 8 to 10 minutes until they are slightly tender. Scoop the beans into a sieve, run cold water over them and set them aside in a separate bowl. Finally, drop the turnip and carrot strips into the boiling water and boil for 8 to 10 minutes, or until the vegetables are tender. Then scoop them into a bowl of cold water and reserve separately.

Remove the tough or bruised outer leaves of the cabbages, wash the heads under cold running water, and cut each head lengthwise into quarters. Blanch the quarters by dropping them into boiling water for 1 minute, then place them in a colander and run cold water over them.

Combine the salt pork and 1 quart of cold water in a 2- to 3-quart saucepan, bring to a boil over high heat, and boil for 3 minutes. Drain the pork and run cold water over it. Then pat it dry with paper towels.

In a heavy 10-quart enameled cast-iron casserole, cook the salt pork over moderate heat for 4 or 5 minutes until it is lightly browned on all sides. Stir in the reserved partridge bones, necks, hearts, gizzards and livers, the onion, garlic, chopped carrots, celery, thyme, cloves, bay leaf and peppercorns, and continue cooking until the partridge pieces are delicately colored and the vegetables soften slightly. Set the cabbage quarters side by side over the meat-and-vegetable mixture, pour in the chicken stock and bring to a boil over high heat. Cover tightly and braise in the middle of the oven for 1 hour and 45 minutes.

Prick the sausages in 5 or 6 places with the point of a small skewer or sharp knife and add them to the casserole. Braise tightly covered for 30 minutes longer.

Transfer the sausages and salt pork to a cutting board, and place the cabbage quarters on a large plate or platter. Strain the liquid remaining in the casserole through a fine sieve set over a saucepan, pressing down hard on the remaining vegetables and partridge pieces with the back of a spoon to extract all their juices before discarding them. Stir in the reserved sauce from the roasted partridges, then skim the fat from the surface of the liquid. Boil briskly until the sauce is reduced to about 1½ cups and then set it aside.

To assemble the *chartreuse de perdreaux,* raise the oven temperature to 450°. With your fingers, spread the remaining 6 tablespoons of softened butter generously and evenly over the bottom and sides of a 5-quart ovenproof bowl. If the butter is very soft, refrigerate the bowl for several minutes until the butter becomes firm.

With a sharp knife, skin the sausages and cut them diagonally into ovals slightly less than ¼ inch thick. Line the bottom of the buttered bowl with a slightly overlapping ring of sausage ovals, then cover the sides with alternating rows of beans, carrot strips, peas and turnip strips,

The vegetable mosaic that envelopes a *chartreuse de perdreaux (below)* is made up of alternating rows of green peas and turnip, string bean and carrot strips. The pattern is assembled by pressing each vegetable piece firmly in place against the side of a bowl lavishly coated with butter *(above).* For a fancier effect, the vegetables may be cut even more precisely and arranged in a more complex design.

pressing them gently into the butter to secure them. Spread half of the cabbage in a layer over the entire inside of the bowl, being careful not to disturb the arrangement you have just created. Press the leaves down gently. Prop the partridge halves on end around the sides of the bowl. Cut the salt pork into slices ¼ inch thick. Stand a slice against each half bird and set all but 12 of the remaining slices of the sausage at random around the inside of the bowl. Fill the bowl with the remaining cabbage, pressing it down gently over the birds. (Drape foil over the remaining sausage and salt pork slices to keep them warm.)

Cover the bowl tightly with foil and set it into a large, shallow pan. Place the pan in the middle of the oven and pour in enough boiling water to come 1½ inches up the sides of the bowl. Bake the *chartreuse* for 15 to 20 minutes. Meanwhile, drop the potatoes into enough lightly salted boiling water in a saucepan to cover them completely and boil briskly until they are tender. Drain the potatoes in a sieve or colander. Return them to the dry saucepan, cover and keep them warm off the heat.

To unmold and serve the *chartreuse de perdreaux,* remove the foil and place an inverted heated serving plate over the bowl. Grasping plate and bowl together firmly, carefully invert them. The mold should slide out easily. If any of the decorations stick to the sides of the bowl, pick them off and restore them to their original places on the mold. Arrange the remaining sausage and salt pork slices around the mold and place a potato on top of each sausage. Sprinkle the potatoes with the parsley. Reheat the reserved sauce briefly, stirring frequently. Taste for seasoning, and swirl in the 2 tablespoons of butter bits. Pour the sauce into a sauceboat and serve it at once with the *chartreuse.*

Bavarois Clermont
VANILLA-FLAVORED BAVARIAN CREAM WITH GLACÉED CHESTNUTS

BAVAROIS (BAVARIAN CREAM) : Brush the inside of a 2½-quart decorative mold with oil and remove the excess with a paper towel. Sprinkle the gelatin into ⅓ cup of water in a heatproof cup. When the gelatin has softened for 2 or 3 minutes, set the cup in a skillet of simmering water and stir over low heat until the gelatin dissolves. Remove from the heat but leave the cup of gelatin in the water to keep warm. In a heavy 3-quart enameled-iron or copper saucepan, bring 3 cups of milk and the vanilla bean to a boil over moderate heat. Cover and set aside.

With a wire whisk or a rotary or electric beater, beat the 5 egg yolks and 1½ cups of sugar together in a deep bowl for 3 or 4 minutes, or until the yolks fall in a slowly dissolving ribbon when the beater is lifted from the bowl. Remove the vanilla bean from the milk and reserve it. Whisking constantly, pour the milk into the egg yolks in a slow thin stream. When thoroughly blended, return the mixture to the saucepan. Stir over low heat until the custard thickens enough to coat a spoon evenly or reaches 180° on a candy thermometer. Do not let it come to a boil or the custard will curdle. Add the gelatin and stir until it is completely absorbed. Strain the custard through a fine sieve into a stainless-steel bowl.

With a wire whisk or a rotary or electric beater, whip the cream in a chilled bowl until it forms almost firm peaks. Then set the bowl of cus-

To serve 10 to 12

BAVAROIS
Vegetable oil
2 envelopes unflavored gelatin
⅓ cup water
3 cups milk
1 vanilla bean
5 egg yolks
1½ cups sugar
3 cups heavy cream, chilled
1 cup finely chopped *marrons glacés*
  (glacéed chestnuts, not the
  chestnuts packed in syrup)

tard into a larger bowl filled with crushed ice or ice cubes and water and stir until the custard is just cool. Do not let it chill enough to become the least bit lumpy.

Remove the bowl of custard from the ice and scoop the whipped cream over it. With a rubber spatula, fold the two quickly but gently and thoroughly together, using an over-under cutting motion rather than a stirring motion, until no trace of white remains. Fold in the chestnuts, then pour the mixture into the oiled mold and smooth the top with the spatula. Cover with foil or plastic wrap and refrigerate for at least 6 hours, or preferably overnight until the Bavarian cream is firm.

CRÈME ANGLAISE (ENGLISH CUSTARD): Combine 2 cups of milk and the reserved vanilla bean in a 3-quart enameled saucepan. Bring to a boil and immediately remove the milk from the heat. Cover and set aside.

Beat the 4 egg yolks and ½ cup of sugar together with a wire whisk or a rotary or electric beater until they are thick enough to form a slowly dissolving ribbon when the beater is lifted. Remove the vanilla bean and pour the hot milk gradually into the yolks, whisking all the while. Return the mixture to the saucepan and stir over low heat until the *crème anglaise* thickens lightly. (Do not let it come near a boil or it will curdle.) Pour the *crème anglaise* into a bowl, and cool to room temperature. Cover tightly and refrigerate until ready to serve.

CRÈME ANGLAISE
2 cups milk
1 vanilla bean (re-use the bean above)
4 egg yolks
½ cup sugar

MARRONS CARAMÉLISÉS (CARAMELIZED CHESTNUTS): In a heavy 2- to 3-quart saucepan, bring 2 cups of sugar, 2 cups of water and the cocoa to a boil over high heat, stirring until the sugar dissolves. Bring the syrup to a boil, then reduce the heat to low and simmer the syrup for 25 to 30 minutes until it reaches 300° on a candy thermometer. As soon as the syrup reaches the proper state, remove the pan from the heat and place it in a pot half-filled with hot water to keep the caramel fluid and warm.

To make each caramelized chestnut, impale one chestnut half on a thin long skewer. Holding the skewer vertically, submerge the chestnut in the hot syrup and twirl it around until it is heavily coated with caramel. Lift the chestnut and, holding the skewer horizontally over wax paper, let the excess caramel drip off. The caramel will form a thin iciclelike thread as it drips. With scissors, keep this thread to a length of about 6 inches, cutting it repeatedly until the caramel stops dripping and becomes firm.

Place the chestnut on a sheet of buttered aluminum foil and carefully pull out the skewer. Repeat the entire procedure with all of the remaining chestnut halves. Set the caramelized nuts aside.

MARRONS CARAMÉLISÉS
2 cups sugar
2 cups water
2 tablespoons unsweetened imported cocoa
7 whole *marrons glacés* (glacéed chestnuts), 6 cut in half and rounded with a knife and one reserved

FINAL ASSEMBLY: To unmold the *bavarois,* run a thin knife or spatula carefully around the inside rim of the mold and briefly dip the bottom of the mold into hot water. Wipe the mold dry, place a chilled serving plate upside down over the top and, grasping the mold and plate securely together, quickly invert them. The *bavarois* should slide out easily.

Spoon the chilled *crème anglaise* around the base of the *bavarois* and arrange the caramelized chestnuts in a ring surrounding it. If you like you may decorate the *bavarois* or outline the details of its form by piping melted semisweet chocolate onto it with a pastry tube fitted with a very small plain pastry tip. A few spoons of chopped *marrons glacés* may be stirred into the *crème anglaise.* Place the remaining whole glacéed chestnut decoratively on the top of the *bavarois* and serve.

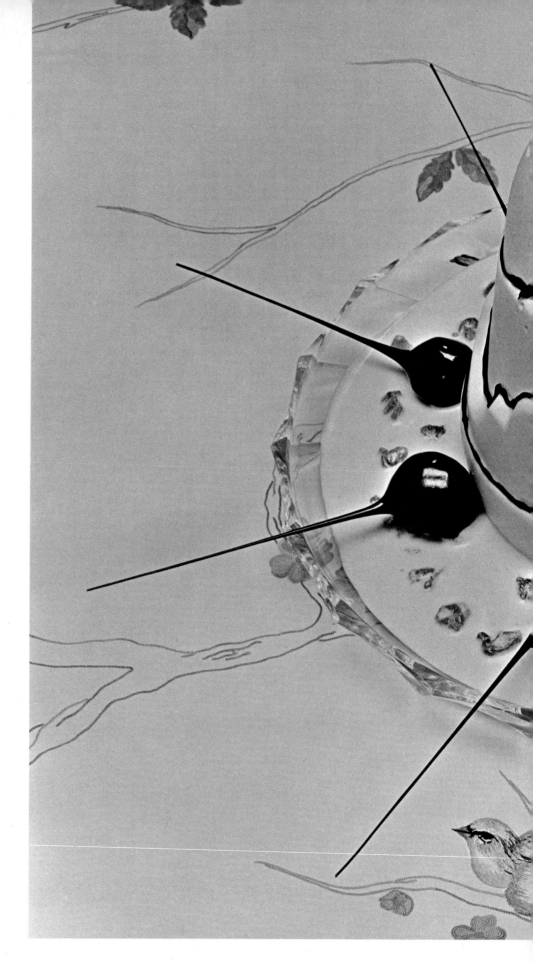

The *bavarois Clermont,* a molded vanilla-flavored Bavarian cream with glacéed chestnuts *(Recipe Index),* is believed to have made its appearance before the days of Antonin Carême. To decorate the dish, chestnuts are dipped in hot caramel, then held up in the air while a thin strand of caramel descends from them and hardens like an icicle. The hardened caramel forms the "spokes" radiating out from this dessert.

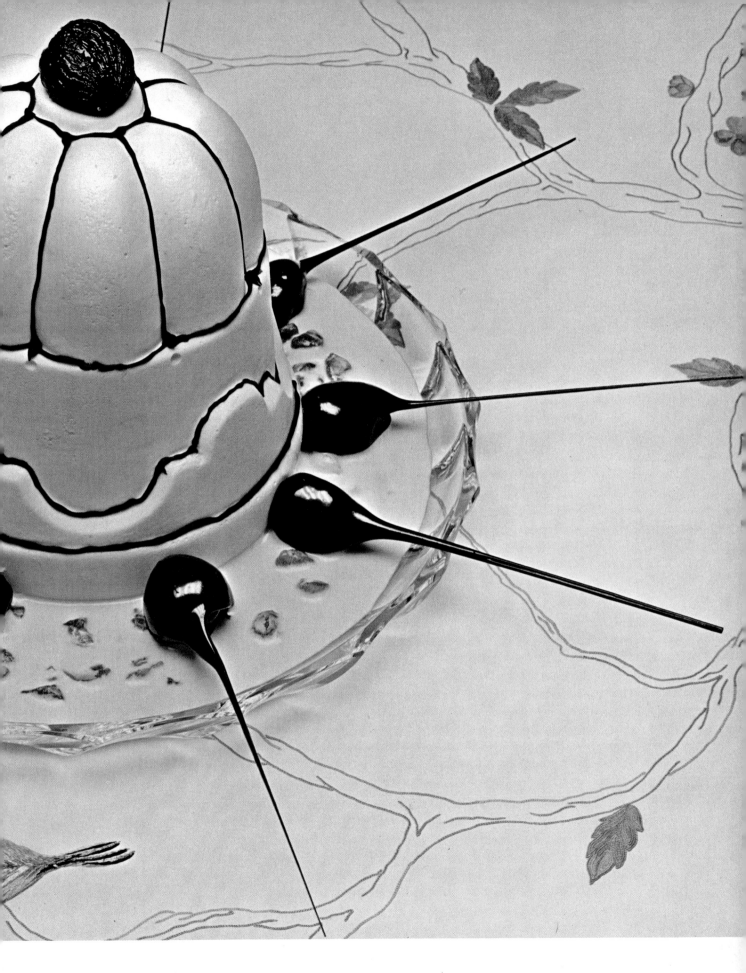

To serve 10

PÂTE SUCRÉE

1 cup plus 2 tablespoons all-purpose
   flour
1 tablespoon sugar
¼ teaspoon salt
6 tablespoons unsalted butter,
   chilled and cut into ½-inch bits
   plus 1 tablespoon butter, softened
2 tablespoons vegetable shortening,
   chilled and cut into ½-inch bits
3 to 4 tablespoons ice water

PÂTE À CHOUX

6 eggs
1½ cups water
12 tablespoons unsalted butter, cut
   into ½-inch bits plus 1
   tablespoon butter, softened
1 tablespoon sugar
¼ teaspoon salt
1½ cups plus 2 tablespoons all-
   purpose flour

Gâteau Saint-Honoré
CREAM PUFF AND PASTRY CREAM CAKE

PÂTE SUCRÉE (SWEET PASTRY): In a large mixing bowl combine 1 cup of flour, 1 tablespoon of sugar, ¼ teaspoon of salt, the 6 tablespoons of butter bits and the vegetable shortening. With your fingertips rub the flour and fat together until they look like flakes of coarse meal. Do not over-blend or let the mixture become oily.

Pour 3 tablespoons of ice water over the mixture all at once, toss together lightly and gather the dough into a ball. If the dough crumbles, add up to 1 tablespoon more ice water by drops until the particles adhere. Dust the pastry dough with a little flour and wrap it in wax paper. Refrigerate for at least 30 minutes before using.

With a pastry brush, spread the tablespoon of softened butter over a large baking sheet. Sprinkle 2 tablespoons of flour over the butter, tipping the sheet to coat it evenly. Then invert the sheet and rap it sharply to remove the excess flour.

On a lightly floured surface, pat the dough into a rough circle about 1 inch thick. Dust a little flour over and under it and roll it out, from the center to within an inch of the far edge of the pastry. Lift the dough and turn it clockwise about 2 inches; roll again from the center to within an inch or so of the far edge. Repeat—lifting, turning, rolling—until you have created a rough circle about 10 to 11 inches in diameter and no more than ¼ inch thick.

Roll the dough loosely over the rolling pin, lift it and unroll it carefully on the buttered baking sheet. With a pastry wheel or sharp knife, and using a pie tin or plate as a guide, cut the dough into a 9-inch round. Remove and discard the excess dough, then prick the pastry all over with the tines of a table fork, but do not pierce through it completely. Refrigerate the pastry while you make the *pâte à choux*.

PÂTE À CHOUX (PUFF PASTE): Break one egg into a small bowl, beat lightly with a fork and set aside. In a heavy 2-quart saucepan, bring 1½ cups of water, 12 tablespoons of butter bits, 1 tablespoon of sugar and ¼ teaspoon of salt to a boil over high heat, stirring occasionally. As soon as the butter has completely melted, pour in the 1½ cups of flour all at once, remove the pan from the heat, and beat vigorously with a wooden spoon for 2 or 3 minutes until the paste moves freely with the spoon and pulls away from the bottom and sides of the pan in a mass.

Use the spoon to make a well in the center of the paste. Break an egg into the well and beat it into the paste. When this egg has been completely absorbed, add the 4 remaining eggs, one at a time—beating well after each egg is added. The finished paste should be smooth, shiny and just thick enough to fall slowly from the spoon in a thick strand when it is lifted out of the pan. To achieve this consistency, add as much of the reserved beaten egg as necessary, beating it in by the tablespoonful. (The paste, covered with plastic wrap, may be safely kept at room temperature for several hours before baking if you like.)

When you are ready to bake the *pâte à choux*, preheat the oven to 425°. Brush a large baking sheet with the tablespoon of softened butter. Sprinkle 2 tablespoons of flour over the sheet, invert and rap the sheet sharply to remove the excess flour.

Threads of spun sugar wreathe the candle-decked *gâteau Saint-Honoré (below)*—itself a fanciful composition of caramel-coated cream puffs, liqueur-laced pastry cream and whipped cream ribbons assembled on a crisp pastry base. (Fittingly, the *gâteau* is named for the patron saint of bakers.) As the pictures at right show, spinning sugar is a process straight out of Disneyland. A shaker made from a cut-down whisk or a nail-studded wooden square is dipped into hot boiled syrup. As it is whipped and whirled through the air, the syrup spins off the points of the shaker as shining filaments of candy.

Spoon the *pâte à choux* into a pastry bag fitted with a ½-inch plain tip and pipe the paste onto the *pâte sucrée* base, creating a ring about ½ inch wide and ¼ inch or so from the outside edges of the base. Pipe the remaining *pâte à choux* onto the buttered baking sheet into puffs about 1½ inches in diameter and 1 inch high, spacing them approximately 2 inches apart. (There should be about 15.)

Place the baking sheets side by side on the middle shelf of the oven if it is wide enough to accommodate them. If the oven is too narrow, bake the *pâte sucrée* base first, then bake the individual cream puffs later. Keep the puffs at room temperature while waiting. In either case use the following sequence of oven temperatures. Bake at 425° for 8 minutes, reduce the heat to 350° and, with the point of a small knife, prick the bubbles that have formed in the *pâte sucrée*. Continue baking for 15 to 20 minutes longer, or until the crust base is golden brown and the ring and puffs are firm and dry to the touch. Turn off the oven and let the pastry rest for 15 minutes to allow it to become dry and crisp. With a wide metal spatula, carefully slide the crust base and the individual puffs onto wire cake racks to cool to room temperature.

CARAMEL: When the base and puffs have cooled completely, prepare the caramel. In a 1- to 1½-quart enameled cast-iron or copper saucepan, bring the 2 cups of sugar, ½ cup of water and cream of tartar to a boil over moderate heat, stirring until the sugar dissolves. Boil the syrup briskly until it turns a rich golden tealike color. This may take 10 minutes or more. Watch carefully and do not let the sugar burn; it colors very quickly. (As the syrup bubbles up around the sides of the pan, brush the sugar crystals back down with a hair bristled [not nylon] pastry brush that has been dipped into cold water.)

As soon as the syrup reaches the proper color, remove the pan from the heat and place it in a wide pot half filled with hot water. This will keep the caramel fluid and warm.

Working quickly but carefully, pick up one puff at a time with tongs and submerge the top in the caramel. Hold the puff in place over the ring on the pastry crust and let the excess caramel drip off the puff onto the ring. When the caramel stops flowing freely, carefully set it glazed side up over the drops of caramel on the ring. (The whole procedure is somewhat like anchoring a candle in hot wax.) Place the glazed puffs side by side completely around the ring. There should be several puffs left over; glaze one of the extra puffs to decorate the center of the cake and set it aside on a plate. The cake may now be kept at room temperature for 3 or 4 hours.

CRÈME SAINT-HONORÉ (SAINT-HONORÉ PASTRY CREAM): In a 2- to 3-quart enameled cast-iron or copper saucepan, heat the milk and vanilla bean over moderate heat until small bubbles appear around the edge of the pan. Remove the pan from the heat and cover to keep the milk warm.

With a wire whisk or a rotary or electric beater, beat the egg yolks and ½ cup of sugar together until the yolks are thick enough to fall in a ribbon when the beater is lifted from the bowl. Beating constantly, gradually sift in ⅓ cup of flour. When the flour is absorbed, remove the vanilla bean from the milk and pour in the warm milk in a thin stream, beating all the while. Immediately pour the mixture back into the saucepan.

CARAMEL
2 cups sugar
½ cup water
⅛ teaspoon cream of tartar

CRÈME SAINT-HONORÉ
2 cups milk
1 whole vanilla bean, or substitute
 2 teaspoons vanilla extract
6 egg yolks
½ cup sugar
⅓ cup flour
A pinch of salt
6 egg whites
¼ cup Grand Marnier or other
 orange-flavored liqueur
1 envelope unflavored gelatin
⅓ cup water
1½ cups heavy cream, chilled
½ cup confectioners' sugar

Stirring deeply along the sides and into the bottom of the pan with a whisk or a wooden spoon, bring to a simmer over moderate heat. Do not let the pastry cream come near a boil at any point, but simmer it long enough to remove any taste of raw flour, about 5 minutes. Remove the pan from the heat and strain the hot pastry cream into a large bowl.

Then, working quickly, add a pinch of salt to the egg whites in another bowl and, with a wire whisk or a rotary or electric beater, beat until they are just stiff enough to form unwavering peaks on the beater when it is lifted from the bowl. Scoop about ¼ of the egg whites at a time over the hot pastry cream, stirring after each addition until no trace of white shows. Stir in the Grand Marnier and set the pastry cream aside to cool to room temperature.

Complete the pastry cream no more than an hour before you plan to serve the cake. Sprinkle the gelatin into a heatproof measuring cup or small bowl filled with ⅓ cup of cold water. When the gelatin has softened for 2 or 3 minutes, set the cup or bowl in a small pan of simmering water and, stirring constantly, cook over low heat until the gelatin dissolves completely. Remove the pan from the heat but leave the cup or bowl of gelatin in the water to keep it warm.

With a wire whisk or a rotary or electric beater, whip 1½ cups of chilled heavy cream until it begins to thicken. Sprinkle in the ½ cup of confectioners' sugar and continue beating until the cream is stiff enough to form soft peaks on the beater when it is lifted from the bowl. Beat in the dissolved gelatin.

Scoop the whipped-cream mixture over the pastry cream and, with a rubber spatula, fold them together gently but thoroughly, using an over-under cutting motion rather than stirring. Taste for flavoring and refrigerate for at least 30 minutes.

CRÈME CHANTILLY (CHANTILLY CREAM): In a large chilled bowl, beat ½ cup of chilled heavy cream with a wire whisk or a rotary or electric beater until it begins to thicken. Sprinkle the top with 1 tablespoon of confectioners' sugar and ½ teaspoon of vanilla extract, and continue beating until the cream is very stiff and stands in firm peaks on the beater when it is lifted from the bowl. Refrigerate until ready to use.

FINAL ASSEMBLY: Carefully slide the puff-topped cake onto a serving plate with a large metal spatula.

With the point of a skewer gently make a hole near the base of each individual cream puff from the inside edge of the ring. Spoon one third of the pastry cream into a pastry bag fitted with a ¼-inch plain tip and carefully fill each puff with a little of the cream. To prevent the puffs from crushing or loosening at this stage, hold each one lightly with one hand while filling it with the other. (Fill the reserved glazed cream puff with *crème Saint-Honoré* and set it aside.)

Fill the center of the cake with the remaining *crème Saint-Honoré,* smoothing it evenly with a spatula and mounding the center slightly.

Decorate the top of the cake as fancifully as you like with the *crème Chantilly* piped through a pastry bag fitted with a star tip. Set the reserved cream puff in the center. If you like, surround the edge of the cake with spun sugar *(Recipe Index)*. (To serve *gâteau Saint-Honoré* as a birthday cake, insert a small candle in the center of each cream puff.)

CRÈME CHANTILLY
½ cup heavy cream, chilled
1 tablespoon confectioners' sugar
½ teaspoon vanilla extract

La bonne cuisine est la
base du véritable bonheur

A. Escoffier

Mai 1911

IV

King of Chefs, Chef of Kings

The celebrated classic chef Auguste Escoffier wears the *toque blanche* of his trade in this portrait, which is now displayed at the Escoffier Museum in his hometown of Villeneuve-Loubet, in southern France. Appropriately, the inscription reads "good cooking is the basis of true happiness."

Carême's most illustrious successor was Georges Auguste Escoffier, who was known in his own lifetime as the "king of chefs and chef of kings," and has been widely recognized since then as the greatest culinary artist of the modern age. Escoffier acknowledged the classic cuisine's debt to Carême and the bygone era when "every meal was a ceremony and a celebration." But the world was changing rapidly, the pace of life was accelerating and by the end of the 19th Century a culinary revolution was under way—with Escoffier carrying its banner.

The call was sounded by a young rebel named Prosper Montagné, who was himself to become one of the most celebrated chefs of French history. Montagné argued that everything that was not a part of the food itself—*pièces montées,* nonedible superfluous garnishes and decorations —should be discarded from the table. Nothing that did not contribute directly to the enjoyment of the food should be tolerated there.

Escoffier resisted this simplistic-sounding revolutionary doctrine at first. Montagné, he scoffed, was a mere *sous-chef,* an underling and an upstart. But then—largely through the persuasive powers of another outstanding chef, Philéas Gilbert—he became convinced of the rightness of Montagné's argument. And as so often happens, the convert became a zealot. Escoffier called for reform and refinement to bring the classic cuisine up to date in an age "when life is active, when a thousand worries of industry and business occupy the mind of man, and he can devote only a limited place to eating well."

Escoffier's creed became "tasteful simplicity," and he extended it to every area of the cuisine. He invented scores of outstanding new dishes, streamlined the art of decorating food, reduced menus to manageable proportions, speeded up service and organized his kitchens along more efficient lines.

Yet Escoffier, like Carême, made his greatest mark in his writings, which documented and codified the cuisine in its modern form. These works included *Le Livre des menus, Ma Cuisine* and *Le Guide culinaire* (which contained 5,000 recipes and was written in collaboration with Philéas Gilbert). They were to classic cooking what Blackstone was to the law. Once they appeared even the most complicated culinary arguments could readily be resolved. Chefs who disagreed could settle their differences by resorting to Escoffier instead of coming to blows.

Escoffier was born in 1846 in the picturesque Provençal village of Villeneuve-Loubet, 10 miles from Nice. His father was a blacksmith and tobacco grower, and the family lived in an ageless stone house that today is a brightly lighted museum in Escoffier's honor. To reach it, you walk along a narrow freshly washed street, then turn up a flight of stone stairs that is bordered in summer with rambler roses and hanging geraniums. The air is filled with the pungent scent of rosemary and thyme, and around midday you can smell the good warm odor of roasting meats waft-

Escoffier's inspired invention, *poularde Derby,* is a roasted chicken with rice, truffle and foie gras stuffing. The garnish is of truffles and cylinders of bread topped with foie gras and truffle slices.

ing upward from the neighborhood kitchens just as it must have in Escoffier's time. The three-story house has a trellised arch leading onto a terrace where stands a gnomelike ceramic figure of St. Fortunat, the patron saint of chefs. Inside the house one of the first things you notice is a deeply recessed fireplace with a spit large enough to accommodate a whole lamb. The fireplace holds a *crémaillère,* the maneuverable metal rod from which an iron *marmite* is suspended, and it was here no doubt that Escoffier was first exposed to good cooking.

People who knew Escoffier in those days later recalled him as an obedient, active child, handsome but slightly built. In this region of sunshine and olive trees, where Cézanne and Van Gogh produced many of their masterpieces, the young Escoffier preferred paint brushes and a palette to saucepans and *marmites,* but a career as an artist was not to be. For Escoffier's uncle owned a restaurant in Nice called the Français, and when the boy was 13, his father took him out of school and apprenticed him in the kitchen there.

Kitchens were cauldrons then—there was no electricity and stoves were fired by wood, charcoal and coal—but Escoffier thrived on his work and showed such an aptitude for cooking and kitchen management that he was hired by the nearby Hôtel Bellevue. While he was there, the owner

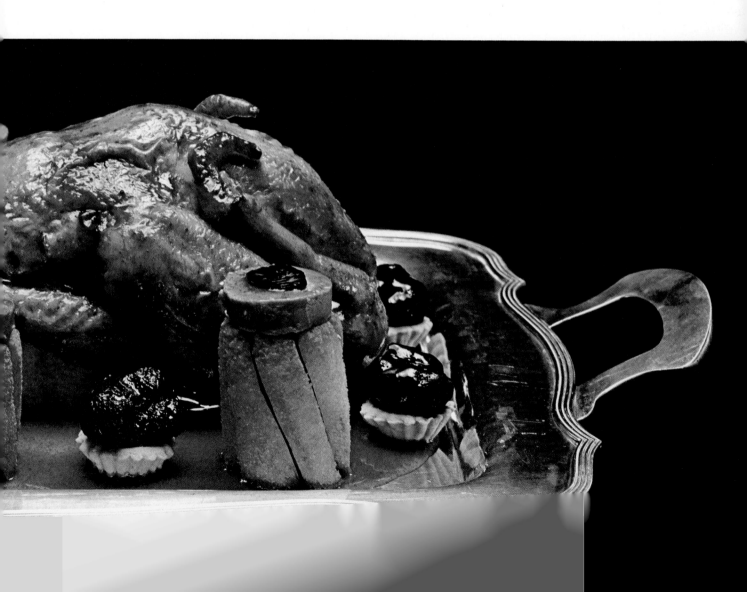

Chez Ritz

In the sumptuous turn-of-the-century setting of the Ritz Hotel in Paris, chic patrons such as these soon made the word "ritzy" a synonym for a snobbish and ostentatious life style.

of a fashionable Paris restaurant, Le Petit Moulin Rouge, offered him a job as *commis-rôtisseur* (apprentice roast cook). Since Paris was the center of the universe for any young, aspiring chef, Escoffier accepted. The year was 1865, he was 19, on the verge of manhood, and already he had created the mold that was to fit him for the rest of his days—gentleman from sole to crown, mild-mannered, soft-voiced and impeccably dressed. He was just over five feet tall, and according to one biographer wore special high heels "to put that much more distance between his head and the heat of the ovens."

A position at Le Petit Moulin Rouge was an auspicious beginning for a young man fresh from the provinces, but only a few months after Escoffier's arrival he was called to active army duty. For five months he was stationed in a barracks at Villefranche-sur-Mer, only a little over three miles from his old haunts in Nice, and he made the most of this happy accident. A *niçois* craftsman introduced him to the art of making wax flowers, and Escoffier was so intrigued that after arduous hours of drilling by day, he would walk to Nice and practice flower-making by night, returning to the camp on foot at dawn. Later he was to write a book on wax flower decorations *(Les Fleurs en cire)* and he would often decorate his tables with these lifelike objects.

Off and on, Escoffier spent nearly seven years in the army. The Franco-Prussian War broke out in 1870, and he was assigned to duty at Metz as *chef de cuisine* at the Rhine Army's headquarters. His innate resourcefulness helped him out of a number of tight situations which he later recalled in his memoirs. Once, when his food stocks were low, he found a rabbit, cut it up, browned it in hot lard, then added six finely chopped onions, pepper and salt. Then he poured a glass of cognac and a glass of white wine over the rabbit and let it simmer for twenty minutes. Few men in any army have been blessed with a cook of Escoffier's talents, and the headquarters' officers were delighted with his improvisation.

On another occasion he bought some suckling pigs and made a delicious pâté. "I used the flesh from the thighs and fattest parts to make a well-seasoned stuffing," he recalled with a recipe writer's precision. "I then boned the remains and divided the fillets and leanest parts into strips with the skin." After seasoning the pork well, he cooked it briskly over a high flame. Then he added a few herbs, a glass of cognac, a glass of wine and some truffles and left it all to cool in an earthenware dish. "I lined with pastry a mold which I borrowed," Escoffier noted. "Inside I placed first a layer of stuffing, then another composed of the strips of bacon, truffles and pork skin. I continued alternating the layers until I had used up everything, I covered the dish with a thin layer of pastry, slightly moist as I had no egg mixture with which to paint it, and left it to cook. The skin of the pork melted during the cooking process and formed a most delicious jelly when the pâté cooled."

When the Germans laid siege to Metz and cut off French lines of supply Escoffier served his men horse meat, stewed or braised, with macaroni. Sometimes he prepared it with lentils, haricot beans or a purée of peas, scalding the meat and letting it cool before cooking to remove the bitter taste. On other occasions, he served it minced, as an accompaniment to boiled eggs. In later years he was to say with unimpeachable authority that "horse meat is delicious when one is in the right circumstances to appreciate it."

After the war ended in 1871 Escoffier worked at a number of restaurants, mostly in Paris, then opened his own place, Le Faisan Doré, in Cannes, where he made the most fateful acquaintance of his life.

By now the Riviera was becoming a fashionable resort area, favored by wealthy French and British aristocrats, and it was here that Escoffier met César Ritz who came to Monte Carlo to assume the position of general manager of the Grand Hôtel. Ritz was 30 years old and his meteoric career was already well under way. Like Carême and Escoffier, he had started life under humble circumstances, the 13th child of Swiss peasants who herded cattle for his father.

Ritz had left his homeland for Paris in 1867, the year of the international exposition. The first job he got was menial enough: he polished boots and scrubbed floors at the Hôtel de la Fidelité on the boulevard du Prince Eugène. Later he worked as a waiter at the prestigious Voisin restaurant. After the Franco-Prussian War, he became maître d'hôtel of the aptly named Hôtel Splendide. Still later his peregrinations led him to Vienna, the South of France, Switzerland and eventually the Grand Hôtel in Monte Carlo. By this time he had mastered "the art of catering exquisitely to the rich," as one of his biographers described his calling, and he had come to appreciate the value of a fine cuisine to a luxury hotel.

Ritz brought along to the Grand one of the finest chefs of France, Jean Giroix, who had worked with Escoffier at Le Petit Moulin Rouge in Paris. Giroix' sauces were marvels, his game preparations superb, his meals an unvarying success from hors d'oeuvres to petits fours. As customers flocked to the Grand its glittering nearby rival, the Hôtel de Paris, began to feel the pinch. And so the Hôtel de Paris made the logical move: it hired Giroix away by offering him more money.

Ritz was too proud to bargain. Besides, he had heard from many sources —including Giroix himself—of a brilliant young chef named Auguste Escoffier. Ritz dispatched an emissary to Escoffier, who accepted the post of chef at the Grand Hôtel, and thus began the most renowned association in hotel history.

CÉSAR RITZ
(1850-1918)

Ritz rose from cattle herder to keeper of the world's most sophisticated hotels. Convinced of the importance of a fine cuisine, he hired Escoffier to organize the kitchens for his hotels in Monte Carlo, Paris and London.

The team of Ritz and Escoffier was to be associated in a string of luxury hotels in Lucerne, Rome, Paris, London, Budapest, Madrid, Montreal, New York, Pittsburgh and Philadelphia. The two men complemented each other perfectly. Ritz spent long hours studying hotel plans, simplifying the decor, eliminating needless ornaments and dust-gathering fabrics. He saw to it that dining rooms were properly lighted and his staff properly attired—white tie and aprons for the waiters, black tie for the maître d'hôtel and morning coats for the hotel manager and his staff.

Meanwhile Escoffier was reorganizing the kitchens, eliminating mammoth *pièces montées* and useless garnishes. And the two men often helped each other: Ritz would sample Escoffier's sauces and give his opinion of them, while Escoffier pitched in on the purchase of tableware, china, porcelain, crystal and silver.

Escoffier was chef at the Grand for six years. During that time Richard

NELLIE MELBA
(1861-1931)

This famous Australian soprano struck a pair of culinary high notes by having two of Escoffier's most famous creations—*pêche Melba* and Melba toast—named after her.

D'Oyly Carte, the Gilbert and Sullivan impresario, visited the Riviera. D'Oyly Carte was an Irishman who thought that something should be done to improve the quality of British hotels. He planned to open a hotel in London to be called the Savoy, and he wanted César Ritz for its manager. Ritz was reluctant at first, but he agreed to go to London for the hotel's opening in 1889, and everything went so well that he accepted the managership and took Escoffier to London to organize the kitchens. As Madame Ritz later recalled in a biography of her husband, "the success of the Savoy was brilliantly assured, reservation for rooms had to be made weeks in advance, and the restaurant was crowded every night with the élite of society. The most brilliant stars of the theatrical firmament, Sarah Bernhardt, Henry Irving, Ellen Terry, Beerbohm Tree; world-famed singers from Covent Garden, the brothers De Reszke, Patti, Melba, Eames; patrons of the musical and theatrical world who were also members of the most exclusive society . . . new-made millionaires . . . exiled princes . . . 'professional' beauties from the inner circle of the Marlborough House set, Lily Langtry, Mrs. Keppel, Rachel Gurney, Mrs. Wheeler, adorned with princely jewels, [all] found at the Savoy the food and the ambiance that were congenial to them."

The Prince of Wales held a party at the Savoy, and for the occasion Escoffier prepared a dish called *cuisses de nymphes à l'aurore*—frogs' thighs served cold in a jelly with cream, Moselle wine and paprika to add the rosy hue of dawn. Escoffier promptly became known as the man who taught the English to eat frogs. But he created an even greater stir when the Australian coloratura Nellie Melba appeared at the Covent Garden Opera House in *Lohengrin,* opposite a stentorian tenor who glided over the Teutonic waters in a swan-drawn boat and bellowed an aria. Melba became the toast of the town. Escoffier went to hear her and was so entranced that he decided to create a new dish in her honor—peaches on vanilla ice cream, served between the wings of a swan carved out of ice and covered with spun sugar. He called this *pêche Melba,* but it was not until some time later that he gave the dish its distinctive flavor by covering the peaches and ice cream with raspberry purée.

Another Escoffier invention was born when Madame Ritz complained that the toast she was served never was thin enough to suit her. So Escoffier grilled a piece of toast, split it through the middle and cooked it a second time until it was browned on each side. At first he was inclined to name this novelty "toast Marie," after Madame Ritz, but then the great Melba arrived at the hotel from an American tour. She happened to be on a diet that included toast, and in deference to her Escoffier called his thin, crunchy creation "Melba toast."

In June 1898 César Ritz, with Escoffier's help, opened the Hôtel Ritz in Paris on the Place Vendôme. The Ritz was the last word in modernity, with electric lights tinted apricot pink to flatter the ladies' complexions and dresses. Among the many other special features were the large bathrooms, built-in cupboards and wardrobes, Baccarat crystal and furniture copied after pieces at Versailles, Fontainebleau and the Louvre. The hotel housed a wine cellar so solidly built that no traffic vibration from aboveground could disturb its 4,000 bottles of vintage wine.

A reserve cellar a few blocks away held an additional 180,000 bottles.

Escoffier planned the kitchen for the Paris Ritz. One of his requirements called for stoves that burned coke and wood; he insisted that only with the natural heat from these fuels could a beefsteak be well grilled and a chicken or lamb well roasted. The kitchen walls were lined with copper pots and pans, which have always been preferred by chefs for their efficiency as heat conductors, but which must be polished and retinned at frequent intervals. "Aluminum and enamel are used in kitchens where manpower is wanting," Escoffier conceded, but, he added, "as that is not the case here, we aim only at perfection of the cuisine."

The Paris Ritz was scarcely a year old when the Ritz-Escoffier team opened a second hotel in London, the Carlton. The hotel served as many as 500 guests per meal, and Escoffier directed a staff of 60 cooks. Keeping a careful eye on supplies, he purchased sole, turbot, salmon-trout and Scotch salmon in London, but had fowl, foie gras, lambs, early vegetables and fruit brought over from Les Halles in Paris. Escoffier's pupils and biographers, Eugène Herbodeau and Paul Thalamas, have given us a picture of the great chef in action at the Carlton. In the mornings he rose at 6:30, dressed himself in an elegant tail coat and had breakfast in his office. He supervised the drawing up of the day's menus, then went to the kitchen to oversee every detail of its operation, reprimanding anyone who was smoking or drinking—both of them practices he had strictly forbidden in the proximity of food preparation. He also visited the Carlton restaurant to talk with the manager and head waiter. "Every detail was important," his biographers say, "the nationality of the guests, their favorite dishes, the numbers at each table and the proportion of men and women, and the approximate amount they proposed to spend." He usually had lunch with César Ritz or with some of his guests, then divided his afternoons between reading, writing and visiting food suppliers. He would be back in the kitchen by 6 o'clock, drawing up dinner menus and supervising the preparations, inspecting each dish carefully before it was carried into the dining room. Around 9 o'clock he would dine alone—unless he had been invited to join some particularly important guest. Like most chefs, he ate sparingly, usually taking only a light supper of soup with a sprinkling of rice, and fruit.

The team of Ritz and Escoffier was separated in 1901 when the energetic Ritz, at 51, suffered a nervous breakdown. Although he lived until 1918, he never resumed management of his hotels. Escoffier remained at the Carlton Hotel until 1919, retiring when he was 73. That year the President of France, Raymond Poincaré, came to London and made him a Chevalier of the Legion of Honor. Later he was elevated to the rank of *Officer* of the order.

Yet even after Escoffier "retired," he stayed active. He served as consultant to numerous hotels, and became a sort of chef emeritus and ambassador at large for the world of gastronomy, traveling to Copenhagen, Stockholm, New York, London, Paris, Frankfurt, Grenoble, Zurich, Marseilles and countless other towns and cities where he felt his presence would further the cause of classic cooking.

On January 28, 1935, Escoffier, long ailing, entered a clinic in Nice

SARAH BERNHARDT
(1844-1923)

The French actress inspired Escoffier to scramble eggs with garlic and to create a soup, a strawberry dessert and a soufflé with strawberries, as well as Curaçao and macaroons.

A Close Cousin to Peach Melba

For the ornate *pêches Ninon*, a molded vanilla-flavored pudding is encircled by poached fresh peaches coated with apricot glaze. Escoffier used a similar combination for *pêche Melba*, poaching fresh peaches and covering them with raspberry purée. He served the peaches on vanilla ice cream.

suffering from uremia, but doctors decided that his case was hopeless. He died two weeks later in his home in Monte Carlo, the Villa Fernand, and is buried next to his wife in the cemetery of Villeneuve-Loubet, his birthplace in the Maritime Alps.

It is not easy to assess the elusive qualities that make a great chef. Beyond doubt Escoffier had an exquisiteness of palate that few can boast. He knew as by instinct when to add an extra grain of salt, an extra thread of meat glaze, or a simple garnish that yielded perfection. He often prepared scrambled eggs for his friend Sarah Bernhardt, and when he stirred the eggs, he would use a knife with a clove of garlic on the tip. This gave the eggs a special fillip that Bernhardt loved, but he never told her the secret. It has been said that he could have made a thistle palatable.

Of the scores of famous dishes Escoffier created, many were far more inspired than his universally acclaimed dessert, *pêche Melba*. One of his earliest creations, for example, was *poularde Derby (Recipe Index)*—roasted chicken stuffed with a pilau of rice mixed with foie gras and truffles, and served tender and moist in a sauce of its own juices and veal stock, flavored with truffles and thickened with arrowroot.

Escoffier was forever creating new dishes to mark an event or honor a celebrity. When the Arctic exploration ship *Jeannette* became stuck in the ice on its way to the North Pole, he devised *suprême de volaille Jeannette*. To prepare this he boiled some chicken breasts, then made an aspic from the chicken broth, perfumed it with tarragon and poured it over the chicken. He served the chicken cold with slices of fresh foie gras, and, as a tribute to the *Jeannette,* encrusted the dish with ice.

Another flight of Escoffier's imagination resulted in *filets de sole Otero,* named after the well-known Parisian courtesan, La Belle Otero. Escoffier baked potatoes and scooped out their shells. Then he poached some sole fillets in a fish *fumet,* and garnished the bottom of each potato shell with a tablespoon of shelled shrimp tails combined with a white wine sauce. He placed a poached sole fillet over this garnish, then covered the fish with enough Mornay sauce to fill the shell. Finally he sprinkled grated cheese over the sauce, glazed the stuffed potato shells in the oven and served them piping hot.

Next to *pêche Melba* and Melba toast, Escoffier's most famous creation was *tournedos Rossini (Recipe Index),* named for the great Italian composer, who was a gastronome with a special passion for foie gras. Escoffier sautéed some *tournedos* (tender round slices from the heart of the fillet of beef) in butter, and arranged them in the form of a crown on fried bread slices. On each of the *tournedos* he set a slice of foie gras that had been seasoned and fried in butter. Then he set a fine slice of truffle on top of each slice of foie gras and covered this new creation with a Madeira-flavored brown sauce. The result was as satisfying as a Rossini overture.

Yet Escoffier's achievements went far beyond the invention of dazzling dishes. One of his most notable feats was to simplify the menus of his day. This process was facilitated in the mid-19th century when another innovative French chef, Urbain Dubois, instigated the adoption in France of the Russian style of serving—course by course, to the individual diner. Up to that time, vast numbers of dishes were displayed simultaneously on the table, where most of them got cold before they could be eaten, and a guest had no way of knowing beforehand what was going to be served. Escoffier listed the food and beverages for a meal on a single card, offering his guests a simple, easily mastered bill of fare, as well as a pleasant souvenir of the occasion. While some of his meals sound elaborate today, it should be remembered that he lived in an age when people still consumed vast quantities of food—although by comparison with Carême's menus, Escoffier's were simple indeed.

Escoffier believed that "the meals remembered with the greatest pleasure are those where one leaves the table with a satisfied appetite without overloading one's stomach." Moreover, he added: "It is far better to serve a short, well-balanced, perfectly executed menu that the guests can unhurriedly enjoy than to parade before them a long litany of dishes they haven't time to eat."

Carême served scores of dishes at a single meal, but Escoffier limited the number to a dozen or so, choosing them carefully as components of a perfectly orchestrated whole. His menu for a dinner for 16 to 20 people, served at the Savoy in London on December 16, 1897, began with assorted hors d'oeuvres, then proceeded from caviar with *blinis* to clear turtle soup to young turbot with a red wine sauce. Next he offered a fillet of chicken with truffles, shallots, tomatoes and white wine, or a saddle of venison with a *sauce chasseur* and soufflé of chestnuts. Then there was woodcock that had been cooked on a spit accompanied by a salad of celery with truffles, asparagus and foie gras poached in Rhine wine. The meal concluded with a Sicilian bombe, pastries and fruit. It sounds staggering, but the food was served in sensible portions and by past standards the meal would have seemed almost spartan.

Escoffier was determined that food be served as quickly as possible without in any way detracting from its quality. To achieve this speed he reorganized the kitchen staff—precisely defining the duties of each man—into groups to prepare sauces, fish, side dishes, soups, roasts, pastry, ices and sweets. In the old days a dish such as *oeufs Meyerbeer* had been prepared by a single chef, who needed fifteen minutes to make it, but by dividing the responsibilities Escoffier made a group operation of it. The *entremettier* cooked the eggs, the *rôtisseur* grilled the kidney garnish and the *saucier* prepared the truffle sauce. In this way the dish was prepared in a few minutes, the patron's waiting period was reduced to a minimum and the food was served at exactly the right temperature.

Escoffier not only reorganized the kitchen; he assembled and trained highly efficient teams or *brigades* of cooks. These crack teams could be quickly dispatched to new hotels, restaurants and ocean liners to get the kitchens going. Escoffier's disciples brought a special distinction to the hotels and restaurants where they worked. In later years many of them became missionaries for the classic French cuisine as they established themselves in such faraway lands as North and South America, Russia and the Transvaal. For a generation after Escoffier died, the highest recommendation a chef could bear was that he had trained under the master, and the highest recommendation a classic dish could receive was that it had been prepared (with proper care) from one of his recipes.

For copper pots and pans—and, for that matter, casseroles, molds and virtually every other utensil used in the classic cuisine—no shop in the world is so well stocked as the 150-year-old Maison Dehillerin in the heart of Paris' former market district, Les Halles.

Tournedos Rossini
TOURNEDOS WITH FOIE GRAS, TRUFFLES AND MADEIRA SAUCE

Combine ½ cup of the Madeira and the truffle juice in a small enameled saucepan and boil briskly until reduced to ¼ cup. Add the *fond lié* and stir over moderate heat for 2 or 3 minutes. Set aside off the heat and cover the pan to keep the sauce warm.

In a heavy 12-inch sauté pan or skillet, warm 3 tablespoons of the clarified butter over moderate heat for 10 seconds. Add the bread rounds and, turning them frequently with a slotted spoon, fry until they are crisp and golden brown on both sides, adding more butter to the pan if necessary. Arrange the croutons side by side on paper towels to drain, then transfer them to a large heated platter.

Add 3 more tablespoons of clarified butter to the skillet and raise the heat. Pat the *tournedos* completely dry with paper towels and season them with salt and pepper. Then sauté them in the hot butter for 3 to 4 minutes on each side, or until they are cooked to the state of doneness you prefer. Ideally they should be rare.

Place a *tournedos* on top of each crouton and set a round of foie gras and then a truffle slice on each one.

Working quickly, pour off the fat remaining in the skillet and in its place add the remaining ¼ cup of dry Madeira. Scrape in the browned particles clinging to the bottom and sides of the pan, stir in the reserved *fond lié* mixture, and cook over moderate heat for a minute or so to heat the sauce through.

Strain the sauce through a fine sieve into a small saucepan, swirl in the 2 tablespoons of butter bits and then taste for seasoning. Pour the sauce over the *tournedos* and serve at once.

To serve 4

½ cup plus ¼ cup dry Madeira
2 tablespoons truffle juice *(see Glossary)*
1 cup *fond lié (page 35)*
6 to 10 tablespoons clarified butter *(page 34)*
4 slices homemade-type white bread about ¼ inch thick, cut into rounds 2½ inches in diameter
4 six-ounce *tournedos,* each about 1½ inches thick
Salt
Freshly ground black pepper
4 round slices of foie gras *en bloc,* each about 2 inches in diameter and ¼ inch thick, at room temperature *(see Glossary)*
4 round slices of black truffle, each about 1 inch in diameter and ⅛ inch thick, thinly peeled *(see Glossary)*
2 tablespoons unsalted butter, chilled and cut into ½-inch bits

Poularde Derby
ROAST CHICKEN WITH RICE, FOIE GRAS AND TRUFFLE STUFFING

FARCE (STUFFING): First prepare the *farce* in the following fashion: Preheat the oven to 375°. Melt 4 tablespoons of butter in a heavy 2- to 3-quart casserole over moderate heat. Add the 2 teaspoons of chopped onion and, stirring frequently, cook for 1 or 2 minutes. When the onion is soft, add the rice and stir for a few minutes until the grains glisten with butter, but do not let the rice brown. Then pour in the stock, add the ½ teaspoon of salt and ¼ teaspoon of white pepper and bring this mixture to a boil over high heat.

Cover the casserole tightly and bake in the middle of the oven for about 20 minutes, or until the grains are softened but still somewhat resistant to the bite. Drain the rice in a sieve, fluffing the grains with a fork to remove excess moisture, then place it in a bowl and stir in the chopped truffles and chopped foie gras. Taste for seasoning.

MIREPOIX: Meanwhile, in a heavy copper or enameled cast-iron cas-

To serve 6

FARCE
4 tablespoons unsalted butter
2 teaspoons finely chopped onions
1 cup uncooked converted long-grain white rice
1½ cups *fond blanc de volaille (page 31),* or substitute 1½ cups canned chicken stock, chilled, then degreased
½ teaspoon salt
¼ teaspoon freshly ground white pepper
5 tablespoons finely chopped black truffles *(see Glossary)*
5 tablespoons finely chopped foie gras *en bloc (see Glossary)*

Tournedos Rossini, Escoffier's tribute to the Italian composer, consists of slices from a beef fillet, topped with foie gras and a truffle slice.

MIREPOIX

3 tablespoons unsalted butter
1¼ cups finely chopped onions
½ cup finely chopped carrots
⅓ cup finely chopped celery
2 tablespoons finely chopped lean
  cooked ham
1 tablespoon finely chopped fresh
  parsley
½ large bay leaf
1 sprig fresh thyme, finely cut, or
  ¼ teaspoon crumbled dried
  thyme
½ teaspoon salt
⅛ teaspoon freshly ground white
  pepper

POULARDE

Two 3½-pound roasting chickens
2 tablespoons softened butter
Salt
3 cups *fond brun de veau (page
  33)*
1 tablespoon arrowroot dissolved in
  ¼ cup dry Madeira
2 tablespoons chilled unsalted
  butter cut in ½-inch bits

GARNITURE

Six ½-inch-thick slices foie gras *en
  bloc (see Glossary)*
Six ⅛-inch-thick slices of black
  truffle, thinly peeled *(see Glossary)*
6 large whole black truffles *(see
  Glossary)*
6 cylinders cut out of a loaf of stale
  homemade-type white bread, each
  about 1½ inches in diameter
  and 3 inches long
6 two-inch *pâte brisée* tartlet shells
  (Recipe Booklet)
6 tablespoons melted butter
3 large green leek leaves

serole large enough to hold the two birds comfortably, melt 3 tablespoons of butter over moderate heat. When the foam begins to subside, add the 1¼ cups of chopped onions, the carrots, celery, ham, parsley, bay leaf, thyme, ½ teaspoon of salt and ⅛ teaspoon of white pepper. Stirring frequently, cook the mirepoix mixture for about 5 minutes, or until the vegetables are soft but not brown. Set the casserole aside off the heat.

POULARDE (CHICKEN): Reduce the oven heat to 350°. Pat the chickens completely dry inside and out with paper towels. Spoon the *farce* loosely into the chickens. Close the openings by lacing them with skewers or by sewing them with heavy white thread. Fasten the neck skin to the back of each chicken with a skewer and truss the birds securely *(see Recipe Booklet)*. Rub the entire outside surface of each bird with 1 tablespoon of softened butter and lightly salt them.

Place the chickens on their backs side by side on top of the mirepoix and pour ½ cup of the *fond brun de veau* into the casserole. Bring to a simmer on top of the stove, then cover the casserole tightly and braise the chickens in the middle of the oven for about 45 minutes, basting them every 15 minutes with the cooking liquid.

Increase the oven temperature to 500°. Carefully transfer the chickens from the casserole to a rack set in a large, shallow roasting pan and roast in the middle of the oven for about 10 to 15 minutes, or until both of the birds are richly browned.

Meanwhile, strain the liquid remaining in the casserole through a fine sieve set over a heavy 1- to 2-quart saucepan, pressing down hard on the vegetables with the back of a spoon to extract all their juices before discarding them. Let the liquid rest for a minute or so, then skim as much fat as possible from the surface. Add 2½ cups of *fond brun de veau* to the roasting liquid and boil briskly until reduced to 2 cups. Lower the heat. Stirring constantly, pour in the arrowroot-and-Madeira mixture in a thin stream and simmer for several minutes until the sauce thickens lightly. Swirl in the 2 tablespoons of butter bits. Taste for seasoning. Add the slices of foie gras and both the sliced and whole truffles for the garniture and simmer for a few minutes, basting them constantly with the sauce.

GARNITURE: To garnish and serve, arrange the previously prepared *socles (below)* and the tartlet shells around the birds. Top each *socle* with a slice of foie gras and a slice of truffle and moisten them with a little of the sauce. Place a whole truffle in each tartlet shell. Pour the remaining sauce into a bowl and serve at once.

SOCLES (PEDESTALS): With a sharp knife, cut diagonal grooves about ¼ inch deep and ¼ inch wide around the long sides of each bread cylinder. Stand the cylinders side by side on a baking sheet and brush them evenly with 6 tablespoons of melted butter. Toast in a preheated 375° oven until they are golden.

Blanch the leek leaves by dropping them into boiling water and letting them boil for 1 or 2 minutes. Drain in a sieve or colander under cold water to set their color, then pat them dry with paper towels and cut them into fine strips about 4 inches long and ⅛ inch wide. Slide a strip of the blanched leek into each groove of the *socles* and trim off any excess top and bottom. These "pediments" of toasted bread may be served at room temperature and can be made hours in advance if necessary.

Canard à l'orange
ROAST DUCK WITH ORANGE SAUCE

With a small, sharp knife, remove the peel from one of the oranges in long strips as wide as possible, without cutting into the bitter white pith. Cut the peel into julienne strips 1½ to 2 inches long and no more than 1⁄16 inch wide. You should have ¼ cup. If less, use part of the peel of the second orange. Drop the peel into boiling water and boil for 1 or 2 minutes, then drain the julienne in a sieve and run cold water over the strips to set their color. Spread the strips on paper towels to dry. Squeeze enough juice from the oranges to make ⅓ cup and set aside.

Preheat the oven to 450°. Pat the ducks completely dry inside and out with paper towels. With a sharp knife, cut off each wing tip at the joint. Rub the cavities of both ducks with salt and pepper and sprinkle the skin of the ducks lightly with salt. Truss the ducks *(see Recipe Booklet)*, and prick the skin around the thighs, the backs and the lower part of the breasts with the point of a skewer or small, sharp knife.

Place the ducks breast side up, as far apart as possible, on a rack set in a large, shallow roasting pan. Roast in the middle of the oven for 20 minutes until the skin browns lightly. Draw off the fat from the pan with a bulb baster, and turn the ducks on one side.

Reduce the heat to 350° and roast for about 30 minutes; turn the birds on the other side and continue roasting for about 30 minutes more. Place the ducks breast side up again and continue roasting for about 30 minutes longer, occasionally removing the fat as it accumulates in the pan. To test for doneness, pierce the thigh of each bird with the point of a small, sharp knife. The juice that trickles out should be a clear yellow; if it is slightly pink, roast the ducks for another 5 to 10 minutes. Lift each duck off the rack with a wooden spoon inserted in the tail opening, letting the juices from the cavity drain back into the pan. Arrange the ducks on a heated platter and drape them with foil while you prepare the sauce.

Tilt the pan and, with a large spoon, remove and discard all the fat from the juices that remain. Pour in the *fond lié* and bring to a simmer over moderate heat, meanwhile scraping in the browned particles clinging to the bottom and sides of the pan. Set aside off the heat.

In a 2- to 3-quart enameled cast-iron or copper saucepan, stir the sugar and vinegar together and bring to a boil over high heat. Cook briskly until the mixture thickens to a tealike gold syrup. Be careful not to let the sugar burn; it will color very quickly. Pour in the warm *fond lié,* reduce the heat to low and, stirring all the while, simmer 3 or 4 minutes. Stir in the reserved orange juice, the lemon juice and the currant jelly, if you are using it. Continue to simmer for 3 to 4 minutes longer.

Strain the sauce through a fine sieve into another saucepan. Swirl in the 3 tablespoons of butter bits and when they are completely absorbed, add the Grand Marnier. Season to taste with salt and pepper. If you wish, pour some of the sauce around the birds and serve the remainder in a sauceboat. Scatter the orange peel attractively over the ducks and serve.

Or, garnish the ducks with peeled orange segments and orange baskets cut as fancifully as you like. You may also insert into the ends of each bird decorative silver skewers *(attelets)* garnished with artfully cut oranges, lemons and miniature oranges.

2 medium-sized oranges
2 five- to six-pound ducks
Salt
Freshly ground black pepper
4 cups *fond lié (page 35)*
⅓ cup sugar
⅓ cup white wine vinegar
⅓ cup fresh lemon juice
2 teaspoons red currant jelly (optional)
3 tablespoons unsalted butter, chilled and cut into ½-inch bits
1 tablespoon Grand Marnier or other orange-flavored liqueur

The Spectacular, Delicious "Canard à l'orange"

As Webster defines it, a canard is a false report, but in France it also means duck. And *canard à l'orange,* when properly prepared, is one of the truest joys of the French cuisine. The roast duck must be tender and juicy and its skin must be crisp. Its sauce contains caramel, with orange juice added to lend tartness. The ducks shown here are decorated with orange segments, festooned with strips of orange peel and speared with *attelets* holding other garnishes.

To serve 8

GÂTEAU DE SEMOULE
Vegetable oil
2 cups milk
1 vanilla bean
1 teaspoon finely grated fresh lemon
   peel
¼ cup farina or cream of rice
5 egg yolks
½ cup sugar
1 envelope plus 1 teaspoon
   unflavored gelatin
1½ cups heavy cream
2 tablespoons confectioners' sugar

PÊCHES POCHÉES
2 cups sugar
The yellow peel of 2 lemons, cut in
   long strips
8 firm ripe peaches, each about
   2½ inches in diameter

CRÈME CHANTILLY
1½ cups chilled heavy cream
3 tablespoons confectioners' sugar
1 crystallized violet (*see Glossary*)

Pêches Ninon
POACHED FRESH PEACHES WITH MOLDED VANILLA-FLAVORED PUDDING AND
APRICOT GLAZE

Brush the inside of a 6-cup shallow ring mold with vegetable oil. Then rub it with paper towels to remove the excess.

In a 2- to 3-quart enameled-iron or copper saucepan, bring the milk, vanilla bean and grated lemon peel to a boil over moderate heat. Remove the pan from the heat and let the flavorings steep for 10 or 15 minutes. Strain the milk through a fine sieve and return it to the pan. Wash off the vanilla bean and set it aside. Then bring the milk to a simmer over moderate heat and, stirring constantly, pour in the farina or cream of rice in a slow, thin stream. Reduce the heat to low and, still stirring to prevent any lumps from forming, cook for about 5 minutes, or until the mixture thickens enough to coat a spoon. Set aside off the heat.

In a deep bowl, beat the egg yolks, the ½ cup of sugar and the gelatin together with a wire whisk or a rotary or electric beater for 3 or 4 minutes, or until the mixture forms a slowly dissolving ribbon when the beater is lifted from the bowl. Slowly pour the beaten eggs into the farina mixture, stirring continuously until no streaks of yellow show. Still stirring, bring to a simmer over low heat and cook slowly for 1 or 2 minutes. Do not let the mixture come anywhere near the boiling point. Remove the pan from the heat to cool.

With a whisk or a rotary or electric beater whip the cream in a chilled mixing bowl until it forms soft peaks. Beat in 2 tablespoons of confectioners' sugar. Set the farina mixture into a pot filled with crushed ice or ice cubes and water, and stir for 4 or 5 minutes, or until it is cool but still fairly fluid. Beat with a whisk to be sure it is perfectly smooth.

With a rubber spatula scoop the whipped cream over the farina mixture and fold them together gently but thoroughly. Pour the entire contents of the bowl into the oiled mold, smoothing the top with the spatula. Cover with foil or plastic wrap and refrigerate for at least 6 hours, or until very firm.

PÊCHES POCHÉES: Meanwhile, combine 2 quarts of water, 2 cups of sugar, the strips of lemon peel and the reserved vanilla bean in a heavy 3- to 4-quart saucepan. Bring to a boil over high heat, stirring until the sugar dissolves. Reduce the heat to low and simmer for about 10 minutes. Place the peaches in the syrup, cover the pan partially and poach the peaches for 10 to 15 minutes, or until they are barely tender and show only slight resistance when pierced deeply with the tip of a small skewer. Let the peaches cool completely in the syrup. Then peel and return them to the syrup. Covered with foil or plastic wrap, they can be kept at room temperature for several hours or in the refrigerator for a day or more.

About half an hour before serving, unmold the pudding ring. Run a knife around the sides of the mold to a depth of about 1½ inches and dip the bottom in hot water for a few seconds. Place a serving plate upside down over it and, grasping plate and mold together, invert them. Rap the plate on a table; the pudding ring should slide out easily. Drain the peaches and arrange them around the pudding.

CRÈME CHANTILLY (CHANTILLY CREAM): In a chilled bowl whip 1½ cups of chilled heavy cream with a whisk or a rotary or electric beater until it begins to thicken. Add 3 tablespoons of confectioners' sugar and continue beating until the cream is firm enough to form stiff, unwavering peaks on the beater when it is lifted from the bowl. Using a pastry bag with a decorative tip, pipe decorative rosettes or spirals of whipped cream into the center of the pudding ring. Center the candied violet on top of the cream. (Lacking a pastry bag, spoon the cream into the center of the ring and create fanciful swirls on its surface with a small spatula.)

SAUCE D'ABRICOTS (APRICOT SAUCE): Bring the apricot jam, ⅓ cup sugar and ¼ cup water to a boil over moderate heat, stirring until the sugar dissolves. Reduce the heat to low and, stirring from time to time, simmer for 5 minutes, or until the sauce clears. With the back of a spoon, rub the sauce through a fine sieve set over a bowl. Stir the kirsch into the warm apricot sauce and pour it around the ring. Serve at once.

SAUCE D'ABRICOTS
1½ cups apricot jam
⅓ cup sugar
¼ cup water
3 tablespoons imported kirsch

Like many other elegant French desserts, *pêches Ninon* may be garnished as fancifully as you like. The peaches may be topped by sugar leaves, or leaflike shapes cut from angelica. The pudding ring may be festooned with chocolate leaves and flowers made of semisweet chocolate melted in a double boiler and piped through a wax paper cone of your own fashioning. The flowers may be tinted with apricot glaze.

Cailles aux raisins en timbale
QUAIL WITH GRAPES IN A PASTRY SHELL

To serve 6

TIMBALE (PASTRY SHELL): In a large chilled bowl, combine the flour, a pinch of salt and 12 tablespoons of butter bits. With your fingertips rub the flour and fat together until they look like flakes of coarse meal. Do not let the mixture become oily.

TIMBALE
3 cups all-purpose flour
A pinch of salt
12 tablespoons unsalted butter,
   chilled and cut into ¼-inch bits
   plus 1 tablespoon butter, softened
2 egg yolks
¼ to ½ cup ice water

Add the egg yolks and ¼ cup of ice water, toss the mixture together lightly but thoroughly and gather the dough into a ball. If the dough crumbles, add up to ¼ cup more ice water, 1 tablespoon at a time, until all the particles adhere. Cover the bowl with wax paper and let the dough rest at room temperature for about 30 minutes.

Preheat the oven to 400°. With a pastry brush, spread the tablespoon of softened butter evenly over the bottom and sides of an 8- to 9-inch-square baking pan about 2 inches deep.

On a lightly floured surface, pat the dough into a rough square about 1 inch thick. Dust a little flour over and under it and roll it out into a large square, at least 15 to 16 inches, and ¼ inch thick. If the dough sticks to the board or table, lift it gently with a metal spatula and sprinkle a little flour under it.

Roll the dough gently around the rolling pin, lift it and unroll it slackly over the buttered pan. Press the dough against the bottom and sides and then into the corners of the pan, taking care not to tear it. With a pair of scissors cut off the excess dough from the edges, leaving a ¼-inch overhang all around the outside rim. Turn the overhang under the edge and crimp it attractively.

Spread two sheets of buttered heavy-duty aluminum foil across the pan at right angles to each other and press into the edges to support the sides of the pastry as it bakes.

Bake on the middle shelf of the oven for 20 minutes. Remove the foil,

The name of the game in *cailles aux raisins en timbale* is quail, combined with grapes, cognac and a sauce in a pastry shell.

CAILLES

1½ cups seedless or other green
    grapes, peeled and seeded
⅓ cup cognac
Six 6-ounce quail
4 tablespoons melted clarified butter
    (page 34), plus 2 tablespoons
    unsalted butter, chilled and cut
    into ½-inch bits
½ teaspoon salt
¼ teaspoon freshly ground black
    pepper
1½ cups *fond lié (page 35)*

pick through any bubbles in the dough and continue baking for 20 minutes, or until the rim is golden brown. Let the pastry cool for 5 minutes to room temperature and then unmold it.

Run a thin knife around the sides to loosen them. Place an inverted wire cake rack over the pan and, grasping plate and rack together firmly, carefully turn them over. The pastry should slide out easily. Turn it over and set it aside on a serving platter.

CAILLES (QUAIL): Combine the grapes and cognac in a small bowl and turn them about with a spoon until the grapes are well coated. Marinate at room temperature for at least 1 hour, stirring occasionally.

If you have freshly killed quail, remove the feathers and clip off the wing tips. Singe the feet over an open flame and rub off the skins. With a small, sharp knife, make an incision down the length of the back of the neck of each bird, cutting through to the neck bone. Free the bone from the surrounding skin with your fingers and then snip it out with scissors. Pull out the intestines through the same incision at the base of the neck.

Discard the hearts, livers and gizzards. Truss the quail securely with kitchen string *(see Recipe Booklet)*. Then push the head of each bird back against the body and anchor it deeply on both sides with wooden toothpicks. (If you buy quail from the butcher, they will already be eviscerated with the heads and feet removed. Pat the birds dry inside and out with paper towels and truss them securely.)

Preheat the oven to 500°. In a 12-inch skillet warm the clarified butter over high heat until a drop of water flicked into it splutters and evaporates instantly. Season the quail with the salt and pepper and place them in the skillet, turning them about with tongs or a spoon until they are evenly coated with butter.

Regulating the heat as necessary, continue to turn the birds until they color richly and evenly. As soon as the birds are brown, place the skillet on the middle shelf of the oven and roast the quail for 8 to 10 minutes. To test for doneness, pierce the thigh of a bird with the point of a small knife; the juices that trickle out should be pale pink. If they are still red, roast the birds for 2 or 3 minutes longer. Transfer the quail to a heated platter and quickly prepare the sauce.

Drain the grapes in a sieve over a bowl and put them aside. Pour off the fat from the skillet and in its place, add the liquid from the grapes. Bring to a boil over high heat, stirring constantly and scraping in the browned particles that cling to the bottom and sides of the pan.

Pour in the *fond lié* and, still stirring, continue to cook for 3 or 4 minutes until the sauce is smooth and thoroughly heated. Taste for seasoning and strain the sauce through a fine sieve into a small saucepan. Swirl in the 2 tablespoons of butter bits.

Arrange the quail attractively in the pastry shell and spoon the reserved grapes around them. Pour the sauce evenly over the birds and serve at once.

Consommé Célestine
CHICKEN CONSOMMÉ GARNISHED WITH HERB-SEASONED CRÊPES

"Fines herbes" literally means small savory herbs—and the term is often confused with finely chopped fresh parsley. More precisely, "fines herbes" is a mixture of fresh parsley, tarragon, chervil and chives, all finely chopped (or cut). The proportions used may be varied to suit your taste, and one or more of the herbs may be omitted if unavailable. One half teaspoon of dried tarragon can be substituted for 1 teaspoon of fresh tarragon if necessary, but the other herbs must always be fresh.

Prepare the crêpe batter with the ingredients listed and fry them, following the technique described in the recipe for *coulibiac (page 154)*. Covered with plastic wrap, the crêpes may safely be kept at room temperature for 2 to 3 hours before they are used.

Just before serving, bring the consommé to a simmer over moderate heat. Stack 3 or 4 crêpes on top of each other and roll them into a cylinder. With a sharp knife, slice it crosswise into fine strips. Place the crêpe strips in a heated tureen or in eight heated individual soup plates. Pour in the consommé and serve at once.

To serve 8

CRÊPES AUX FINES HERBES
½ cup plus 2 tablespoons all-purpose flour
2 eggs
½ cup milk
½ cup plus 2 tablespoons cold water
1½ tablespoons unsalted butter, melted and cooled plus 3 tablespoons melted clarified butter *(page 34)*
¼ teaspoon salt
¼ cup *fines herbes*

Consommé de fond blanc de volaille (page 31)

V

The Restaurant's Inimitable Role

In the main dining room of the famous Maxim's, the classic saddle of veal Orloff is displayed (*foreground*). Here, in the *belle époque,* celebrated courtesans cavorted with their ardent admirers. Subsequently, the restaurant changed hands and became so exclusive that to be admitted and merely recognized by the super-snobbish maître d'hôtel, Albert Blaser, was to have lived—at least until the check arrived.

For the past two centuries the restaurant has played a key role not only in the development of classic cooking, but in the whole social, artistic and political life of France. If we could stroll through the streets of Paris and arrive at each of the city's leading restaurants—past and present—at the peak of its glory, we would encounter the country's most renowned artists, writers, statesmen, politicians, courtesans and boulevardiers. And while making these rounds, we could enjoy some of the world's finest food. For the French restaurant has produced a legion of distinguished chefs, and these talented men have created many of the most tantalizing dishes of the classic cuisine.

The restaurant was a French invention of the 18th Century that came to flower in the years after the revolution of 1789. By then the old aristocratic households with their elaborate kitchen staffs had disappeared. Many of the talented cooks who had served these households found employment in the newly emerging culinary institutions that were known as restaurants. As a result the food in these uniquely democratic establishments, where anyone could dine who could afford to pay the bill, improved immensely. And from that time to this, French restaurants have outshone all others in the world. This is partly because of the genius of France's chefs, partly because of the French talent for organization, and mostly because the French apparently *care* about food—its quality, its preparation and its service—more than anybody else.

The first restaurant is believed to have opened on the rue des Poulies in Paris in 1765. Its owner was one M. Boulanger. (The word means baker, and some authorities claim that he was a baker whose real name has been lost.) The institution got its name from the restoratives or *restaurants*—soups and broths—that he served. Before Boulanger's day there were inns and hostelries where meals were served to overnight guests, as well as cafés where drinks were dispensed; there were also *traiteurs*—caterers—who sold cooked whole joints of meat, fowl and stews. But Boulanger's was the first public place where people went simply to eat a meal. His menu featured soups and dishes prepared with the finest poultry and the freshest eggs, and Boulanger evidently understood his business in all its essentials. Diderot, the encyclopedist, visited the eating emporium and reported, "I went to dine at the restaurateur's place in the rue des Poulies; one is treated well there but has to pay dearly for it."

Yet Boulanger's restaurant—as the menu indicates—was modest by modern standards. The first luxury restaurant in Paris was the Grande Taverne de Londres on the rue de Richelieu, run by a man named Beauvilliers. It opened in 1782 and reached its zenith in the Napoleonic era, when carriages of all nations drew up to its door. Beauvilliers became the most celebrated culinary artist of his time; he wrote a cookbook called *L'Art du cuisinier* that was the standard work on high-class French cooking for many years. Moreover, he was an accomplished host. Brillat-Savarin, who often dined at his restaurant, reported that he ":was the possessor of a prodigious memory; he would recognize and greet, after the lapse of more than twenty years, persons who had only eaten once or twice in his establishment. . . . When he became aware that a party of wealthy folk had sat down at one of his tables, he would approach . . . with the most marked attention." Beauvilliers would recommend special dishes and suggest vintage wines to accompany them and, when the meal was over, he would present his guests with a suitably swollen check.

It was during the Napoleonic era that French restaurants really came into their own, even though Napoleon himself was not much of an eater. The Emperor dined absentmindedly, and drank little, usually a glass of Chambertin diluted with water. He obviously had other things on his mind. An observer reported that "Never did one manage to make him eat his dinner while it was hot, for once he had settled himself to work no one knew when he would leave it. . . . When dinnertime arrived, chickens were placed on the spit for him at half-hourly intervals, and I have personally seen dozens of them so roasted before coming to the one finally presented to him."

Even so, Napoleon's rule brought a new affluence and luxury to France, and the number and quality of restaurants greatly increased. The culinary and commercial center of Paris at this time was the Palais Royal, the colonnaded, tree-lined area adjacent to the Louvre. Around the garden there were 15 restaurants and 29 cafés, as well as billiard parlors, jewelry shops, bookstores, wig shops, gambling houses and houses where nothing was left to chance.

The best place to eat in the Palais Royal was a restaurant called Véry. Grimod de la Reynière, the literary gastronome, frequented it and reported that it was "certainly the finest restaurant in the whole of France, probably in all Europe." Furnished with marble-topped tables and gilded candelabra, the Véry was crowded with swashbuckling cavalrymen of Napoleon's army and their feminine companions. The menu at this popular establishment offered a dozen different soups, 15 entrées of beef, 20 of mutton and 30 of game.

Honoré de Balzac, the great novelist, went there, and in his novel, *La Comédie humaine,* one of the first things the famous character, Lucien de Rubempré, did on his arrival in the capital from the provinces was to dine at Véry. He ordered a bottle of Bordeaux, a plate of Ostend oysters, some fish, partridge, macaroni and fruit. The dinner cost him 50 francs, and Balzac makes the point that his hero could have lived a month on that amount back home in Angoulême.

Balzac once invited his editor, Werdet, to dine at Véry. Werdet later reported that he was suffering from acute gastritis and ate very little, but that Balzac—as monumental a trencherman as he was a writer—put away a prodigious meal: 100 Ostend oysters, a dozen lamb cutlets, a duckling with turnips, a pair of roast partridges, a *sole à la normande* (sole with oysters, mussels, shrimp tails and mushrooms), as well as hors d'oeuvre, fruits, wines, coffee and liqueurs.

When the meal was finally over Balzac whispered to Werdet, "Have you any money?" The editor leaned forward and pretended to be picking something off the floor as he slipped Balzac a five-franc note. Balzac summoned the waiter, took the check and scrawled something across the bottom. Then he handed the waiter the check and gave him the five-franc note as a tip. With that he rose majestically and left the restaurant with his guest. Werdet asked Balzac what he had written across the bottom of the check and was told: "What I wrote, my friend, you will find out tomorrow." The next morning a man from Véry appeared at Werdet's office with the check, which came to the impressive sum of 62 francs 50 centimes. Balzac's inscription at the bottom informed the restaurant that the editor would be glad to pay the check if it were presented at his office.

In the years after Napoleon's downfall and exile to St. Helena in 1815, the best place to go in Paris for a fine meal was the Rocher de Cancale on the rue Montorgueil, not far from the Palais Royal. A favorite haunt of poets and writers, this restaurant served the best fish and oysters in town. Grimod de la Reynière, with his flair for grandiloquent phrases, called it the "peak of Tenerife in the world of gastronomy," and a visitor to the restaurant reported: "We don't hesitate to place the salon dinners of our best restaurants above those of the best private houses in town. . . . At Rocher de Cancale, we began with six little Marennes oysters and as many spoonfuls of soup which neutralized the cold sensation of the oysters; we sampled several soups, followed by a glass of Madeira. . . . It is not the number of dishes that was great; but they were so well graduated and the manner, appearance, freshness, vitality and flavor were so excellent that everyone had to admire them."

Brillat-Savarin used to visit the Rocher de Cancale once a week to enjoy the *turbot à la broche* (turbot cooked on a spit), while Alexandre Dumas père and Victor Hugo were frequent guests. The main attraction was the chef, whose name was Langlais. His specialty was one of the great dishes of the classic cuisine, *sole à la normande,* which he adapted

PROSPER MONTAGNÉ
(1865-1948)

While only an assistant chef at the Grand Hôtel in Monte Carlo, he proclaimed a revolution that would eliminate all superfluous decorations and garnitures from the classic cuisine. One of France's greatest chefs, his lasting legacy is the *Larousse gastronomique,* basic encyclopedia of French cooking.

One of the oldest and best-known restaurants in Paris is the Grand Véfour in the Palais Royal. The restaurant was opened in 1740 as the Café de Chartres. Today it is run by Raymond Oliver, a well-known television personality and gastronome. The specialties at the Grand Véfour are *lamproie bordelaise* (lampreys with a Bordelaise sauce), fresh foie gras and *pigeon Prince Rainier III* (a stuffed pigeon cooked with wine, cognac and a meat glaze).

from a recipe for sole ragout by Carême. To prepare this fine seafood medley, he took the fillets of a large sole, seasoned them with salt and pepper and cooked them in white wine. Then he combined the cooking liquid with a velouté sauce, reduced this mixture and thickened it with an egg. When the fish was done, he garnished it with oysters, mushrooms and mussels. Finally he poured the sauce over the garnished fish and topped the dish with fried smelts and croutons.

In the reign of Napoleon III (1852-1870)—the Second Empire, as it was known—the social and gastronomic center of Paris shifted from the Palais Royal to the Grands Boulevards, the spacious thoroughfares newly laid out in a program to beautify the capital. A popular spot of this period was the Restaurant Durand, whose chef, Joseph Voiron, invented *sauce Mornay,* the delicious classic white sauce with cream and grated Gruyère and Parmesan cheese. A few blocks away near the boulevard des Italiens stood the Café Foy, often called Chez Bignon after its owner. Gioacchino Rossini, the great Italian composer, lived upstairs. By mid-century he had finished writing his operas and was devoting himself to wining and dining with the same gusto that characterized his music; Chez Bignon proved a handy outlet for this preoccupation. The English novelist William Makepeace Thackeray also liked to dine there, and one dish

122

that he commended without reservation was the steak. Another notable diner one might have encountered was the opéra-bouffe composer Offenbach. In the mid-19th Century his operettas—among them *La Belle Hélène* and *La Vie parisienne*—were the rage of Paris. Napoleon III's regime was a repressive one, with secret police, censorship and infringement of personal liberties, but the Emperor and his Empress Eugénie themselves were high livers, and there was a kind of forced gaiety about the era, a deliberate desire to look the other way to forget the harsh realities of authoritarian rule. Offenbach's frivolous music and the mocking, impish dance, the cancan, perfectly symbolized the era.

Another restaurant that flourished at this time—one of the most famous in Parisian history—was the Café Anglais, on the rue Marivaux. The private dining room here, known as the Grand Seize, was a hangout for the most determined *bon vivants* of the day. The fame of the place was considerably enhanced by Cora Pearl, the daughter of an English music teacher, who had become a leading Paris courtesan. One night four waiters brought in an outsize serving dish, uncovered it and revealed Cora —herself a classic dish—without a stitch, blowing kisses at the clientele. Supper was served at midnight in the Grand Seize and habitués played a card game called baccarat—until morning. Offenbach immortalized the Grand Seize in *La Vie parisienne* with these lines:

> *They talk, they shout*
> *As loud as they can shout.*
> *When they can't shout any more,*
> *They must perforce be quiet*
> *And gaiety slips away bit by bit.*
> *This one is asleep on his feet, that one on the floor.*
> *And that is how the party ends.*

The main reason for the restaurant's popularity, however, was the chef, Adolphe Dugléré, who created the celebrated classic dish known as *sole Dugléré (Recipe Index)*. It was a fillet of sole baked with chopped onion, tomatoes, seasonings and white wine, which Dugléré served with a sauce prepared from the fish's cooking liquid, thickened with a velouté, butter and a few drops of lemon juice. Another of his inventions was the equally famous *potage Germiny (Recipe Index),* the classic consommé with shredded sorrel leaves enriched with egg yolks and cream.

Probably the most important meal ever served at the Café Anglais, outstripping even the Cora Pearl event, was the "Three Emperors" dinner on June 7, 1867. The guests, who were visiting Paris for the Universal Exposition of 1867, included the King of Prussia (later Germany's first emperor), Czar Alexander II of Russia, and his son the Czarevich, subsequently Alexander III. They dined on *soufflés à la reine* (soufflés with creamed chicken), fillet of sole *à la vénitienne,* sliced turbot *au gratin,* chicken *à la portugaise,* lobster *à la parisienne,* ducklings *à la rouennaise,* ortolans on toast and eight different wines (a Madeira, a sherry, a Château d'Yquem, a Chambertin, a Château Margaux, a Château Latour and a Château Lafite as well as champagne). The Café Anglais has long since passed into memory, but the table setting for this historic meal can be seen in Paris at the Tour D'Argent restaurant today.

PHILÉAS GILBERT
(1857-1934)

A friend of Escoffier and his collaborator on *Le Guide culinaire* and other works, Gilbert was a leading chef and gastronomic writer. Founder and editor of a famous periodical called *La Revue de l'Art Culinaire,* he persuaded Escoffier that his friend Prosper Montagné was right in calling for reform of the classic cuisine.

Three years after the "Three Emperors" dinner the Franco-Prussian War broke out. The French army was overwhelmed by the Germans at Sedan; Napoleon III surrendered, was taken prisoner by the Germans and later retired to England after the war. The Third Republic was installed, and a new era began. Although 99 different governments came to power within the next 70 years, this was a period of relative stability in French life. Industrialization proceeded rapidly and by the end of the century a new period of prosperity was at hand. The final decade of the century had ushered in the madcap era known as *la belle époque.* The heart of Paris at this time was the area around the church of the Madeleine. Nearby, at Weber's restaurant, a visitor might have run into the incomparable chronicler of the times, Marcel Proust, emaciated, sickly, bundled in a large overcoat; or the great impressionist composer, Claude Debussy; or the celebrated gastronome, Curnonsky.

Yet the city's epicenter—from a social and a gastronomic point of view —was not Weber's but Maxim's, the world-famous establishment on the rue Royale. The restaurant was opened in 1893 by Maxime Gaillard, who took over the location from an Italian named Imoda, who had run it as an ice-cream parlor. For some unaccountable reason, on Bastille Day in 1890 Imoda had hung a German flag in front of his shop. Parisians were so enraged they all but tore the building down. Gaillard, a waiter at a nearby bar, bought the place, converted it into a restaurant and named it after himself, dropping the "E" in the process. The new owner lived a little more than a year after the restaurant opened, but in that time he hired a chef named Chauveau and a maître d'hôtel named Cornuché, and this proved to be the smartest thing he ever did.

One night not long after Maxim's opened, a voluptuous creature named Irma de Montigny dropped in with a few of her friends. In the course of the evening, they drank 36 bottles of champagne, and Cornuché decided that the key to the restaurant's success lay in attracting more such creatures with well-heeled friends who liked champagne. He bought a piano, hired a musician to play it and encouraged the courtesans of Paris to regard Maxim's as a house away from home.

Emilienne d' Alençon came in from the circus, bringing her rabbit act with her. The rabbits were dyed pink and wore paper collars, and Emilienne would stop at the cloakroom and check the rabbits before going on to more productive pursuits. Jeanne Derval came in carrying a small dog in her chastity belt—which was hardly a standard item of equipment at Maxim's. Other decorative guests included the identical twins Jeanne and Anne de Lancy, so much alike that the morning after no one knew —or cared—which one he had been sleeping with. Princess Caraman-Chimay, who had been christened Clara Ward in her home town of Detroit, usually came straight from the Folies Bergère, where she was appearing in pink tights and a pair of well-placed rosebuds.

Respectable ladies did not dine in restaurants at this juncture. But there were plenty of demimondaines who were happy to frequent Maxim's. The most devastating of all was the Spanish dancer, La Belle Otero, a Carmen-come-to-life who was the daughter of a Greek nobleman and a Spanish gypsy. La Belle Otero was a precocious child who had three lovers and one Italian husband by the time she was 15 years old. A few years later, she had shed the husband and was dancing in a waterfront café in Marseilles. From there La Belle Otero went to Paris, where she was welcomed into the Maxim's set and also reputedly enjoyed the favors of the Prince of Wales, Grand Duke Peter of Russia and nearly all the crowned and uncrowned heads of Europe. Even Kaiser Wilhelm II of Germany, normally a phlegmatic fellow, was not immune to her charms. An explorer named Payen, who had been almost everywhere, offered her $8,000 to spend the night with him. History does not record why she turned him down, but it does claim he was so upset he blew his brains out, which may or may not have been much of a feat.

Money meant nothing to the patrons of Maxim's. Grand Duke Serge offered a cocotte named Augustine a dozen oysters, each containing a pearl worth $2,000. The American James Gordon Bennett, owner of the *Paris Herald,* paid a flower girl 500 francs for a bunch of violets. A New Yorker named Todd flung a fistful of gold louis in the air, and they came down he knew not where, causing a memorable melee among the cocottes. Tossing money around became the thing to do at Maxim's, and 40 years later, when workmen tore up the seats to renovate the place, they found gold louis in almost every crack and cranny.

People also *ate* at Maxim's, as Cornelia Otis Skinner has noted in a delightful book about the *belle époque* felicitously called *Elegant Wits and Grand Horizontals.* As Miss Skinner recounts, a comedy writer named Georges Feydeau once was served a lobster with only one claw. When he complained that he was not getting his money's worth, the waiter patiently explained that the lobster probably had lost its claw while tangling with another crustacean in the tank. "Ah?" replied Feydeau, "then take this away and bring me the victor."

Those were the days, but World War I wiped them out forever. The old clientele disappeared, and Maxim's went into a decline. Then in 1931, Octave Vaudable bought the place. He installed Albert Blaser as maître d'hôtel, and Albert lifted Maxim's face. Sole Albert was the favorite dish, and Albert was the soul of Maxim's, a symbol of arrogance and icy reserve who made everyone who was given a table there feel that he had been admitted to the sanctum sanctorum. Explaining the secret of Albert's success, Countess Guy de Toulouse-Lautrec, a regular patron of Maxim's, wrote: "I knew Albert well. For years, I watched him preside over the entrance to the main room at Maxim's. Impassive and solemnly penguinlike, he turned his cold blue eyes upon newcomers and identified every face with a name drawn from the recesses of his infallible memory. I would not go so far as to say we were friends. Albert had no friends. All he had were connections, but he had them all, from the Aga Khan to the Duke of Windsor, not to mention the innumerable duchesses, film stars and millionaires on his roster. . . . Albert's success in his career and in the comeback of Maxim's was based on his art of snobbing the snobs." A highly successful Paris lawyer put it more succinctly: "I knew I had succeeded in life the day that Albert called me by name."

But Maxim's also achieved a lasting reputation for the superlative food served there. The best-known dish, of course, was and is the sole Albert

EDOUARD NIGNON
(1865-1934)

Nignon was a leading French chef who gratified the appetites of many world-famous figures. He presided over the kitchen of a restaurant favored by Emperor Franz Josef of Austria, still later was chef to Czar Nicholas II of Russia and after World War I cooked for Woodrow Wilson during the President's peacemaking mission to Paris.

There are many good reasons for dining at the Tour d'Argent when you are in Paris. One is pressed duck, being prepared above by a *canardier* (duck presser), who puts a duck carcass in a viselike press and squeezes the blood from it. The blood is combined with duck consommé, Madeira and cognac to provide a sauce for the duck's meat and liver. This makes *caneton Tour d'Argent,* the specialty of the house. The Tour d'Argent, established in 1582 as an eating house for royalty, is the oldest restaurant in Paris. It overlooks the Seine, and one can contemplate Notre Dame while the waiter serves the *caneton.*

—sole dipped in butter and fresh bread crumbs, then baked in vermouth until crisp and brown. Another fine entrée is saddle of veal Orloff, the veal cooked with shallots in white wine and port, and served with a mushroom purée, a purée soubise (onion sauce) and wine sauce.

If you visit Maxim's today (making sure to have a reservation), you can sit among the gilt-framed mirrors and the red plush seats and imagine that La Belle Otero will pop in at almost any minute. If you are persistent, you may even get to see the two large dining rooms upstairs that used to be intimate salons in the *belle époque,* when dalliance was the order of the day. (In the same mood, if you wander over to the Left Bank you can visit Lapérouse, another fine Paris restaurant, and see the *salons particuliers,* private rooms where—when Maxim's palled—the courtesans of the *belle époque* and their companions cavorted between courses.)

Anyone who stopped in at these leading restaurants during the *belle époque* or the years before World War II might well have run into the fabled Curnonsky. For he was a professional, untiring, peripatetic gastronome, an institution that is almost as French as Maxim's itself or the Eiffel tower.

Curnonsky was born in Angers and came to Paris when he was only 12. His real name was Maurice Edmond Sailland, but when he went into journalism while still in his teens he adopted the pseudonym Curnonsky (from the Latin *cur non,* meaning Why Not?). Later he decided to combine the two great interests of his life—creative writing and a passion for fine food. Ultimately he became the culinary czar of France,

spending the better part of his life eating and often taking as much as five hours for a meal. His palate was so finely attuned that he once correctly identified 12 champagnes and their vintage years while blindfolded. A prodigious eater, he weighed 277 pounds in his prime (and once reached 300, he said). In a Paris restaurant in 1946, for example, he started with a thick slice of foie gras with a Tokay 1942. He then devoured an enormous fillet of sole garnished with truffles, surrounded with huge red crayfish and golden-fried gudgeon—a small freshwater fish—in a glorious white wine sauce with mussels, mushrooms and shrimp. He drank a bottle of Bâtard-Montrachet 1943 with the sole and then consumed a roast partridge stuffed with truffles and washed it down with a Beaune Grèves 1929, a fine red Burgundy.

So great were Curnonsky's appetite and reputation that in 1927, when the newspaper *Paris-Soir* polled 5,000 gastronomes, chefs and restaurant owners, he was elected prince of all gastronomes in France. In the years that followed there was hardly a banquet or a meal of importance in France that he did not attend. Restaurants implored him to dine on their premises. Cookbook authors begged for prefaces under his name, and he became one of the first gastronomes to appreciate the relationship between the automobile and food. With a companion, Marcel Rouff, he traveled throughout France, visiting restaurants and writing articles on them. Together they produced *La France gastronomique,* 28 paper-bound volumes, that told everyone where to go and what to eat.

At this point it might well be asked: Having toured the great French restaurants past and present, which one would you choose above all others? If you could dine at *any* restaurant that ever existed in France, which one would you pick? Beauvilliers? The Café Anglais? Maxim's?

There are many fine restaurants today that I might choose from. In Paris I might go to Lasserre, which has come up in recent years. Or I might pick any of the other three-star restaurants *(page 129):* La Tour d'Argent, Maxim's, or the Grand Véfour. I might even try a two-star restaurant. Some of them are excellent, possibly because they try harder.

In picking the setting for this momentous, all-time meal, I might be tempted to go outside Paris. Nowadays some of the finest restaurants are in the provinces. I might select the Pyramide in Vienne, Paul Bocuse's near Lyon or the Troisgros in Roanne. Still another place that I might choose is the Baumanière in Les Baux-de-Provence. The setting here is almost enough in itself. You drive out from Arles past gnarled cypress trees that almost seem to have been painted there by Van Gogh. Then, around Les Baux the country looks old geologically, with bare, weathered stone mountains. The restaurant is on a terrace with a weeping willow and other shade trees, and there is a swimming pool close by. The woodcock pâté and the *gigot d'agneau en croûte* (boned, stuffed leg of spring lamb in pastry crust) are excellent, and on a sparkling day with a bottle of good Burgundy, you may want to sit there forever.

Still I suspect my choice of all the French restaurants would be one that no longer exists and is not included in most chronicles of outstanding eating establishments: Montagné, Traiteur, which used to stand in Paris on the rue de l'Echelle near the Palais Royal. The reason for the choice would be the chef Prosper Montagné, one of the most remarkable men in the history of French cuisine. Montagné was an evangelist. As Dr. Alfred Gottschalk, the gastronomic authority, has noted, Montagné preached "that the basis of all good cooking must be good taste and common sense, and not mere fancy and make-believe." As a young man he worked at the Grand Hôtel in Monte Carlo. Then he went to Paris to the Restaurant Ledoyen and the Pavillon d'Armenonville in the Bois de Boulogne. He produced the great encyclopedia of food, wine and cookery, *Larousse gastronomique,* and he was an incomparable chef, so good in fact that in 1920 a group of affluent gourmets offered to set him up in business at Montagné, Traiteur. Curnonsky acclaimed the restaurant, and the way Dr. Gottschalk described it is enough to make me wish I could have gone there. "There never was better food nor better service anywhere in Paris," Gottschalk said. "Montagné served . . . none but the finest classical dishes. . . . Everybody who went was enchanted, and would not have missed it for anything."

Montagné's menu included pheasant pâté with foie gras, saddle of lamb with stuffed squashes, breast of veal Curnonsky, quail, young partridge, woodcock, thrush and chicken. Unfortunately, the great chef was not much of a businessman; his restaurant closed after a decade and its failure left him penniless. Yet considering the recommendations of those who knew the place, I would like nothing better than to be able to have a meal at Montagné, Traiteur at the peak of its glory. I am not sure what dishes I would choose, but this is a problem I would like to tackle.

MAURICE EDMOND SAILLAND
(1872-1956)

Sailland, better known as Curnonsky, was elected "prince of gastronomes" in France in 1927. A professional food connoisseur, he spent a large part of his life eating in restaurants and writing about his gastronomic experiences. His articles on restaurants in Paris and the provinces were a forerunner of the *Guide Michelin (opposite).*

The Ups and Downs of France's Top Restaurants

In France the best way to get a good line on a restaurant or a hotel before you go there is to look it up in the *Guide Michelin*. The *Guide* evaluates restaurants and hotels in more than 3,400 towns and cities. Its top rating is three stars, which means, as the *Guide* puts it, that the establishment is "well worth the journey." A new *Guide* is issued every year, and even the most illustrious restaurants may lose their rating. As seen here, in the decade 1960-1970 four restaurants lost their three-star rating and six others climbed to the top. Below are listed the three-star restaurants for 1960 and 1970, with their locations and some pertinent information about each establishment.

1960

PARIS
MAXIM's, 3 rue Royale Tel: ANJ 27-94, closed Sunday. Lunch à la carte 25 to 35 francs; dinner à la carte 30 to 45 francs.

TOUR D'ARGENT, 15 quai Tournelle Tel: ODE 23-31, closed Monday. A la carte 26 to 52 francs.

GRAND VEFOUR, 17 rue Beaujolais Tel: RIC 58-97, closed Sundays and August. A la carte 27 to 50 francs.

LAPEROUSE, 51 quai Grands Augustins Tel: DAN 68-04, closed Sundays in June, July, August. A la carte 20 to 31 francs.

AVALLON
POSTE, 13 place Vauban Tel: 4.48, closed January 15-February 5. Set price meal 35 francs and à la carte.

LES BAUX-DE-PROVENCE
BAUMANIERE, Tel: 7, closed November 2-December 5. A la carte 22 to 35 francs.

NOVES
LA PETITE AUBERGE, Tel: 2.21. Set price meal 24 francs and à la carte.

SAULIEU
CÔTE D'OR, 2 rue Argentine Tel: 0.18, closed October 10-November 15. A la carte 16 to 38 francs.

TALLOIRES
AUBERGE DU PERE BISE, Tel: 45.88.01. Set price meal 35 francs and à la carte.

VIENNE
PYRAMIDE, boulevard Pyramide Tel: 85.00.96, closed Tuesdays and November. Set price meals 30 or 35 francs.

1970

PARIS
LASSERRE, 17 ave. Franklin D. Roosevelt Tel: 359.53.43, closed Sundays and August 2-31. A la carte 56 to 95 francs.

MAXIM's, 3 rue Royale Tel: 265.27.94. A la carte 55 to 100 francs.

TOUR D'ARGENT, 15 quai Tournelle Tel: 033.23.32, closed Monday. A la carte 70 to 90 francs.

GRAND VEFOUR, 17 rue Beaujolais Tel: 742.58.97, closed Sundays and August 8-26. A la carte 55 to 100 francs.

LES BAUX-DE-PROVENCE
OUSTAU DE BAUMANIERE
Tel: 7, Telex 42203 Baucabro Baux. A la carte 55 to 85 francs.

ILLHAEUSERN
AUBERGE DE L'ILL, Tel: 47.83.23, closed Tuesdays and January 15-February 15. Set price lunch 38 francs (weekdays only) or 58 francs; dinner à la carte only.

LYON
PAUL BOCUSE, Collonges-au-Mont-d'Or, 50 quai Plage Tel: 47.00.14. Closed August 9-23. Set price meals 50 or 60 francs and à la carte.

LA NAPOULE-PLAGE
L'OASIS, Tel: 38.95.52. Closed Tuesdays from January to Easter and November 1-December 15. Set price meals 35 or 45 francs and à la carte.

ROANNE
TROISGROS, place de la Gare Tel: 71.26.68, closed January 3-13. Set price meals 36 francs (weekdays only) or 66 francs and à la carte.

TALLOIRES
AUBERGE DU PERE BISE, Tel: 45.88.01. Set price meal 70 francs and à la carte.

TOURS
BARRIER, 101 ave. Tranchée Tel: 53.20.39, closed Wednesdays and July 6-26. Set price meals 45 or 55 francs and à la carte.

VIENNE
PYRAMIDE, boulevard F. Point Tel: 85.00.96 closed Tuesdays and November 1-December 15. Set price meals 60 or 70 francs.

Côtes d'agneau sautés
SAUTÉED LAMB CHOPS

Pat the lamb chops completely dry with paper towels and season them evenly on both sides with salt and a few grindings of pepper.

In a heavy 12-inch skillet, heat the clarified butter over high heat until a drop of water flicked into it splutters and evaporates instantly. Add the lamb chops and sauté them for 3 to 4 minutes on each side, or until they are cooked to the state of doneness you prefer. Ideally they should be medium rare. Arrange the chops attractively on a heated platter and serve at once accompanied, if you like, by any of the potato recipes that follow.

8 rib lamb chops, 4 to 5 ounces each, cut 1 inch thick and French style *(see opposite page)*
Salt
Freshly ground black pepper
¼ cup clarified butter *(page 34)*

Pommes sarladaise
POTATO SLICES MOLDED WITH TRUFFLES

To serve 8

Preheat the oven to 475°. With a pastry brush, spread the oil over the bottom and sides of a 9-inch cast-iron skillet or a 9-inch round cake pan with a nonstick cooking surface. The pan must be at least 1½ inches deep.

With a swivel-bladed vegetable parer or a small knife, peel and shape the potatoes into neat ovals, dropping them into cold water as you proceed. Then cut the potatoes into ⅛-inch-thick rounds, using a *mandoline* or other vegetable slicer; ideally the thickness of the slices should be as uniform as possible. Rinse the slices as you proceed and then wrap them in a dampened towel. (There should be about 6 cups of potato slices.)

In a heavy 10- to 12-inch skillet, warm ¼ cup of the clarified butter over moderate heat for 10 seconds. Pat a handful of the potatoes completely dry with paper towels and fry them in the butter for 3 or 4 minutes, turning the slices from time to time with a spatula until they are translucent and pale yellow on both sides. Transfer the potatoes to a large platter and proceed with the remaining slices, adding more butter to the skillet when necessary.

Ring the bottom of the 9-inch skillet or cake pan with a row of alternately overlapping potato and truffle rounds. Fill the space in the center with concentric rings of overlapped potato slices and line the sides of the pan with more potato rounds. Then fill the pan completely with the remaining potato and truffle rounds, at random. (The top layer of potatoes may rise slightly above the rim of the pan but the potatoes will settle and shrink as they bake.)

Bake in the middle of the oven for 40 minutes, pressing gently down on the top with a wide spatula every 10 minutes or so. When finished, the potatoes should show no resistance to the point of a sharp knife.

Remove the potatoes from the oven and run a thin metal spatula around the inside edges of the pan. Place a heated serving plate upside down over the pan and, grasping plate and pan together, invert them quickly. The *pommes sarladaise* should slide out in a cake. If any slices stick to the pan, carefully lift them out and return them to their original places.

1 tablespoon vegetable oil
4½ to 5 pounds baking potatoes
½ cup clarified butter *(page 34)*
3 black truffles, thinly peeled and cut into ⅛-inch-thick rounds *(see Glossary)*

Artfully arranged French-style lamb chops are accompanied by tricky *pommes soufflées* in this *côtes d'agneau pommes soufflées en nids.* The potatoes are fried in oil once, then fried again at a hotter temperature.

INGREDIENTS FOR POTATO RECIPES

To serve 6

3 pounds firm baking potatoes, all
   of the same size
Vegetable oil or shortening for deep
   frying
Salt

The ubiquitous "French-fry" in the United States is only one version of France's *"pommes frites"*—and not the most interesting one by any means. In France, potatoes are sliced, slivered, ruffled and cut in strips of many sizes before they are fried. For best results, potatoes should be shaped uniformly—and sliced on a French *mandoline* with adjustable blades. Precise frying requires a large, heavy pan that will hold 3 inches of fat when half-full, a wire frying basket, a slotted spoon or skimmer, and a thermometer to keep the fat at the exact temperature required. On these pages are some recipes for authentically French deep-fried potatoes.

Pommes allumettes
MATCHSTICK POTATOES

Peel and shape the potatoes into rectangles about 2½ to 3 inches long, dropping them into cold water as you proceed. With an adjustable-blade *mandoline,* cut the rectangles lengthwise into sticks about ¼ inch thick and ¼ inch wide, or cut the potatoes with a sharp knife. Rinse in cold water and wrap the potatoes in a dampened towel to prevent discoloring.

Pour vegetable oil to a depth of at least 3 inches into a deep-fryer or large, heavy saucepan lined with a basket. Heat until the oil reaches a temperature of 330° on a deep-frying thermometer.

A handful at a time, pat the potato strips dry with paper towels. Lift the basket, drop the strips into it, and plunge them into the hot oil. Turning the strips constantly with a skimmer or slotted spoon, fry for about 3 minutes, or until the potatoes are pale gold on all sides. As they are finished, transfer them to paper towels to drain.

Just before serving, heat the oil to 360°. Deep-fry the matchsticks, in the basket by the handful, again, for 1 or 2 minutes, or until lightly browned. Drain on paper towels, add salt to taste and serve at once.

Pommes gaufrettes
WAFFLED DEEP-FRIED POTATO SLICES

Peel and shape the potatoes into neat ovals, dropping them into cold water as you proceed. With the ruffled blade of a *mandoline* adjusted to make ¼-inch-thick slices, cut one potato at a time crosswise into rounds, turning at right angles after each stroke so that one side of the slice is ruffled horizontally and the other side vertically. Rinse the slices in cold water and wrap them in a dampened towel to prevent discoloring.

Pour oil into a deep-fryer or large, heavy saucepan lined with a basket to a depth of at least 3 inches. Heat until the oil reaches a temperature of 375° on a deep-frying thermometer.

A handful at a time, pat the wafflelike slices completely dry with paper towels. Lift the basket, drop the slices in it and plunge it into the hot oil. Turning the slices frequently with a skimmer or slotted spoon, deep-fry for 2 or 3 minutes until they color lightly and evenly. As they are finished transfer the *pommes gaufrettes* to paper toweling. Sprinkle with salt and serve the *pommes gaufrettes* while they are still warm.

Pommes soufflées
PUFFED DEEP-FRIED POTATO SLICES

Peel and shape the potatoes into smooth ovals about 2 inches in diameter at the widest part, dropping them into cold water as you proceed. With an adjustable-bladed *mandoline* or other slicer, cut the potatoes into ⅜-inch-thick rounds. Wrap the slices in a damp towel to prevent discoloring.

Pour vegetable oil into two large, heavy saucepans at least 8 inches deep, filling them both to a depth of 3 inches. Heat the oil in one pan until it reaches a temperature of 325° on a deep-frying thermometer, and the oil in the second pan until it reaches 375°.

A handful at a time, pat the slices completely dry with paper towels and drop them one by one into the 325° oil. Sliding the pan gently back and forth on the burner so that the potatoes cook evenly, deep-fry them for 6 minutes. Transfer the slices to the 375° oil with a skimmer. They should puff up almost immediately. As they puff, place them on a linen towel to drain. (Set the potatoes which have not puffed aside separately to serve as plain *pommes frites;* there may be a few in each batch.) Proceed in similar fashion with the remaining slices. At this point, the potatoes can wait for several hours before final cooking.

Just before serving, heat one pan of oil to 385°. Drop in the potatoes a few at a time and deep-fry for 1 minute or until they puff up again and are golden. Remove them from the oil with a skimmer, drain briefly on paper towels, salt to taste and serve.

Pommes pailles
STRAW POTATOES

Peel the potatoes, dropping them into cold water as you proceed. Adjust the blade and cross-cutting mechanism of a *mandoline* to produce the thinnest, narrowest strips possible. Rinse in cold water and wrap the strips in a dampened towel to prevent discoloring.

Pour vegetable oil to a depth of at least 3 inches in a deep-fryer or large, heavy saucepan. Heat until the oil reaches a temperature of 375° on a deep-frying thermometer. A handful at a time, drop the potato strips into the basket. Plunge it into the hot oil. Turning the strips constantly with a skimmer or spoon, fry them for about 3 minutes until golden. As they brown, transfer them to paper towels to drain. Season with salt and serve the *pommes pailles* while they are still warm.

To make nests, cut the strips as described above. Without rinsing them, wrap in a dampened towel. When the oil reaches 375°, pat half of the potato strips evenly against the bottom and sides of the larger section of a nest-shaped frying basket, letting enough strips extend above the rim of the basket to create a nestlike effect. Set the smaller section of the basket over them and clamp the handles securely together. Plunge the basket into the hot oil and deep-fry the potatoes for about 3 minutes, until they are golden brown. Remove the basket from the oil, and slip out the inside section. Invert the larger section over paper towels and slide out the potato nest. Set aside while you prepare the second nest in the same fashion as the first. Serve the potato nests filled with any of the deep-fried potatoes on these pages.

To serve 8

SOUBISE

4 tablespoons unsalted butter

2 cups coarsely chopped onions

½ cup uncooked long-grain
    regular-milled white rice

1 cup *fond blanc de volaille (page
    31)*, or substitute 1 cup canned
    chicken stock, chilled then
    degreased

PURÉE DE CHAMPIGNONS

1 pound fresh mushrooms

2 tablespoons clarified butter *(page
    34)*

1 cup heavy cream

1½ tablespoons strained fresh
    lemon juice

Beurre manié made from 2
    tablespoons unsalted butter,
    softened and rubbed to a paste
    with 2 tablespoons flour

½ teaspoon salt

Freshly ground white pepper

SELLE DE VEAU

A 5½- to 6-pound saddle of veal
    (a short double loin), with inner
    fat removed and all but ⅛ inch
    of fat trimmed from the surface

2 teaspoons salt

½ teaspoon freshly ground black
    pepper

3 tablespoons butter, softened

1 pound veal bones, sawed into
    1-inch lengths

1 large onion, peeled and cut into
    ¼-inch-thick rounds

½ cup thinly sliced scraped carrots

½ cup thinly sliced celery

1 medium-sized firm, ripe tomato,
    coarsely chopped

A *bouquet garni* made of ½ cup
    parsley stems, 1 medium-sized
    bay leaf and 2 thyme sprigs or
    ½ teaspoon dried thyme *(see
    Glossary)*

¼ cup dry white wine

2 tablespoons *glace de viande (page
    34)*

2 large black truffles *(see Glossary)*,
    cut into ⅛-inch-thick rounds

Selle de veau Orloff
SADDLE OF VEAL WITH SOUBISE, MUSHROOMS, TRUFFLES AND MORNAY SAUCE

SOUBISE (ONION-AND-RICE MIXTURE): Preheat the oven to 325°. In a heavy 1½- to 2-quart casserole, melt the 4 tablespoons of butter over moderate heat. When the foam begins to subside, add the chopped onions and, stirring frequently, cook for about 5 minutes until they are soft and translucent but not brown. Watch carefully for any sign of burning and regulate the heat accordingly.

Stir in the rice and stock and bring to a boil over high heat. Cover the casserole tightly and bake in the middle of the oven for 45 minutes, or until the grains are soft and have absorbed all of the liquid. Purée the onion-and-rice mixture through the finest blade of a food mill, or rub it through a fine sieve with the back of a spoon. Set the mixture aside.

PURÉE DE CHAMPIGNONS (MUSHROOM PURÉE): Wipe the mushrooms with a damp cloth and trim off and discard the base of the stems. Then put them through the finest blade of a food grinder or chop both caps and stems as fine as possible. A handful at once, place the mushrooms in the corner of a towel or double thickness of cheesecloth and squeeze vigorously to extract as much of their juice as possible.

In a heavy 8- to 10-inch skillet, heat 2 tablespoons of butter over moderate heat for 10 seconds. Add the mushrooms and, stirring constantly, cook over low heat for 3 or 4 minutes. The mushrooms are done when the liquid accumulated in the pan evaporates. Do not let them brown.

Pour in 1 cup of heavy cream and simmer for 5 minutes, stirring occasionally. Then stir in the lemon juice, the butter-and-flour paste *(beurre manié)*, salt and a pinch of white pepper. Continue cooking for 4 or 5 minutes longer, still stirring occasionally until the *beurre manié* has been absorbed. Stir the purée into the onion-and-rice mixture, cool to room temperature, cover with foil or plastic wrap and set aside.

SELLE DE VEAU (SADDLE OF VEAL): Ask the butcher to prepare the veal for roasting in the following fashion, or do it yourself: Trim the bone at the base of the front end of the saddle with a cleaver so that the saddle will lie perfectly flat. Then trim any ragged edges from the flaps. Sprinkle the underside of the veal with 1 teaspoon of salt and ¼ teaspoon of the black pepper. Tuck the flaps under and, with white kitchen cord, tie the saddle crosswise in at least 3 places.

Preheat the oven to 400°. Sprinkle the top of the saddle evenly with 1 teaspoon of salt and ¼ teaspoon of pepper and rub it with 3 tablespoons of softened butter. Spread the bones as evenly as possible in the bottom of a shallow roasting pan large enough to hold the saddle comfortably and set the saddle, fat side up, on top.

Roast the veal uncovered and undisturbed in the middle of the oven for 30 minutes. Then reduce the oven heat to 350°. Scatter the onion, carrots, celery and tomato around the saddle and add the *bouquet garni*. Cover the pan snugly with heavy foil and braise the veal undisturbed for 30 minutes. Then remove the foil and roast for 30 minutes longer. Transfer the veal to a cutting board and let it cool to room temperature.

With tongs or a slotted spoon remove and discard the bones from the roasting pan and pour in the wine and *glace de viande*. Bring to a boil over high heat, stirring constantly and scraping in the browned particles

134

that cling to the bottom and sides of the pan. Strain the mixture through a fine sieve into a bowl, pressing down on the vegetables with the back of a spoon to extract all their juices before discarding them. Set the strained liquid aside. When it cools, skim all the fat from the surface.

TO ASSEMBLE THE VEAL: Cut off the trussing strings and carve the veal into ¼-inch-thick slices following the diagram in the Recipe Booklet. In order to reassemble them easily, keep the slices from each side in separate stacks, and in the order in which you have cut them. Spread one slice at a time with about a ¼-inch-thick layer of the onion-and-mushroom mixture, place a truffle round in the center of the slice and return the slice to its original place on the saddle.

When the saddle is completely reassembled, carefully place it on a rack in a shallow roasting pan. With a metal spatula spread the remaining onion-and-mushroom mixture over the entire surface of the saddle, smoothing and masking it completely.

At this point the saddle, covered with foil, may safely wait at room temperature for 2 to 3 hours. The Mornay sauce also may be made 2 or 3 hours in advance and finished at the last minute. Half an hour before serving preheat the oven to 375°.

SAUCE MORNAY: In a heavy 8- to 10-inch skillet, combine the *sauce béchamel* and ¼ cup of heavy cream. Stirring constantly with a wire whisk, cook over low heat until the sauce is heated through, but do not let it come to a boil. Whisk in the egg yolks, one at a time, add the cayenne, and, stirring constantly, simmer for about a minute longer. Remove the skillet from the heat and stir in half of the grated cheese. At this point the sauce may be dotted with butter to prevent a skin from forming on the top, then covered and kept for 2 or 3 hours before finishing. Just before using fold in the whipped cream.

FINAL COOKING: Spoon the Mornay sauce on top of the saddle of veal, and smooth it evenly with a spatula, again masking it completely. Sprinkle the remaining grated cheese evenly over the sauce. Roast in the middle of the preheated 375° oven for 15 to 20 minutes, or until the topping is a delicate golden brown.

Transfer the saddle to a large heated platter. Arrange the previously prepared garniture of salsify and cucumber-filled tartlets *(below)* attractively around the veal. Quickly reheat the reserved roasting liquid, spoon some of it onto the platter and pour the remaining liquid into a sauceboat and serve.

GARNITURE: The fresh salsify may be poached hours in advance and reheated at the last minute; canned salsify needs only to be drained, washed under cold water and patted dry before it is heated for serving. The tartlets may be made a day ahead of time; the cucumbers to fill them can be poached several hours ahead of time but they must be sautéed and sauced at the last minute.

SALSIFIS (SALSIFY): Poach the fresh salsify, if you are using it, in the following fashion *(à blanc)*: In a heavy 2- to 3-quart saucepan, whisk the flour and ½ cup of the cold water together to make a smooth paste. Beat in the remaining 5½ cups of water, the ¼ cup of lemon juice and 1 teaspoon of the salt. Add the fresh salsify and spoon the liquid over it. Bring to a boil, then reduce the heat to low and simmer for about 20 minutes,

SAUCE MORNAY
1½ cups *sauce béchamel (page 35)*
¼ cup heavy cream, plus ¼ cup heavy cream whipped into soft peaks
2 egg yolks
Ground hot red pepper (cayenne)
¼ cup finely grated imported Parmesan combined with ¼ cup finely grated imported Gruyère cheese

SALSIFIS
¼ cup flour
6 cups cold water
¼ cup fresh lemon juice
1¼ teaspoons salt
2 pounds fresh salsify (or oyster plant), peeled, cut into 1½-inch lengths and dropped immediately into cold water, or substitute one 15-ounce can imported salsify
2 tablespoons clarified butter *(page 34)*
⅛ teaspoon freshly ground white pepper

Continued on page 138

A High-Riding Saddle of Veal

The *selle de veau Orloff*, a longtime favorite at Maxim's and other leading French restaurants, is a roast saddle of veal with puréed mushrooms, a *soubise* (onion sauce) and Mornay sauce. This version of the dish serves eight and is garnished with cucumber-filled tartlets and strips of salsify.

or until the salsify is tender and shows only slight resistance when pierced with the point of a small knife. Set the salsify aside to cool to room temperature in its poaching liquid.

Just before serving, drain the fresh salsify or the canned salsify in a sieve or colander, and run cold water over it. Pat the pieces dry with paper towels. In a heavy 8- to 10-inch skillet, warm 2 tablespoons of clarified butter over moderate heat for 10 seconds. Drop in the salsify and, turning it about frequently with a spoon, sauté for about 5 minutes, or until it is heated through. Do not let it brown. Season with ¼ teaspoon salt and ⅛ teaspoon white pepper and serve at once.

TARTLETTES DE CONCOMBRES (CUCUMBERS IN TARTLET SHELLS): With a small, sharp knife, peel the cucumbers and cut them lengthwise into quarters. Scrape out the seeds with a spoon and cut the cucumber strips into olive shapes about 1 to 1¼ inches long and ¾ inches in diameter.

Drop the cucumber-olives into enough lightly salted boiling water to cover them completely. Let the water return to a boil, then reduce the heat to low and simmer uncovered for 5 minutes. Remove from the heat, and pour off all the water. Cover the pan and set the cucumbers aside at room temperature. (They can wait in this state for 2 or 3 hours.)

Just before serving, spread the cucumbers on paper towels and pat them dry. In a heavy 8- to 10-inch skillet, warm 2 tablespoons of clarified butter over moderate heat for 10 seconds. Add the cucumbers and, turning them about constantly with a spoon, cook for 2 or 3 minutes until they are heated through. Do not let the cucumbers brown. Pour in ½ cup of heavy cream and add the ½ teaspoon salt and ⅛ teaspoon white pepper. Stirring all the while, continue cooking for 3 minutes. Taste for seasoning and stir in the tarragon. Immediately spoon the cucumbers and cream into the tartlet shells and serve.

Filet de boeuf Richelieu
ROAST FILLET OF BEEF WITH FILLED MUSHROOM CAPS, BRAISED LETTUCE, CHÂTEAU POTATOES, AND TOMATOES

FILET: Preheat the oven to 450°. Sprinkle the fillet evenly with 2 teaspoons of salt and ½ teaspoon of pepper and rub the 2 tablespoons of softened butter into all sides of the meat. Insert a meat thermometer at least 2 inches into one end of the beef. Place the fillet on a rack in a large, shallow pan and roast in the middle of the oven for 30 minutes, or until the thermometer reaches a temperature of 120° to 125°. (The fillet will continue to cook internally after it is removed from the oven.) Transfer the fillet to a heated platter, and let it rest at room temperature for 5 to 10 minutes before serving.

Prepare the sauce in the following fashion: Combine the Madeira, truffles and truffle juice in a small, heavy skillet and bring to a boil over high heat. Stirring occasionally, cook briskly for 2 or 3 minutes. Add the *fond lié* and bring to a simmer, reduce the heat to low and cook for 8 to 10 minutes, stirring from time to time. When the sauce is as thick as heavy cream, remove the skillet from the heat, add the remaining 1½ teaspoons salt and 3 or 4 grindings of fresh pepper and swirl in the 4 tablespoons of butter bits and the cognac.

TARTLETTES DE CONCOMBRES

3 medium-sized cucumbers

2 tablespoons clarified butter *(page 34)*

½ cup heavy cream

½ teaspoon salt

⅛ teaspoon freshly ground white pepper

8 three-inch *pâte brisée* tartlet shells *(Recipe Booklet)*

1 teaspoon finely cut fresh tarragon or ½ teaspoon crumbled dried tarragon

To serve 8

FILET

A 4-pound fillet of beef, center cut, trimmed and tied at equal intervals in 4 places around the meat

3½ teaspoons salt

½ teaspoon freshly ground black pepper

2 tablespoons softened butter, and 4 tablespoons unsalted butter, chilled and cut into ½-inch bits

¼ cup dry Madeira

⅓ cup thinly peeled and finely chopped black truffles *(see Glossary)*

¼ cup truffle juice *(see Glossary)*

1 cup *fond lié (page 35)*

2 tablespoons cognac

To serve, arrange the previously prepared garniture *(below)* of filled mushroom caps, braised lettuce, château potatoes and tomatoes in an attractive pattern around the beef. Moisten the fillet with a little sauce and serve the rest separately in a sauceboat.

GARNITURE: The mushroom caps and *duxelles* filling may be prepared 3 or 4 hours ahead of time and then reheated. Braise the lettuce and parboil the potatoes at the same time. However, the final cooking of the potatoes and the tomatoes must be done while the fillet is roasting.

CHAMPIGNONS FARCIS (MUSHROOM CAPS FILLED WITH DUXELLES): To prepare ½ cup of *duxelles,* warm the 2 tablespoons of clarified butter over moderate heat for about 10 seconds. Add the shallots and onions and stir for 2 or 3 minutes until they are soft but not brown. Then drop in the chopped mushrooms, add the lemon juice and, stirring constantly, cook for about 3 to 4 minutes, or until they have released some of their liquid. Reduce the heat to low and, stirring from time to time, simmer for 10 to 15 minutes or even longer. The mushroom mixture is done when all its liquid has evaporated and the *duxelles* is fairly dry. Do not let the mushrooms brown. Stir in the teaspoon of parsley.

Wipe the mushroom caps clean with a damp cloth and brush them evenly with 3 tablespoons of the melted clarified butter. Arrange the caps stem side up in a lightly buttered baking dish just large enough to hold them comfortably, and then sprinkle them with ½ teaspoon salt and ¼ teaspoon of pepper. Bake in a preheated 450° oven for about 10 minutes, or until the mushrooms are tender but still firm. Remove them from the oven and fill each cap with about 1 tablespoon of the *duxelles,* mounding the top slightly. Sprinkle with bread crumbs and moisten with the remaining 2 tablespoons of melted clarified butter. Cover with foil and set aside. Just before serving reheat for 2 or 3 minutes in a 450° oven.

LAITUE BRAISÉE (BRAISED LETTUCE): Remove any wilted outer leaves from the lettuce and cut off the bottoms of the lettuce heads, but take care not to cut so deeply that the leaves separate. Rinse the heads in cold water, spreading the leaves apart gently to remove any traces of sand. Drop the lettuce in 3 or 4 quarts of boiling water and cook briskly for 2 or 3 minutes, or until the leaves are limp. Immediately remove the lettuce with tongs and plunge it into cold water for a few minutes to set its color. Gently squeeze each head, pat it dry with paper towels, and cut each head into quarters. (The inner leaves may have become somewhat brown after cooking.) Flatten each quarter by pressing it gently with the side of a cleaver or large knife blade. Trim the ragged side edges of the lettuce quarter with a knife to form a smooth-sided triangle, then cut off the heavy white stem at the core. Place the lettuce so the inside leaves are facing down, fold under the tops of the leaves and shape each triangle into an oblong packet. Set the lettuce aside on paper towels.

In a heavy 10- to 12-inch skillet, melt the 2 tablespoons of butter over moderate heat. Add the carrot, onion, bay leaf, thyme, salt and a liberal grinding of black pepper. Stirring frequently, cook for 3 or 4 minutes until the vegetables are slightly soft but not brown. Arrange the lettuce packets, inside leaves down, in one layer on top of the vegetables and pour the ¾ cup of *fond lié* over them. Cover with a circle of buttered wax paper or parchment paper cut to fit snugly into the skillet, reduce

CHAMPIGNONS FARCIS
2 tablespoons clarified butter *(page 34)*
2 tablespoons finely chopped shallots
2 tablespoons finely chopped onions
1 cup finely chopped fresh mushroom stems and caps (about ¼ pound)
2 teaspoons lemon juice
1 teaspoon freshly chopped parsley
8 fresh mushroom caps, each about 2 inches in diameter
5 tablespoons melted clarified butter *(page 34)*
½ teaspoon salt
¼ teaspoon pepper
2 teaspoons soft fresh crumbs made from homemade-type white bread, trimmed of crusts and pulverized in a blender or finely shredded with a fork

LAITUE BRAISÉE
5 firm 5- to 6-inch heads Boston lettuce
2 tablespoons butter
1 medium-sized carrot, scraped and finely chopped
1 medium-sized onion, peeled and finely chopped
1 medium-sized bay leaf
⅛ teaspoon finely chopped fresh or crumbled dried thyme
1 teaspoon salt
Freshly ground black pepper
¾ cup *fond lié (page 35)*

the heat to low and braise the lettuce for about 20 minutes until tender.

If you plan to use the lettuce at once, transfer it with a slotted spatula to a heated platter. Strain the sauce through a fine sieve set over a bowl and spoon it over the lettuce. If you make the lettuce earlier (it may safely be kept at room temperature for an hour or so), leave it undisturbed in the skillet. Just before serving, warm the lettuce over low heat for 3 to 4 minutes, basting it once or twice with its braising liquid.

POMMES CHÂTEAU (CHÂTEAU POTATOES): With a small, sharp knife, peel the potatoes and cut them into egglike shapes about 2½ inches long and 1½ inches in diameter at the middle. Trim a ¼-inch slice off each end, then shape each potato into a faceted but slightly rounded oval by removing 7 thin lengthwise slices. Drop the potatoes into enough slightly salted water to cover them completely and boil briskly for 2 or 3 minutes. Drain the potatoes, then pat them completely dry with paper towels.

Just before serving, preheat the oven to 450°. In an 8-inch ovenproof skillet, heat the ¼ cup of clarified butter for about 10 seconds. Add the potatoes and, turning them frequently with a spatula, sauté over moderate heat for 4 or 5 minutes until they are lightly browned on all sides. Place the skillet in the oven and, turning the potatoes over occasionally, bake for 25 minutes, or until they are crisp and golden brown.

TOMATES ÉTUVÉES AU BEURRE (BAKED TOMATOES): Drop the tomatoes into a pan of boiling water and boil briskly for about 10 seconds. Run cold water over them and peel them with a small, sharp knife. Cut out the stems. Squeeze the tomatoes gently to remove the seeds and juice. One at a time, place a tomato on a kitchen towel. Pull the towel up tightly around the tomato, enclosing it completely. Twist the ends of the towel together close to the tomato and squeeze gently to shape the tomato into a compact ball. Brush the tomatoes with the clarified butter, set them in a baking dish and lightly salt and pepper them. Cover with foil and set aside for an hour or so before baking. Bake the tomatoes for 8 to 10 minutes in a 450° oven or until they are tender but still intact. Serve at once.

POMMES CHÂTEAU
8 medium-sized boiling potatoes
¼ cup clarified butter *(page 34)*

TOMATES ÉTUVÉES AU BEURRE
8 large firm ripe tomatoes, each
    about 3 inches in diameter
6 tablespoons clarified butter *(page 34)*
½ teaspoon salt
Freshly ground white pepper

Crêpes Suzette
DESSERT CRÊPES WITH GRAND MARNIER-FLAVORED SAUCE

CRÊPES: To make the batter with an electric blender, combine the flour, 3 tablespoons sugar, eggs, milk, ¼ cup Grand Marnier and 2 tablespoons melted, cooled butter in the blender jar. Blend at high speed for a few seconds. Turn off the machine, scrape down the sides of the jar with a rubber spatula and then blend again for about 30 or 40 seconds. Pour the batter into a deep mixing bowl.

To make the crêpe batter by hand, stir the flour, sugar and eggs together in a mixing bowl and gradually stir in the milk and Grand Marnier. Beat with a wire whisk or a rotary or electric beater until the flour lumps disappear, then rub through a fine sieve into another bowl and stir in the melted, cooled butter.

Cover and refrigerate the batter for at least two hours before using it. To fry the crêpes, warm a 4- to 5-inch crêpe pan or skillet over high heat until a drop of water flicked into it splutters and evaporates instantly. With a hair bristled (not nylon) pastry brush, lightly grease the bottom

To serve 8

CRÊPES
1¼ cups all-purpose flour
3 tablespoons sugar
4 eggs
1¾ cups milk
¼ cup Grand Marnier, Cointreau
    or other orange-flavored liqueur
2 tablespoons unsalted butter,
    melted and cooled, plus 6
    tablespoons melted clarified
    butter *(page 34)*

and sides of the heated pan with a little of the melted clarified butter.

Stir the crêpe batter lightly with a wire whisk or a spoon; then, using a small ladle, pour about 2 tablespoons of the batter into the pan. Tip the pan from side to side so that the batter quickly covers the bottom; the batter will cling to the pan and begin to firm up almost immediately. At once tilt the pan over the bowl and pour off any excess batter; the finished crêpe should be paper-thin.

Cook the crêpe for a minute or so until a rim of brown shows around the edge. Turn it over with a spatula and cook the other side for a minute longer. Slide the crêpe onto a plate. Brush clarified butter on the pan again and make the remaining crêpes similarly. As the crêpes are finished, stack them one upon the other. The crêpes may be made hours ahead of time and kept, covered with plastic wrap, at room temperature.

SAUCE SUZETTE: One at a time, infuse 3 of the sugar cubes with lemon oil by pressing and rubbing them into the surface of the lemon, turning each cube about to coat it on all sides. Similarly, infuse 3 sugar cubes with orange oil by rubbing them into the orange. Set the lemon aside for another use, but squeeze the orange. Strain the juice into a measuring cup; there should be ½ cup, if necessary squeeze another orange. Drop the 6 flavored sugar cubes into the orange juice and mash and stir until they dissolve completely. Set aside at room temperature.

In a deep bowl, cream the ¼ pound of softened butter with 1 tablespoon of sugar, beating and mashing them together against the sides of the bowl with the back of a large spoon until the mixture is light and smooth. Cover the bowl tightly with plastic wrap and refrigerate until it is ready to use.

FINAL ASSEMBLY: When you are ready to serve the crêpes suzette, complete them at the dinner table. Light an alcohol burner or table-top stove and set a 12-inch copper crêpe suzette or flambé pan over the flame. Place the plate of crêpes, the remaining ¼ cup of Grand Marnier and the dark rum conveniently beside the pan. (You may also measure the liqueur and rum ahead of time and combine them in a pitcher or cruet.)

Warm the creamed butter and sugar in the crêpe pan, stirring from time to time so that the mixture melts evenly without burning. Add the orange juice mixture and, stirring frequently, cook briskly until the sauce has been reduced to ½ cup.

With a serving fork in one hand, and a serving spoon in the other, lift up a crêpe and lay it in the sauce. Quickly turn the crêpe over and when both sides are moistened with sauce, fold it in half and then in half again to make a triangular shape. Push the finished crêpe to the side of the pan and repeat the procedure with the remaining crêpes, arranging them attractively in overlapping rows as they are sauced.

When you have folded as many of the crêpes as you plan to serve, carefully pour the Grand Marnier and rum into the sauce remaining in the pan. It may burst into flame spontaneously. If not, ignite the sauce with a match. Gently slide the pan back and forth over the heat until the flames die. Then spoon the sauce over the crêpes and serve at once. (Any extra unsauced crêpes may be wrapped tightly in foil and frozen. Defrost thoroughly and let them come completely to room temperature before separating and using them.)

SAUCE SUZETTE
6 large sugar cubes
1 large lemon
1 or 2 large juice oranges
¼ pound unsalted butter, softened
1 tablespoon sugar
¼ cup Grand Marnier
2 tablespoons dark rum

141

VI

A Favorite Gastronomic Game

At the stylish Lasserre
restaurant in Paris,
headwaiter Jacques
Serreperrot, since
appointed maître d'hôtel,
carefully serves *canard à
l'orange* during the
luncheon hour. The three-
star restaurant on the
avenue Franklin Roosevelt
also features truffles in
pastry and a dish
particularly enjoyed by the
author *(page 146):* a
salmon mousse encased in
brill fillets and poached.

One of the most intriguing games gastronomes play begins with the question: if you were ordering a classic meal, what—given ample funds—would you choose? The rules of this game are, happily, relaxed. You are not bound by any limitations of time or place. You may simply make your selections and assume that everything you order will magically appear on the table. You may even cheat a bit; if you find it hard to fix on any one choice for a particular course, you are allowed an alternate, or even several if you prefer. This is a once-in-a-lifetime feast. The object of the game is to pick anything and everything on the roster of supreme classic dishes that you would like to eat.

My own answer would be easy enough—for the first course, at least. I would begin with fresh foie gras and a Sauternes that was freezing cold. There are many traditionalists who would strongly disagree with my choice of wine, I know. They insist that the wines should always go from light to heavy, and a Sauternes should therefore only be taken at the end of the meal. But fresh foie gras eaten with an icy Sauternes is something to exult over. And if the foie gras happens to be centered in a perfectly made, egg-rich brioche, it is something to pray over. I would choose it for my starter. Another possibility would be galantine of duck *(Recipe Index)* which, when sliced, offers a pink, white, black and green mosaic of meats, truffles and pistachio nuts.

From here on the choices are not so easy, for one of the glories of the classic cuisine is its variety. For my soup course, if it were spring, when the oval-shaped leaves of sorrel are at their greenest and best, I think I might choose a *potage Germiny,* whose principal character comes from the delicate acidity of those leaves, gently stewed in butter before the chicken stock, egg yolks and cream are added.

On the other hand, if I knew my next course was to be a dish with a heavy cream sauce, I would want a clear soup. Of the delicious but bewildering assortment of rich consommés to choose from, I would be more than content to order *consommé Célestine* with shredded *crêpes* (unsweetened, of course, but the same as one makes for *crêpes Suzette*), or *consommé Rachel* with bits of marrow in croutons, or *consommé royale* with bits of custard. If I were in the mood for a more elaborate soup, I would undoubtedly order a *petite marmite,* garnished with small cubes of chicken and beef and finely cut vegetables. *(See Recipe Index for most of these varieties.)*

Selecting my fish course would be even more of a challenge. In no other department is the French chef's imagination more fertile, for fish cookery ranges from a simple poached turbot with hollandaise or a bass with herbs to elegant dishes served with creamy sauces and decorated with elaborate garnishes.

Yet for all these riches, if the meal were in the middle of the day, my choice would be one I consider to be among the finest of all fish dishes in the classic cuisine. I often enjoyed it for luncheon at the late Henri Soulé's Pavillon restaurant in New York where Pierre Franey prepared it when he was chef there. Bearing a Russian origin and title, it is the *coulibiac (Recipe Index),* that superb, involved invention consisting of layers of tender strips of boneless salmon covered with a velouté sauce, matchlessly seasoned with dill and mushrooms and encased in fresh and yeasty brioche dough. The whole thing is formed into a loaf and sealed and baked, and it is almost a complete meal in itself. Coming hot and golden brown from the oven, it is sliced and served with melted butter.

As an alternate to *coulibiac,* or if my hypothetical meal was to be a dinner rather than a luncheon, I might well be swayed in favor of a lobster soufflé *(Recipe Index).* The particular soufflé that I would choose is really two things in one and comes as something of a sumptuous surprise on first encounter. The base of the dish is the piquant lobster *américaine,* lightly tomatoed and seasoned with fresh herbs and a suggestion of cognac. Surmounting this is a gossamer, towering soufflé made with grated cheese. A hot lobster sauce is served with this superb dish.

A classic meal moves always from lighter dishes to heavier ones. After soup and fish the natural progression is to poultry or meat. There are many beautiful chicken dishes that would be appropriate here—the *poulet sauté Boivin (Recipe Index),* with its rich meat glaze, its artichoke bottoms and new potatoes is an excellent choice. Among the meats there are spring lamb, milk-fed veal and tender beef dishes to choose from. The beef dishes include all sorts of fillets and *tournedos,* and one of my favorites is the fillet of beef Richelieu. Named for the Duc de Richelieu, grand nephew of the cardinal, it is prepared by roasting the beef and garnishing it with braised lettuce, château potatoes, tomatoes and mushroom caps filled with *duxelles,* a purée of mushrooms.

If wild game were in season, I might just forget the meat and indulge

Opposite: One of the most luxurious dishes of the classic repertory is pheasant Souvaroff. The bird is placed in a *cocotte* with truffles and foie gras, then sealed with a pastry ring and roasted. To be properly savored it should be accompanied by a red burgundy.

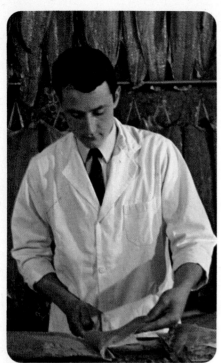

For the finest caviar, smoked sturgeon and trout and other marine delicacies, elite restaurants and gourmets in Paris rely on Petrossian's, a boutique on the avenue de la Tour Maubourg. Claude Moins *(above)*, head of the shop's salmon section, slices a smoked Irish salmon which was selected by a discerning patron.

myself with one of the most luxurious dishes of the classic cuisine—the exalted delicacy called pheasant Souvaroff *(Recipe Index)*. The pheasant is prepared in a brown sauce with foie gras, truffles and Madeira, then sealed in a casserole with a ring of pastry before baking. When it is opened at the table, the medley of entrancing aromas it yields is only the prelude to a truly Lucullan eating experience.

If for some strange reason pheasant Souvaroff did not tempt me at the moment, I might turn instead to *caille aux raisins en timbale (Recipe Index)*, a delicious quail with fresh grapes that is served in a pastry shell and flavored with cognac.

Capping my classic meal with a dessert would pose the most delightful of dilemmas. The range is almost limitless: puddings, soufflés, mousses, *sorbets* (sherbets), *bombes* (fancy molded ice creams) in every conceivable flavor—chocolate, vanilla, mocha, praline and Grand Marnier —crêpes, Bavarian creams, savarins (specially molded rum- or kirsch-soaked cakes) and *beignets* (deep-fried fruit fritters). Some of these desserts are the last word in the pastry-maker's art. I will cite only a few that I would find very difficult to pass up. The *riz à l'impératrice (Recipe Index)*, named after Napoleon III's consort, the Empress Eugénie, is a glorious concoction of sweetened rice molded with custard and glacéed fruits sometimes decorated with a rich, cathedrallike, stained-glass pattern of the fruits. The *bavarois Clermont (Recipe Index)*, is a molded vanilla Bavarian cream, garnished with whole glacéed chestnuts dipped in caramelized sugar with chocolate in it. The *gâteau St. Honoré (Recipe Index)* is a circle of pastry balls dipped in caramelized sugar, the center of which is filled with pastry cream. Another masterpiece I would find quite irresistible is *poires Bourdaloue (Recipe Index)*, a tart with frangipane cream, topped with poached pears, then brushed with apricot glaze and sprinkled with chopped pistachio nuts and crumbled macaroons.

The second question that almost invariably comes up at any gathering of people who know and love food is: What specific dishes or meals (good ones) do you recall most vividly? Even in France the perfect meal is rare, but the perfect dish is another matter. It may be encountered in a small one-chef restaurant in Burgundy or a fully staffed, luxurious restaurant in Paris. Wherever the locale, if the diner happens to be someone who really cares about food, all of the circumstances of the occasion—the setting and the wine as well as the exact details of the dish—become firmly fixed in the mind.

Who could forget the fish course on a sparkling spring day at Lasserre, that gracious dining palace near the Champs Elysées? I remember it well. The setting was brilliant—gleaming mirrors and chandeliers, immaculate napery, fresh flowers (hydrangeas)—and the wine, a Puligny-Montrachet/Drouhin 1964, was perfection. The fish that I ate there was a superb *pain de barbue saumonée*—a poached masterpiece of pink-fleshed salmon mixed with cream and egg whites encased in the white fillets of *barbue* (brill). This had been wrapped in cheesecloth, poached in a court bouillon, then sliced hot and served with a ravishing, creamy white wine sauce, with a julienne of mushrooms and truffles for added luster.

Then there was a meal at Lucas-Carton, that elegant and admirable restaurant near the Madeleine. What a feast, and what attention to detail! Snow-white napkins half the size of tablecloths; fresh rose petals in the finger bowls and velvet footstools for ladies who desired them. The meal began with *langoustines*—large Brittany prawns—in a superbly seasoned *sauce américaine* tempered with rich cream and glazed most appetizingly. My luncheon partner had a first course of lark, boned and filled with foie gras, roasted and served cold. With a bottle of crisp *brut* champagne, either dish would have delighted the most jaded of connoisseurs.

I remember a fresh salmon with its delicate sauce of sorrel and butter at the Troisgros restaurant in Roanne, near Lyons, and I also remember the incredible hot pâté of sweetbreads and green pistachio nuts at Paul Bocuse's lovely restaurant near Lyons. The pâté was baked in a puff pastry and served with a piquant brown sauce. My companion had a *rouget,* a small delicately textured red mullet, cooked in court bouillon, then drained and coated with a sauce of melted butter, chopped herbs and fennel seed. We drank a flinty Pouilly-Fuissé, and I remember thinking that Bocuse's restaurant is far superior to—and far less expensive than—many of the best-known luxury restaurants in New York.

Petrossian's caviar specialist, Ivan Vorotnycev, fills an order, meticulously handling the fragile sturgeon eggs with an oversized wooden fork. Once an aide-de-camp to Czar Nicholas II of Russia, Vorotnycev turned his caviar expertise to practical use after the Bolshevik revolution and has been at Petrossian's since 1930.

One of the feasts most sharply etched in my memory occurred on a fine spring day years ago in, of all places, that once-infamous prison, the 16th Century Château Chillon near Montreux, Switzerland, on the shores of Lake Léman. I was going to hotel school in Lausanne at the time. In one of the castle's vast rooms long dining tables were laid and fires were banked in the tall, deeply recessed fireplaces. Before the coals, spitted barons of tender spring lamb turned until the meat achieved a rare succulence. The meal began with a rich consommé that had simmered throughout the night, and with the lamb there were giant white stalks of asparagus, brought in from the region of Landes south of Bordeaux and served with an impeccable hollandaise. There were fine cheeses and fine wines and the dessert consisted of *friandises* and *mignardises* (petit fours)—served with strawberries from Italy, honey-sweet and large as Iranian medlars. In all there were a dozen courses served on this memorable occasion, and for dramatic effect, each was heralded by trumpet blasts. The waiters, even the students among them—of whom I was one—dined in due time as sumptuously as the guests of honor, who were the elite restaurant owners of Europe.

More recently I remember two sharply contrasting meals when Pierre Franey and I were traveling through France. One of them came about quite unexpectedly on the Riviera. We had flown there to see the Escoffier Museum at Villeneuve-Loubet, and while we were in the area we stopped off to visit a chef of exceptional talent who had retired a few years earlier to a small house near Monte Carlo. The talk, of course, had veered to food—notable catastrophes in the kitchen, the produce of France, restaurants in Paris, the disappearance of the great Parisian market Les Halles and so on. We mentioned that we were setting out the next morning for Vienne to have luncheon with Madame Fernand Point at the world-famous Restaurant de la Pyramide. Our intention was to stop on the road for croissants and coffee. As we said our goodbyes the chef walked into his small, well-equipped kitchen and returned with a

ALEXANDRE DUMAINE
(1895-   )

A superbly talented chef, Dumaine
made the provincial town of Saulieu a
gastronomic shrine during the 32 years
he ran a restaurant there. Apart from
the war years, from 1931 to his
retirement in 1963 his Restaurant de la
Côte d'Or never received fewer than
the maximum three stars from the
Michelin Guide. His admirers dubbed
him "Alexandre the Great."

hamper, which he enjoined us to keep cool and not to open until we were
hungry the next morning.

It was early June and the following morning dawned with penetrating
brilliance. We left our hotel in Nice shortly after dawn without even a
cup of coffee to launch us. From one end of the city to the other, massive
clusters of ivy geraniums cascaded over stone walls in the early sun. Beyond Nice the countryside was an almost painfully beautiful riot of color;
the dazzling red-orange of poppies vied with the pure, innocent yellow
of *genêt* (Genista), the characteristic bush of Provence, blanketing field
after field, hill after hill. We drove past the immaculately tended vineyards of Brignoles and then, in the land of honey, nougat and lavender,
somewhere near the town of St. Maximin, our appetites overcame us.
We turned off the main road onto a dusty path and drove onto a nearby
mountainside. Then, a little farther along, we stopped the car, and beneath an ancient olive tree we sampled the wares that our friend, the chef,
had conferred upon us.

The lid of the hamper was lifted to reveal a feast of the simplest, most
eloquent and unexpected sort. A Charente melon, small and round and
with the chill still on it and with honey in its flesh. A crackling, fresh
loaf of bread and a bottle of prime Pommard. The heart of the feast was
a pâté of rabbit lightly perfumed with rosemary and thyme and a small terrine of woodcock with its profusion of chopped truffles and the delicate
scent and flavor of aged cognac. It was just as well, perhaps, that the
small round of cheese, a *chèvre,* tucked away in a corner of the case, went
unnoticed until a few days later.

We arrived at Vienne and the Pyramide Restaurant early in the afternoon of the next day. I had been there 15 years earlier, when Fernand Point, founder of the Pyramide, was still alive. In those days the
restaurant enjoyed a matchless reputation. The celebrated gastronome
Curnonsky acclaimed it as "one of the great places of the world" and M.

Point as "one of the greatest chefs of our time," noting also: "There are people who have traveled the length and breadth of France to enjoy eating *Chez Point* [as the Pyramide is often called], for even the simplest cooking here attains a unique perfection."

On my earlier visit I had found the Pyramide worthy of Curnonsky's high praise, and now I was anxious to sample the food again. In the years since M. Point's death in 1955, his wife had been running the restaurant. Reports from all sides indicated that the restaurant had not slipped and I wanted to see whether this could be true.

The Pyramide is a remarkably unpretentious place. It sits behind an eight-foot stone wall with only a small plaque bearing the words: "F. Point, Restaurateur" to identify it. We walked through the garden, alive with roses on that June day, and as we entered the restaurant, Madame Point was waiting to greet us—gracious, warm and chic, uniquely and attractively French from the tip of her toes to her auburn hair and with her face and figure belying her 70-odd years.

The interior of the Pyramide was simple, almost austere. The tables were laid with plain white tablecloths, and around the room were vases with tall bouquets of gladiolas. Although the Points have played host to many of the world's most glamorous people, the clientele this day was far from stylish. The ladies were in modest summer dresses; some of the men wore neither ties nor jackets.

The years have produced few changes in the food at the Pyramide. The basic menu is still the one created by Fernand Point. Indeed part of the pleasure of revisiting the restaurant lies in knowing that you are going to start your meal with *foie gras en brioche* and pike mousse and continue through a remembered pattern.

The master chef at the Pyramide today is Guy Thivard, who joined the staff in 1958 while in his early twenties. Trying to describe the glory of M. Thivard's *foie gras en brioche* is like trying to capture a dazzling ray of light. Picture, if you will, a golden square of bread with the most compelling texture. And situated precisely and perfectly in the center, the round foie gras, rich as butter, lightly scented with port, delicately coated with aspic and crowned with two black slices of fresh truffle. It is the sort of dish that should be eaten in silence and with reverence. Then came the hot mousse of pike, custardlike, airy, tender and pyramid-shaped (it is baked in a special mold) with a dark *sauce périgourdine* containing thick slices of chopped truffles and the least suggestion of Madeira. Both dishes came off beautifully with a bottle of 1964 *blanc de blanc* champagne, fresh from the Point cellars.

The fish course offered a choice of salmon with champagne sauce or a fillet of turbot with almonds. I had the salmon, while Pierre chose the turbot, and it would be difficult to say which was superior. Both were marvelously fresh, the salmon bathed in a rose-colored sauce of white wine, fresh tomatoes and mushrooms—and enriched with a spoon or two of hollandaise sauce before glazing. The less complicated boneless turbot was cooked *à la meunière*—browned in butter, the interior remaining impeccably moist, and over all a rain of crisp, toasted, nut-brown almonds.

The true test of a memorable meal lies in not feeling surfeited with

FERNAND POINT
(1897-1955)

In the early 1950s Fernand Point loomed larger than any other restaurateur in France, not only because he weighed 300 pounds, but because his restaurant, the Pyramide in Vienne, was widely regarded as the finest in the world. Leading chefs called him "Le Roi," and he trained many of the country's outstanding culinary artists. When he died in 1955, his wife *(next page)* took charge of the Pyramide.

food at any point. As each of the principal dishes at the Pyramide arrived, I felt an undiminished sense of welcome. My main course was a Bresse chicken with a creamy tarragon sauce, served with a rice pilau. The chicken was a marvel of tenderness and the sauce a savory complement. Pierre chose guinea fowl, filled with a *farce américaine* (the French frequently refer to bread stuffings for fowl as American); the fine, fresh, buttery bread crumbs were seasoned with finely chopped, crisply cooked bacon, thyme, parsley and bay leaf. The fowl was accompanied by a thin, natural *jus* from the roasting pan blended with hot melted butter. The wine for the main dishes was a silken smooth Burgundy, a Romanée-St.Vivant 1961, which had been decanted (the sommelier explained that by decanting he raised the temperature of the wine, which was just a shade too cool).

The cheeses for that dinner included two solid goat cheeses, an excellent Brie and a perfectly ripe Gorgonzola which seemed to have traveled from Italy especially for the occasion. Then the sommelier lifted the champagne out of the cooler to coincide with the appearance of a spellbinding assortment of pastries—small *barquettes* or pastry boats, filled with glazed fresh fruit; tiny tarts with pastry cream; "figs" made of almond paste and flavored with kirsch; cream puffs filled with rum-flavored pastry cream and a "biscuit" or sponge cake with chocolate cream in the center. We followed the pastries with sherbets, one of pineapple, another of lemon, and after that we had fresh strawberries with *crème Chantilly* and a syrup of raspberries. Coffee with a highly chilled pear brandy ended the meal. We left the restaurant and started north for Paris secure in the knowledge that the Pyramide had not lost its touch.

After Fernand Point's death, few people thought the Pyramide could maintain its preeminent position. Yet under the expert direction of Point's widow the restaurant has retained its three-star rating for more than 15 years. With the help of her chef, Guy Thivard, shown with her in the Pyramide garden (*opposite*), she offers such fine specialties as blue trout, which is taken from a tank and immediately cooked in vinegar and water. And in the tradition of her husband, Mme "Mado" Point insists on using only the freshest, finest ingredients. Two of these—white asparagus and fresh strawberries—appear at left.

Faisan Souvaroff
ROAST PHEASANT BAKED WITH TRUFFLES AND FOIE GRAS IN MADEIRA SAUCE

Preheat the oven to 400°. Pat the pheasant dry inside and out with paper towels. Sprinkle the cavity and skin with the salt and pepper, and truss the bird neatly with white kitchen string *(see Recipe Booklet)*. With a pastry brush, coat the entire surface of the pheasant with 2 tablespoons of the clarified butter. Lay the bird on its side on a rack set in a shallow roasting pan.

Roast the pheasant in the middle of the oven for 10 minutes. Turn it over, brush it with 2 more tablespoons of the clarified butter and roast for 10 minutes longer. Then turn the bird breast side up, brush it with the remaining clarified butter and continue roasting for 15 to 20 minutes longer, or until it is golden brown on all sides but still somewhat undercooked. To test for doneness, pierce a thigh with the point of a skewer or small, sharp knife; the juices that trickle out should be pale pink. If they are still red, roast the bird for 5 minutes longer.

Remove the pan from the oven and transfer the pheasant to a platter. Cut off and discard the trussing string and, with a sharp knife, carve the bird into 5 pieces, cutting out the backbone as shown in the Recipe Booklet. Chop the backbone into small pieces and set aside.

Brush the softened butter over the bottom and sides of a 2-quart cocotte or casserole equipped with a tight-fitting cover. Arrange the pieces of pheasant in the cocotte and scatter the foie gras and truffles on top. Set the cocotte aside.

Pour into the roasting pan any juices that have accumulated on the platter around the pheasant. Add the chopped backbone and the uncooked neck and gizzard. Stirring constantly and scraping in the brown particles that cling to the bottom and sides of the pan, cook over moderate heat for 4 or 5 minutes. Then add the Madeira and stir for a minute or so longer. Pour in the *fond lié* and stir until the sauce is smooth and heated through. Skim as much fat as possible from the surface. Strain the sauce through a fine sieve into the cocotte, pressing down hard on the bones to extract all their juices before discarding them. Cover the cocotte and set aside while you make the *repère,* or pastry seal.

Combine the flour and water in a bowl and beat to a smooth paste with a whisk or spoon. Cover with plastic wrap and let the dough rest in the refrigerator for 30 minutes, or until it is firm but malleable.

Preheat the oven to 400°. On a lightly floured surface, roll the dough out ¼ inch thick. With a 1½-inch round cookie cutter—preferably a fluted one—cut the dough into circles. Overlapping them by about ½ inch, arrange the circles of dough in a ring around the lid so they completely seal the cocotte. Lightly moisten the bottom of each circle with water as you proceed. Brush them with egg yolk and bake the *faisan Souvaroff* in the middle of the oven for 15 minutes. Serve at once, directly from the cocotte. Cut through the pastry seal at the table.

To serve 4

A 3- to 3½-pound oven-ready young pheasant
1 teaspoon salt
½ teaspoon freshly ground black pepper
6 tablespoons melted clarified butter *(page 34)* plus 2 tablespoons butter, softened
¾ cup foie gras *en bloc (see Glossary)*, cut into ½-inch dice
⅓ cup coarsely chopped black truffles *(see Glossary)*
The pheasant neck and gizzard
¼ cup dry Madeira
1½ cups *fond lié (page 35)*
4 cups all-purpose flour
1 cup cold water
1 egg yolk, lightly beaten

Terrine of pheasant lends zest to a fancy picnic. The pheasant and pork mixture with truffles is the same used in *pâté en croûte* on page 68.

SAUMON

2 tablespoons unsalted butter,
softened

3 tablespoons finely chopped
shallots

2 teaspoons salt

¼ teaspoon plus ½ teaspoon
freshly ground black pepper

2 pounds center-cut salmon fillets,
boned carefully with tweezers,
then skinned and cut diagonally
into ¼-inch-thick slices

½ pound fresh mushrooms, wiped
clean, trimmed and cut
lengthwise through cap and stem
into ⅛-inch-thick slices (about
2 cups)

¼ cup finely cut fresh dill leaves

1 cup dry white wine

1 cup *sauce velouté (page 36)*
made with *fumet de poisson*

5 egg yolks

2 tablespoons strained fresh lemon
juice

⅛ teaspoon ground hot red pepper
(cayenne)

CRÊPES (to yield 20)

1¼ cups all-purpose flour

4 eggs

1 cup milk

1¼ cups cold water

3 tablespoons unsalted butter,
melted and cooled, plus 6
tablespoons melted clarified
butter *(page 34)*

½ teaspoon salt

3 tablespoons finely chopped fresh
parsley

3 tablespoons finely cut fresh dill
leaves

Coulibiac
BRIOCHE LOAF FILLED WITH SALMON, MUSHROOMS, VELOUTÉ AND CRÊPES

The "coulibiac" is easier to prepare if you allow yourself two days. You can cook the salmon, crêpes, eggs and rice and make the brioche dough a day ahead. The next day combine the eggs and rice with the tapioca, then roll out the dough and assemble the loaf.

SAUMON (SALMON): Preheat the oven to 350°. Spread 2 tablespoons of softened butter on the bottom and sides of a 7½-by-12-by-2-inch glass baking dish. Scatter the shallots over the bottom of the dish and season them with ½ teaspoon of the salt and ¼ teaspoon of the black pepper. Arrange the salmon in two parallel rows the length of the dish, overlapping the slices at the middle of the dish. Spread the mushroom slices over the salmon, and sprinkle them with ¼ cup of dill, 1 teaspoon of salt and ½ teaspoon of black pepper. Pour the wine over the fish. Cover tightly with foil and bake in the middle of the oven for 20 minutes, or until the salmon flakes easily when prodded with a fork.

With a bulb baster or spoon, transfer as much of the cooking liquid as possible to a heavy 10- to 12-inch skillet. Let the salmon rest for about 15 minutes, then draw up any additional liquid that accumulates around it and add it to the skillet. Bring the liquid to a boil over high heat and cook briskly until it is reduced to about ½ cup. Reduce the heat to moderate and, stirring constantly with a wire whisk, slowly pour in the *sauce velouté* and continue to cook for 4 to 5 minutes. Beat the 5 egg yolks lightly with a fork and whisk them into the sauce. Bring to a simmer, stirring all the while with the whisk and remove the skillet from the heat. Stir in the lemon juice, ½ teaspoon of salt and the red pepper. Taste for seasoning and pour the sauce over the salmon, spreading it (smoothly) with a spatula. As the sauce runs into the dish, spoon it back over the salmon until it is collected on the fish. Cool to room temperature, then cover and refrigerate until the fish is firm to the touch; preferably, overnight.

CRÊPES: To make the batter with a blender, combine 1¼ cups of flour, 4 eggs, 1 cup of milk, 1¼ cups of cold water, 3 tablespoons of melted butter and ½ teaspoon of salt in the blender jar. Blend at high speed for a few seconds. Turn off the machine, scrape down the sides of the jar with a rubber spatula and blend again for 40 seconds. Pour the batter into a bowl and stir in 3 tablespoons of parsley and 3 of dill.

To make crêpe batter by hand, stir the flour and eggs together in a mixing bowl and gradually stir in the milk, water and salt. Beat with a whisk or a rotary or electric beater until smooth, then rub through a fine sieve into another bowl and stir in the melted butter, parsley and dill. Cover and refrigerate the batter for at least two hours before using it.

Heat a 6-inch crêpe pan over high heat until a drop of water flicked into it splutters and evaporates instantly. With a hair-bristled (not nylon) pastry brush, grease the bottom and sides of the pan with a little of the clarified butter. Stir the batter lightly. Using a small ladle, pour about 2 tablespoons of the batter into the pan and tip the pan so that the batter quickly covers the bottom; the batter will cling to the pan and begin to firm up almost immediately. At once tilt the pan over the bowl and pour off any excess batter; the finished crêpe should be paper-thin.

Cook the crêpe for a minute or so until the underside turns golden. Turn it over with a spatula and cook the other side for a minute. Slide the crêpe onto a plate. Brush clarified butter on the pan again and make the remaining crêpes similarly, stacking them on the plate. The crêpes may be made a day ahead of time, cooled to room temperature, covered with plastic wrap and refrigerated. (In this case, they should be brought back to room temperature before they are separated and used.) Or they may be made several hours ahead and kept at room temperature.

MÉLANGE D'OEUFS DURS ET DE RIZ (EGG-AND-RICE MIXTURE): In a small saucepan or skillet, sprinkle the tapioca over ½ cup of cold water and set aside to soften for 5 minutes. Then, stirring frequently, bring to a boil over high heat. Reduce the heat to low and simmer uncovered for 6 to 8 minutes, until the mixture is very thick. Pour the tapioca into a fine sieve and let it drain for at least 10 minutes.

Meanwhile, in a heavy 1- to 1½-quart saucepan, melt 1 tablespoon of butter over moderate heat. When the foam begins to subside, add the onions and stir for about 2 minutes until they are soft but not brown. Stirring constantly, add the rice in a slow stream and continue to cook until the grains glisten. Do not let the rice brown. Pour in the chicken stock and, still stirring, bring to a boil. Reduce the heat to low, cover tightly, and simmer for 20 minutes, or until the grains are soft and have absorbed all the liquid. Remove the pan from the heat.

In a mixing bowl, combine the sieved hard-cooked eggs, 3 tablespoons of parsley, 1 teaspoon of salt and ¼ teaspoon of black pepper. Add the tapioca and rice and toss gently but thoroughly together.

BRIOCHE: Pour the lukewarm milk into a small, shallow bowl and sprinkle it with the yeast and sugar. Let the mixture stand for 2 or 3 minutes, then stir well. Set in a warm, draft-free place (such as a turned-off oven) for about 5 minutes, or until the mixture almost doubles in volume.

Place 3½ cups of the flour and the 2 teaspoons of salt in a large deep mixing bowl, and make a well in the center. Add the yeast mixture, 12 egg yolks and ½ cup of softened butter to the well and, with a wooden spoon, gradually incorporate the flour into the center ingredients. Stir vigorously until the dough is smooth and can be gathered into a ball.

Place the dough on a lightly floured surface, and knead by pushing it down with the heels of your hands, pressing it forward and folding it back on itself. Repeat for 10 to 15 minutes. A little at a time incorporate only enough flour to keep the dough from becoming shiny on the surface. It should be smooth and elastic. (You may need as much as 1 cup, depending on the brand of flour you use.)

When blisters form on the surface of the dough, shape it into a ball and place it in a buttered bowl. Drape with a kitchen towel and set in the warm place for about 1 hour, or until the dough doubles in bulk.

Punch the dough down with a blow of your fist. Then knead it for a minute, shape it into a ball and return it to the bowl to rise and to double its bulk once more. Use at once or cover and refrigerate overnight.

FINAL ASSEMBLY: Preheat the oven to 400°. With a pastry brush spread 1 tablespoon of the softened butter evenly over a large baking sheet.

Punch the dough down and, on a lightly floured surface, roll it out into a rectangle 19 inches long, 15 inches wide and ¼ inch thick.

MÉLANGE D'OEUFS DURS ET DE RIZ
1 tablespoon minute tapioca
½ cup cold water
1 tablespoon unsalted butter
1 teaspoon finely chopped onions
½ cup uncooked long-grain white rice (not the converted variety)
1½ cups *fond blanc de volaille (page 31)*, or substitute 1½ cups canned chicken stock, chilled, then degreased
3 hard-cooked eggs, rubbed through a fine sieve with the back of a spoon
3 tablespoons finely chopped fresh parsley
1 teaspoon salt
¼ teaspoon freshly ground black pepper

BRIOCHE
¾ cup lukewarm milk (110° to 115°)
3 packages active dry yeast
½ teaspoon sugar
3½ to 4½ cups all-purpose flour
2 teaspoons salt
12 egg yolks plus 2 lightly beaten egg yolks
½ cup unsalted butter, softened and cut into ¼-inch bits
2 tablespoons soft fresh crumbs made from homemade-type white bread, trimmed of crusts and pulverized in a blender or finely shredded with a fork

6 tablespoons softened butter plus 1½ cups warm melted butter

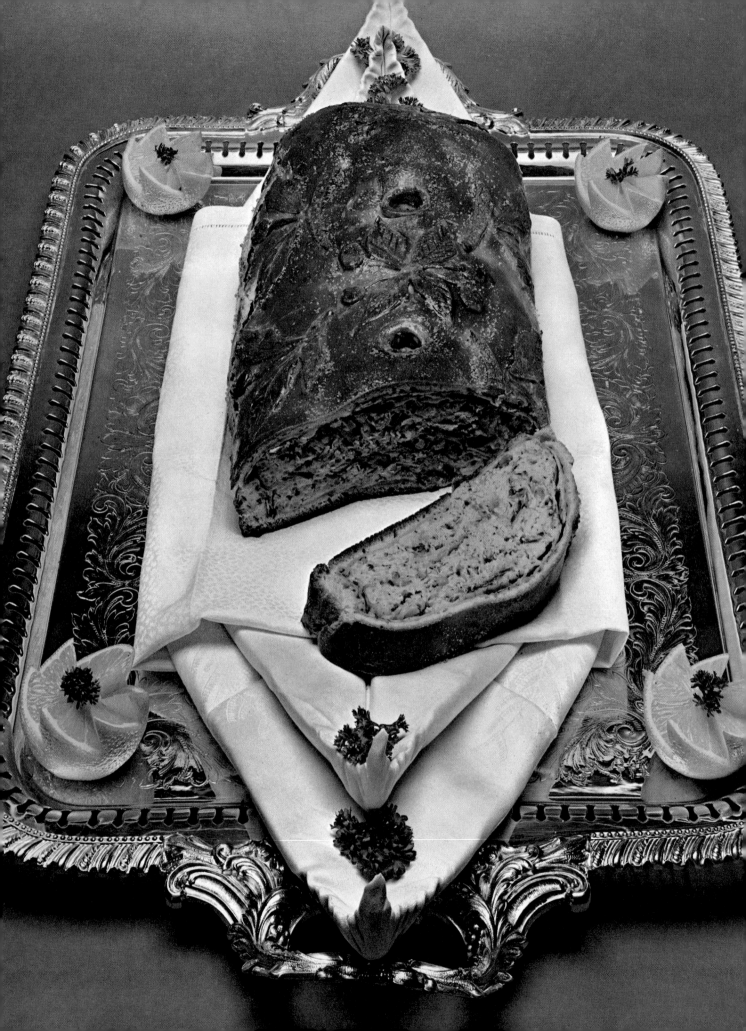

Lay 6 of the crêpes in two parallel rows the length of the rectangle, overlapping the crêpes slightly in the center to leave a 2-inch-wide band of uncovered dough all around the rectangle. Sprinkle the crêpes evenly with about ⅓ of the egg-and-rice mixture.

Cut the salmon in half lengthwise and, with the aid of a large wide metal spatula, gently lift one half from the baking dish and turn it mushroom-coated side down over the center of the crêpes. Arrange 6 more crêpes on top as before, sprinkle them with half of the remaining egg-and-rice mixture, and place the remaining half of the salmon on top with the mushroom-coated side up. Scatter the remaining egg-and-rice mixture over the salmon and cover it with 6 more crêpes.

Lightly brush the edge of one of the exposed long sides of the brioche rectangle with the beaten egg yolk. Lift the opposite side over the filling, then fold the egg-coated side on top of it and press gently to seal the sides together along the top. Trim both ends of the *coulibiac* to extend no more than 3 inches beyond the filling. Brush the tops of the ends with beaten egg yolk and tuck the ends snugly over the top of the filled cylinder.

Carefully turn the loaf upside down on its seam and place it on the buttered baking sheet. With a small, round cookie cutter or sharp knife, make two holes 1 inch in diameter, centered about 3 inches from each end of the loaf. Gather the scraps of brioche dough into a ball and roll out ¼ inch thick. Cut two ½-inch-wide and 4-inch-long strips out of the dough, moisten the bottom of each with egg yolk and fit the strips like collars around the openings, pressing gently to secure them. Score the loaf lightly with a knife in an attractive pattern or, if you prefer, with cookie cutters or a small knife cut the remaining dough into decorative leaf and flower shapes. Moistening the bottom of each decorative piece with egg yolk, arrange them attractively on top of the loaf. Brush the surface with the remaining egg yolk and sprinkle with the bread crumbs.

Cut a strip of aluminum foil about 5 feet long, fold it lengthwise in half and grease one side lightly with 5 tablespoons of softened butter. Wrap the foil around the loaf like a collar and tie it in place with 2 or 3 turns of kitchen string. Place small cylindrical funnels made from a double thickness of heavy foil into each pastry opening. Set the loaf aside in a warm, draft-free place for 30 minutes. Preheat the oven to 400°.

Bake the *coulibiac* in the middle of the oven for 15 minutes. Lower the heat to 375° and continue baking for 30 minutes. Cut off the string and remove the collar of foil and bake for 15 minutes longer, or until the loaf is a rich golden brown. Slide it onto a heated platter and let it rest at room temperature for 15 to 20 minutes before serving. Just before slicing the *coulibiac* pour ¼ cup melted butter into each of the openings in the top of the loaf, and remove the foil funnels. Serve the remaining cup of melted butter separately as a sauce.

NOTE: The tapioca used to thicken the egg-and-rice mixture above is a substitute for the traditional fresh *vesiga,* or sturgeon marrow. If *vesiga* is available, replace the tapioca with 3 ounces of it. Wash the *vesiga* in cold water, then simmer it for 1½ hours in enough lightly salted water to cover it completely. Chop the *vesiga* fine.

The *coulibiac,* which originated in Russia, later came to France and is one of the authors' favorite dishes, consists of fresh salmon and crêpes with dill, mushrooms and a fish velouté, baked in brioche dough.

A Rice Dessert Fit for an Empress

The richly colorful *riz à l'impératrice* is a molded Bavarian cream with rice and glacéed fruits, named after Napoleon III's consort, the Empress Eugénie. The dessert is decorated with glacéed fruits and encircled by raspberry sauce.

To serve 8 to 10

½ cup finely diced mixed glacéed
  fruit
¼ cup imported kirsch
1 envelope plus 1 teaspoon
  unflavored gelatin
¼ cup water
Vegetable oil
½ cup uncooked long-grain white
  rice (not the converted variety)
2½ cups milk
1 cup sugar
2 tablespoons unsalted butter
1 vanilla bean (see Glossary)
5 egg yolks
¼ cup apricot jam, rubbed through
  a fine sieve
2 cups heavy cream
Angelica and assorted thinly sliced
  candied fruits

Riz à l'impératrice
MOLDED VANILLA BAVARIAN CREAM WITH RICE AND GLACÉED FRUITS

Combine the glacéed fruit and the kirsch in a small bowl, stir well and marinate at room temperature for at least 45 minutes. Sprinkle the gelatin over ¼ cup of water and set it aside to soften. Brush the inside of a 2-quart charlotte mold with vegetable oil, then rub it with paper towels to remove the excess.

In a heavy 2- to 3-quart saucepan, bring 1 quart of water to a boil over high heat, drop in the rice and cook briskly for 5 minutes. Pour the rice into a sieve, rinse it under cold water and drain.

Pour 1 cup of the milk into the top of a double boiler, add ¼ cup of the sugar, the butter and vanilla bean. Stirring occasionally, cook over moderate heat until the sugar and butter are dissolved and small bubbles appear around the edge of the pan. Set the pan above simmering (not boiling) water and stir the rice into the mixture. Cover tightly and cook for 25 to 30 minutes, or until the rice is soft. Check from time to time and if the milk seems to be evaporating too rapidly, add a few spoonfuls more. When the rice is finished, however, the milk should be absorbed. To remove any excess moisture, drain the rice in a fine sieve. Remove and discard the vanilla bean.

In a 2- to 3-quart enameled or stainless-steel saucepan, heat the remaining 1½ cups of milk over moderate heat until bubbles form around the edge of the pan. Set aside off the heat and cover.

With a wire whisk or a rotary or electric beater, beat the egg yolks and the remaining ¾ cup of sugar together in a deep bowl for 3 or 4 minutes, or until the yolks form a slowly dissolving ribbon when the beater is lifted from the bowl. Whisking constantly, pour in the milk in a slow, thin stream. When thoroughly blended, return the mixture to the saucepan. Cook over low heat, stirring constantly, until the custard is as thick as heavy cream. Do not let the custard come near a boil or it will curdle. Mix in the softened gelatin and continue to mix until it is dissolved.

Strain the custard through a fine sieve set over a bowl. Stir in the glacéed fruits, kirsch and the apricot jam, then gently mix in the rice.

With a wire whisk, rotary or electric beater, whip the cream in a large chilled bowl until it forms soft peaks. Set aside. Place the bowl of custard in a pot filled with crushed ice or ice cubes and water, and stir for 4 or 5 minutes, or until the custard is cool and begins to thicken very slightly.

Remove the bowl from the ice and scoop the whipped cream over the custard. With a rubber spatula, fold the custard and cream gently together, using an over-under cutting motion rather than a stirring motion until no trace of white remains. Ladle the mixture into the mold, cover with foil, and refrigerate for 6 hours until it is completely firm.

To unmold the *riz à l'impératrice,* run a sharp knife around the sides of the mold and dip the bottom in hot water for a few seconds. Then wipe the mold dry, place a chilled serving platter upside down over the mold and, grasping plate and mold firmly, invert them. Rap the platter on a table and the *riz à l'impératrice* should slide out of the mold.

Decorate this dessert as fancifully as you like with the angelica and candied fruit, pressing the slices gently in place. Refrigerate the *riz à l'impératrice* until ready to serve. Before serving pour some of the raspberry sauce around the edge of the platter, and present the rest in a small bowl.

SAUCE DE FRAMBOISES: Wash the raspberries quickly under a spray of cold water, remove the hulls, and discard any badly bruised or discolored berries. (Frozen raspberries need only to be thoroughly defrosted and well drained in a sieve.)

Combine the raspberries, sugar and kirsch in the jar of an electric blender and blend at high speed for 10 seconds. Turn off the machine, scrape down the sides of the jar with a rubber spatula, and blend again for a minute. Then, with the back of a spoon, rub the purée through a fine sieve set over a small bowl. Cover tightly with foil or plastic wrap and refrigerate until ready to use. (The sauce may be kept for 3 to 4 days.)

Soufflé Rothschild
HOT DESSERT SOUFFLÉ WITH GLACÉED FRUIT

Preheat the oven to 400° and place a large baking sheet on the middle shelf. With a pastry brush, spread 1 tablespoon of the softened butter over the bottom and sides of a 2-quart soufflé dish. Sprinkle the butter with 2 tablespoons of the sugar and tip the dish from side to side to spread it evenly. Invert the dish and rap it gently on a table to remove the excess sugar. Refrigerate the dish until ready to use. Combine the glacéed fruits and liqueur in a small, shallow bowl, turn the pieces of fruit about with a spoon, then set aside to marinate at room temperature while you make the soufflé base.

In a heavy 2½- to 3-quart enameled saucepan, stir the flour and ¼ cup of the milk together with a wire whisk until the flour has completely absorbed the milk, then beat in the remaining ½ cup of milk and ½ cup of sugar. Whisking constantly, cook over moderate heat until the sauce comes to a boil. Lower the heat, and cook for 2 to 3 minutes until it thickens heavily. Remove the pan from the heat and beat in the remaining 3 tablespoons of butter. Let the mixture cool for 5 to 10 minutes.

Drain the marinated fruits into a bowl through a fine sieve, whisk the liquid into the sauce, and reserve the fruit. Beating constantly, add the vanilla and then the egg yolks, one at a time.

With a wire whisk or a rotary or electric beater, beat the egg whites until they are stiff enough to stand in firm, unwavering peaks on the beater when it is lifted from the bowl. Stir 2 large spoonfuls of the egg whites into the sauce; then pour the sauce over the rest of the egg whites and, with a spatula, fold them together gently but thoroughly with an over-under cutting rather than a stirring motion. Fold in the reserved marinated fruits and pour the soufflé into the chilled dish, smoothing the top with a rubber spatula.

Place the dish in the oven on top of the hot baking sheet and immediately turn the heat down to 375°. Bake for 25 minutes, or until the soufflé is golden brown and puffed above the dish.

Meanwhile, roll the strawberries in the superfine sugar to coat them on all sides. When the soufflé has baked its allotted time, without removing the dish from the oven, quickly but carefully arrange the sugared berries in a ring around the top of the soufflé. Bake about 5 minutes more, or until the berries are lightly glazed. Serve at once.

SAUCE DE FRAMBOISES
2 cups fresh raspberries, or substitute 4 ten-ounce packages frozen whole raspberries
¾ cup sugar
¼ cup imported kirsch

To serve 6 to 8

4 tablespoons unsalted butter, softened
2 tablespoons plus ½ cup sugar
⅓ cup finely chopped mixed glacéed fruits
¼ cup gold-flecked *eau de vie de Dantzig* or *Goldwasser,* or substitute imported kirsch
3 tablespoons flour
¾ cup cold milk
1 teaspoon vanilla extract
4 egg yolks
6 egg whites
12 firm ripe strawberries, washed and with hulls removed
¼ cup superfine sugar

VII

World's Greatest Movable Feast

Master Chef Henri Le Huédé of the S.S. *France* considers a wriggling *langouste* on the pier at Le Havre and pronounces it fit to be taken aboard ship. In the kitchens of the *France* (*background*), the spiny lobsters will be prepared in a variety of tempting ways by M. Le Huédé's staff.

At a time when men walk on the moon and jets streak the sky at supersonic speeds, the slow pace of travel aboard an ocean liner is one of life's ultimate time-consuming joys. And if you happen to be traveling aboard the S.S. *France*, there is an extra measure of pleasure. For the first-class dining room of this ship is a showcase of the classic French cuisine. In all my years of sampling food and writing about it, I have never found anything to surpass the variety and the quality of the classic dishes served here. The *France's* versatile, well-equipped kitchen can prepare almost any dish in the classic repertory with a flair and an expertise that simply cannot be beaten.

This amplitude of resources makes it unique. There is no other eating place anywhere—on land, at sea or in the air—where you can order and get, superbly cooked and presented, any dish in the world within reason and without regard to the day's menu. "Within reason" is hardly a hardship; except for oysters and mussels, which are so perishable they are available only a couple of days out of port, and except for such seasonal vicissitudes as the possibility that no springbok was killed anywhere in the world last week, the kitchen of the *France* can serve you just about anything your appetite may desire. No other restaurant that I know can do nearly as much.

If you are coming home from Europe aboard the *France*, the excitement of the trip begins in Paris the moment you board the boat train for Le Havre. The contrast with those abusive, frantic taxicab rides to airports could scarcely be more striking. You sit back and let the French countryside sweep past, and as the train winds through Normandy along the edge of the Seine, picture-postcard vistas flicker by: barges on the river, sleek white cattle grazing in the damp meadows, orchards with gnarled, weather-worn apple trees. The excitement quickens as you reach Le Havre, for here beside the pier is the great ship itself, a splendid white and black floating palace, its top deck crowned by towering, winged, red and black smokestacks.

When Pierre Franey and I went to Le Havre last spring, we made a point of getting there a day early, so we could observe the loading of food onto the ship. This is a serious and exacting process in which some of the world's best raw materials must run a gantlet of some of the world's most exacting palates. I will describe it in some detail because it has a great deal to do with what comes to the tables of the *France*.

We checked in at a hotel near the water front, and arrived at the dock by 7 o'clock the following morning. Already cranes were lowering cargo into the holds. A French Line official led us into a large sky-lighted storage shed where Henri Le Huédé, the master chef of the *France*, immaculate in his starched *toque blanche* and white apron, was passing fastidious judgment on the produce, meats and seafood to be taken aboard. Long tables were spread with white cloths at one end of the room, and next to them stood a tremendous scale which is used to verify the weights of the foods against the orders. One by one, large trucks belonging to suppliers in the Le Havre area drove in through wide doors in a corner of the shed and unloaded crates of fruit, vegetables and

On a buffet in the first-class dining room of the *France,* a sumptuous array of cold dishes awaits service. Included are traditional delicacies such as chicken and quail breasts coated with *chaud-froid* sauce, lobster, salmon and turbot, as well as pork cutlets Taillevent, loin of lamb Rossini and duck *à l'orange*. Custom calls for a guest to admire the display on entering the dining room, then to report his selections to the waiter at his own table.

shellfish, boxes of meat and poultry and styrofoam containers of fish.

Attended by a retinue of inspectors that included the ship's chief provisioner (who kept a check on the quality and weights of various items), a veterinarian (who made sure the meat conformed to health standards) and an agricultural inspector (who checked the produce), M. Le Huédé was examining the meats when we joined him. There were whole baby lambs, barons of lamb, sides of beef and veal, grain-fed chickens from Bresse. As the chef, an intense-looking man, worked his way through the meats from piece to piece, joint to joint, poking at each cut, smelling it, and peering at it closely; it was apparent from his expression whether he liked or disliked a particular item. When he came to the Bresse chickens —a prized delicacy in France—he picked one up, examined it closely, shrugged and pursed his mouth to show his disdain for such a skinny bird. Then he showed his further displeasure as he pulled a half dozen more chickens from a crate. After much discussion, punctuated by waving of the arms, it was decided to order plumper birds.

The meats and poultry were carted away; a truck drove up and disgorged crates of fiery red tomatoes, oranges as golden as dawn, bright red apples, yellow pears, green beans and spinach. M. Le Huédé picked up a small paring knife from a table close by, cut sections from the fruits and offered them around. The apples were perfect, the oranges dripping and sweet, and while the pears were a bit too ripe, they were the very best that could be obtained at that time of year.

The seafood came next. From large crates of lobsters the chef picked up several to make sure they were lively. When he saw their claws tear angrily at the air, he smiled with satisfaction. Then he scrutinized the fish: Dover sole, silver-gray whiting, giant turbot, pike, ling, bass, green pollock, fluke, red mullet, mackerel and eels. The turbot and fluke met with scowls of disapproval. The eyes of the fish were not clear enough, and their gills were too dark—signs that they were not as fresh as they should have been. A substantial part of the order was returned to the supplier, to be replaced before the ship sailed.

All this was only a selective sampling of the produce to be taken aboard. A complete inspection would not be possible, the ship's provisioner explained, because for every round trip between Le Havre and New York, the *France* takes on 15 tons of meat, 5.5 tons of poultry, 5.5 tons of fish, 30 tons of vegetables, 70,000 eggs and 330 pounds of caviar. If the whole does not measure up to the quality of the sample, there is hell for some supplier to pay.

The French Line's young wine master, Georges Palomba, gave us some other impressive statistics. On every round trip, he informed us, 18,000 bottles of ordinary table wine and 4,500 bottles of vintage wines are consumed. Most of the vintage wines are purchased by the bottle from châteaux and estates in Bordeaux and Burgundy, while the table wine is purchased from lesser vineyards in the same areas and brought to Le Havre in tank trucks to be stored in glass-lined vats, later to be bottled and taken aboard ship.

There were certain delicacies—caviar, fresh foie gras, hams and cheeses —that had to be tasted before they went aboard. To appraise these foods

There is nothing perfunctory about the inspection of food destined for the *France*. If some item does not measure up to the high standards of Chef Le Huédé, it is simply not accepted. Above, for example, the chef rejects a shipment of turbot, pointing to gills that are not sufficiently bright red. On the opposite page he examines, with varying degrees of enthusiasm, oranges from Morocco, spiny lobsters from Britain, a sole from the Channel, and some Bresse chickens that he thought too skinny.

a panel of French Line officials and the master chef gather in a company dining room on the dock before each sailing. The judging process, known as a *dégustation,* is marked by great solemnity. On this particular occasion, a large oval table was set with china, silver and wineglasses. Waiters from the ship passed the delicacies and Paul Blet, the *France's* chief provisioner, meticulously tabulated the panel's comments and findings in a large black book for future reference.

The first delicacy was Beluga caviar, served with iced vodka in frosted glasses. The fine black grains were firm and moist. But while the non-panel guests exclaimed their approval, the members of the panel were more reserved, assenting to the quality of the caviar by merely exchanging glances and nodding their heads.

After the caviar and foie gras, five varieties of ham were tasted—a Parma ham, one from York, a smoked Parisian ham, one from Bayonne and one from the Ardennes. There were four sausages and a variety of cheeses including a Pont l'Evêque, Roquefort, Camembert, Port-Salut, a Valençay and a Duc de Bourgogne. The hams were sampled with a Chambertin 1962, an excellent Burgundy, and the cheeses with a Château Haut-Brion 1961, a superb Bordeaux. The panel was unimpressed by the Parisian ham and they rejected all of the sausages. The provisioner made a note in his ominous black book to make sure that better quality items were provided for the next trip.

The *dégustation* lasted two hours—well into the afternoon. After losing a few francs at the casino in Deauville that evening, we boarded the ship in the morning. Passports and boarding passes in hand, we made our way through a mountain of baggage and hordes of milling passengers. First class on the ship is divided into sections named after the provinces of France, and when I reached my cabin I found myself in Champagne—a good gastronomic omen, I felt. The furniture in the cabin was velvet-covered, the rug was a deep-piled yellow and blue, and bright sunlight streamed through the portholes. When I went out on deck to watch the sailing, the day itself sparkled like champagne.

As a fleet of four tugs pulled the *France* out through the calm waters of the channel, thin strips of clouds drifted lazily overhead. Slowly we moved out past the docks lined with moored ships, past storage tanks and factory chimneys and tiny fishing boats. Gradually Le Havre disappeared beyond our foaming wake and all that was left was the open sea.

Shortly after noon we walked down the red-carpeted stairs for luncheon at our assigned table in the first-class dining room. There were fresh gladioli on the table and the napery was beautifully starched. It must be added, however, that the décor of the room as a whole is not one of the glories of the *France*. The room is like a large amphitheater, overly bright and cold, and it needs a lot of people to warm it up. Our appetites had been dulled by a fortnight of heavy eating from one end of France to the other. We settled for a little terrine of duckling, a green salad and a mushroom omelet.

Traditionally, the first night out is always quiet and informal, but on the second night the dining room of the *France* comes into its own. For us the glamor of the occasion began with the ritual of welcoming the

diners. The men in black tie and the women in their floor-length finery came down one staircase to a landing, a doorman admitted them through double glass doors, then they descended a wider staircase that fanned out to the dining-room floor. Maîtres d'hôtel, stewards and waiters were stationed around the room. As each party approached, a maître d'hôtel showed them to their table, and a pair of waiters helped them into their chairs. The tables were a dazzle of crisp white linen, sparkling wine glasses, polished elegant silver and fresh red carnations.

The *France* is renowned for the elegance of its menus. The cover of the menu that evening featured a romantic watercolor depicting three costumed figures at a masked ball, and the back of the menu carried a verse by the 19th Century French poet Verlaine:

> *Your soul is a moonlit landscape fair,*
> *Peopled with maskers delicate and dim,*
> *That play on lutes and dance and have an air*
> *Of being sad in their fantastic trim.*

There was certainly nothing sad about that meal. We began with caviar, savoring the black pearls with iced vodka. The *sole Coquelin,* the next course, was fabulous: the small *paupiettes* or turbans of Dover sole were stuffed with a lighter-than-air salmon mousse. They had been steamed in a delicate fondue of tomatoes with white wine, and were served with medallions of tender lobster meat, fluted mushrooms and a gentle white wine sauce.

Ranged on the afterdeck of the *France* beneath the squinty eye of Maurice Renault, head wine steward, a forest of some 426 wine and liquor bottles suggests the variety available to slake seagoing thirsts. The wine list contains 74 selections of champagne, 50 Bordeaux and 49 Burgundies, as well as scores of other French, Italian, German and Swiss wines.

My next course was *canard rouennais aux oranges d'Espagne,* tender duck from Rouen, garnished with orange segments and encircled by a filigree of croutons. In New York duck *à l'orange* often is a lamentable affair; usually the sauce is too sweet and heavily thickened with cornstarch. But this sauce was magnificent, with just the right touch of natural bitterness from the oranges, and the duck itself was splendid, its skin beautifully brown and crisp.

The salad that followed was of *barbe-de-capucin* (literally, Capucin monk's beard)—wild chicory—in a vinaigrette sauce. The dressing was a bit too acid, but the dessert soon made up for that. It was Bavarian cream Rothschild, an exquisite cold molded vanilla cream served with English custard. It is prepared by lining a mold with ladyfingers, then filling the mold with Bavarian cream flavored with glacéed fruits and kirsch. The molded cream is chilled, unmolded and served with the custard. We ate generously, and yet when the meal was over there was none of that heavy, puffed feeling one often has on leaving so many pretentious restaurants. I was, in fact, in a state of total euphoria.

Throughout the meal, the service had been faultless. Once an order was taken, the food appeared almost magically. There was no clanking of dishes or silverware; every plate that was brought to the table arrived unobtrusively. The ship obviously boasted the elite of captains, waiters and bus boys from all over France. For young Frenchmen aspiring to a place in the culinary world, there surely could be no better training ground.

Later, when I asked how such standards were kept up, I was told that a ratio of one waiter to every six passengers is maintained, and that before every trip a map of the dining room is marked off to indicate the exact positions and responsibilities of every waiter and maître d'hôtel. As a further check against error, every order is signed by the waiter who takes it, and special orders are also signed by a maître d'hôtel.

There was much to enjoy on the *France* when we were not savoring the food. We could play shuffleboard, or swim in the pool, or simply stroll on the upper decks in the sun, filling our lungs with salt air. Sometimes we stretched out on comfortable deck chairs, snugly bundled in bright plaid blankets, and chatted, dozed or watched the ship's wake. And while we were there in the clean open air and ocean breezes, stewards in black suits, crisp white shirts and black hats with shiny visors came around and took our orders for consommé (made in M. Le Huédé's kitchen from a rich golden stock) or for freshly baked cookies and tea.

In the evenings for those who cared for such diversions, there were horse races to wager on and dance contests to enter. Or, if we liked, we could go out on deck where the only sound was the foaming and hissing of the sea, and stand at the rail watching the white wave crests boil up in the blackness of the night. There is something about shipboard life and salt air that arouses hunger. We always seemed to be ravenous, and at midnight we would visit the Cabaret de l'Atlantique on the verandah deck for a snack. The menu here offered smoked Scotch salmon, lobster cocktail, a terrine of foie gras, onion soup, Welsh rabbit, scrambled eggs and sausages—all of it, of course, on the house.

One day in mid-Atlantic, Pierre and I were invited by M. Le Huédé to

Butcher, Baker and Pastry Maker in a Floating Food Factory

The passenger kitchen of the S.S. *France* is a well oiled, highly efficient culinary factory that turns out some of the finest food in the world. Drawing on its own bakery, butcher shop, pastry shop and *garde-manger* (cold storage pantry), it produces seven different kinds of bread (including 4,000 to 5,000 rolls) every day, 175 gallons of soup a day, 9 different kinds of petits fours and dozens of different meat and fish dishes. Meanwhile, its chefs also create a variety of the most beautifully decorated dishes of the classic cuisine, ranging from elegantly garnished, superbly sauced meat to some of the most delectable, intricately designed desserts to be found on land or sea.

Cups and pitchers are conveniently stored over the coffee station.

In the *boulangerie,* bakers fashion rolls from newly risen dough.

The ship's butchers trim cuts of beef and veal in the *boucherie.*

Pastry chefs shape pulled sugar ribbons for petits fours baskets.

A sauce chef flames mushrooms and cognac to accompany a brill.

In the *garde-manger*, baskets of cold fruit, melons and strawberries are ready for serving. The lockers contain cheeses and extra fruits.

inspect the ship's kitchen. We went down to "A" deck in the afternoon, and as the double doors automatically swung open, found ourselves in a gleaming expanse of stainless-steel counters, cabinets and shelves. The ceiling was hung with silver coffee and tea pitchers, long rows of coffee cups, and baskets of fruit tied with pink, green and yellow satin ribbons.

The kitchen of the *France* is equipped with its own bakery, pastry shop, butcher shop, fish kitchen, soup and vegetable kitchen, grills and *garde-manger,* where cold dishes are prepared. About 180 people—chefs, assistants and bus boys—work here turning out thousands of meals every day. (On a recent 20-day Caribbean cruise the kitchen produced 110,000 meals.) Yet even at the peak of activity, with all hands chopping, mixing, grilling, grinding, baking and boiling, the kitchen seems not frenzied but calm. The impression it gives is rather like that of a ballet, where all the movements fall quietly, harmoniously and effortlessly into place.

In the bakery, nine men were standing around a table, waiting in silence as an enormous mass of dough was lifted from a mixing bowl that stood waist-high on the floor. Suddenly the room erupted into activity. At the far end of the table, one man cut small pieces of dough from the great mass in front of him, his metal cutter making a quick, sure, syncopated rhythm on the wooden table surface. As he separated each piece of dough, he quickly flung it to another man. Hands flew as the pieces of dough were rapidly broken in two, shaped into balls and set on huge boards. These were then inserted in racks along the wall. Again a stillness fell over the room, and one was left with the clean, invigorating smell of flour and yeast, as the bakers waited for the dough to rise. One of them told us that the bakery turns out 4,000 to 5,000 rolls a day.

In the butcher shop five men in white aprons were cutting and trimming pieces of meat on large wooden blocks. At the far end of the room great sides of beef and veal, a whole pig and barons of lamb hung from the ceiling. The whole area, with its chrome fixtures, its immaculate glass refrigerator cabinets, and the sea air blowing in through the portholes, was the most impressive butcher shop we had ever seen.

We found M. Le Huédé in the pastry shop, discussing special dessert orders. He told us that the staff never prepares the same dish twice during a voyage, unless it is specifically requested by a guest. The kitchen is open at all hours, ready to take any order in its stride, from a *chartreuse* of partridge, which involves the preparation of a mosaic of hundreds of pieces of carrots, turnips, green beans and peas, to such an exotic, nonclassic dish as *mole poblano,* the Mexican national favorite—turkey served with a chocolate sauce. As M. Le Huédé spoke, a pastry cook was decorating a tray of small cakes with swirls of mocha cream from a pastry tube. In the background, a confectioner was putting the finishing touches on a spun-sugar fantasy, a small world of mushrooms and elves.

For better or worse it is the chef who is the heart of a restaurant, and we wanted to know by what route this one had become the master chef of the *France.* M. Le Huédé's birthplace, he told us, was the little town of Batz-sur-Mer on the Brittany coast, and his first job was as an apprentice in the Duchesse Anne restaurant in the nearby city of Nantes in 1931, when he was 12. In those days—some 40 years ago—apprentices worked without pay, and M. Le Huédé still remembered the experience vividly.

"When I started work at the Duchesse Anne," he recalled, "I was so small I had to stand on a box to put a skillet on the stove. One day the chef asked me to fry some smelts, and as I was draining some of them, I tipped the box over and accidentally knocked a platter of fried fish all over the floor. The chef picked me up by the back of the neck and threw me into the dishwashing tub!"

On another occasion, the young apprentice was making bread crumbs by pounding a loaf of dry bread on a table in front of him. The chef was not popular with the apprentices, and as Le Huédé pounded the loaf, he made believe it was the chef, calling out the man's name as he vigorously whacked the bread. Unhappily, the chef was standing directly behind him, and the result was a beating that M. Le Huédé even today mentions with some feeling.

When he was 14 he joined the staff of Prunier in Paris, which at the time was the most famous seafood restaurant in the world; there he learned the basic techniques of frying, poaching, baking, making sauces and decorating fancy platters. His first taste of seafaring life came a year later when he joined the kitchen staff of the S.S. *Mexique,* a passenger ship of the French Line on the transatlantic run between France and Mexico. With time out for service in the French Navy during World War II, M. Le Huédé has been with the French Line ever since, serving aboard the *De Grasse,* the *Liberté* and the *Ile de France.* The glorious *Ile de France* was in service from 1927 until 1958 (except for wartime troop-transport duty) and she is fondly remembered by all who knew her, including M. Le Huédé. However he did have one harrowing adventure while serving aboard the ship that merits a place among the historic crises of the classic French cuisine.

It occurred the night of the captain's gala, an especially elaborate dinner customarily enjoyed on French Line ships on the next to last night out. On this occasion the captain emerges from his seclusion to dine with the first-class passengers, and the food is more lavish than usual. For this particular gala, the fish course planned for the captain's table was to be something special, *turbot soufflé surprise,* a title that soon proved prophetic.

In the kitchen the chef's assistant had lifted the fish onto a platter and was carrying it to the fish chef, who was to add the sauce. Suddenly the platter slipped from the assistant's hands and the turbot broke in a hundred pieces on the floor. Only the head and tail remained intact. The assistant stood petrified, but the fish chef did some quick thinking. He remembered that the tourist-class menu for that night included fillet of sole. So he put the head and tail of the turbot on another big platter, placed some sole fillets between the head and tail and cut them to the proper shape. Then he added a layer of mushroom purée and another layer of sole fillets and shaped the whole thing to look like a turbot. The platter was whisked off to the fish chef, who poured over it the sauce originally intended for the turbot.

Meanwhile, the maître d'hôtel and the waiter were making anxious inquiries about the fish. They were told that the dish was supposed to be a

Continued on page 178

Culinary Artistry for a First-Class Buffet

The artistic splendors of a first-class buffet aboard the *France* are among the culinary wonders of the world, the end result of painstaking and loving labor by the ship's talented kitchen staff. The cold platters shown here, prepared for the captain's gala dinner on a trip from Le Havre to New York, took two days to prepare and represent the handiwork of two master chefs and a pair of assistants. The talents of such men must include not only a knowledge of every facet of cooking and seasoning, but a highly developed decorative sense. Carved vegetables, truffle "flowers," fully plumed fowls: on the *France* such rarities are routine—to the chefs, that is.

Masked with *chaud-froid* sauce, a colorful *canard à l'orange* is surmounted by a decoration of fruit skewered on an *attelet*.

A pheasant in its splendid plumage, watches over a covey of quail breasts stuffed with foie gras and truffles and coated with aspic.

Turbot froid "petite russe" is decorated with a tomato rose, a radish tulip, an egg-white lily of the valley and an olive delphinium.

Surrounded by stuffed tomatoes and eggs, a pair of spiny lobsters perform a *contredanse* in the dish known as *langoustes à la parisienne*.

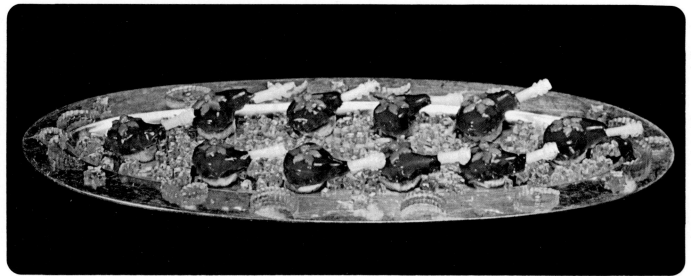

Côtes de pré salé fleuriste are lamb chops coated with brown *chaud-froid* sauce, placed upon croutons and strewn with gems of aspic.

Suprêmes de pigeons à la vigneronne are miniature birds fashioned of pigeon breasts and grapes, accompanied by a pair of partridges.

For a gala dinner aboard the *France,* the ship's *patissiers* turn out a rainbow variety of cakes and petits fours. The little cakes at right are filled and decorated with mocha butter cream. Among the petits fours on the opposite page are such exotic confections as lavender *nicéens* colored with crushed candied violets, the chocolate rose-shaped *dujas (center foreground)* and glacéed chestnuts *(immediately above the "dujas").*

surprise and could be prepared only at the very last moment. Within 15 minutes after the catastrophe, the *turbot soufflé surprise* was on the captain's table. The captain, knowing the kitchen's usual efficiency, suspected that something had gone wrong, but his guests were blissfully unaware. Several even asked for the recipe. The evening was saved, but the *turbot soufflé surprise* was never again served on the *Ile de France.*

In 1962 M. Le Huédé joined the kitchen staff of the *France,* becoming master chef six years later. In this lofty role he spends most of his time in the kitchen, walking among the hot stoves, tasting soups, sampling sauces, taking small nibbles from pastries, and inspecting each dish before it leaves the kitchen for the dining room.

When he is not on duty, he occupies a small cabin one deck below the kitchen. The cabin is large enough to accommodate a desk and a record player, and underneath it are nestled albums of his favorite composers, Beethoven, Mozart and Chopin. On one of the walls hangs a large poster of Napoleon, a particular hero of M. Le Huédé's, and tucked under one side of the poster is a small bunch of dried yellow flowers, which the chef picked on a visit to the island of St. Helena, which was Napoleon's final place of exile.

On a working day M. Le Huédé rises at 7 o'clock, breakfasts in a small staff dining room or in his cabin on coffee and a croissant and then holds a brief meeting with his staff. After that he begins one of his most important and exacting tasks, planning the ship's menus. The breakfast menu is standard throughout the trip—fresh fruits, soups, cereals, fish, grilled meats, cold meats, pancakes, potatoes and eggs—but the luncheon

and dinner menus are different every day, dinner being the more elaborate and varied meal. The chef makes out his menus two days in advance, keeping a running record of a whole trip's meals on a form he has devised specially for the purpose. Then, at the end of each trip, he rips up the menus, to make sure he does not repeat them on later voyages.

His colleagues on the *France* extol M. Le Huédé as the Verlaine or Baudelaire of the menu, and his menus do have a poetic ring, an effect he frequently achieves by adding to the name of each dish the place of origin of its principal ingredient. Thus a slice of foie gras from Adour becomes *médaillon de foie gras de l'Adour,* and lobster Thermidor, prepared with lobsters from the waters around the Cornwall region of Britain, becomes *homard de Cornouailles au gratin Thermidor.* In selecting the names for his dishes, M. Le Huédé will sometimes decide to honor a gastronomic hero or a celebrated culinary establishment. He has called a chicken soup *crème de volaille Curnonsky,* after Maurice Edmond Sailland (1872-1956), the "prince of gastronomes," whose pseudonym was Curnonsky, and he once christened a stuffed pear *poire givrée Carlton,* after the London hotel where Escoffier reigned as chef in the early part of this century.

Next door to the pastry shop in the *France's* kitchen is the *garde-manger,* where some of the most beautiful dishes of the classic French cuisine are created. The food is cold here, and therefore the designs may be worked out more carefully and elaborately than if it were hot and had to be served immediately.

Inside a cold storage locker we saw a dazzling lineup of cold dishes on the shelves. A fully plumed pheasant watched over quail breasts stuffed

179

with foie gras and truffles, and a pair of plumed partridges with fresh purple grapes in their beaks stood gazing over pigeon breasts coated with white *chaud-froid* sauce decorated with a design of grapes. Fierce-looking cold spiny lobsters, with overlapping slices of delicate tailmeat decorating their shells, confronted each other in a fighting stance. There was a whole cold poached salmon, garnished with tomato roses, egg whites in the shape of lilies of the valley and bordered with wedges of clear aspic that glittered like diamonds. And there was a large turbot also decorated with tomato roses, a beautifully garnished ham and an almost endless array of other frigid masterpieces.

Cold buffet dishes from the *garde-manger* are customarily featured at the captain's gala and as we came into the dining room that night, a large table at the foot of the staircase was laden with them. There were the spiny lobsters garnished with their own tailmeat and still poised in their fighting stance, the partridges stuffed with foie gras and garnished with grapes, a pheasant surrounded by quail breasts decorated with truffles and a toy kangaroo poised over an oval mold of foie gras in aspic.

The dining tables were decorated with baskets of petits fours, tied with enormous bright green, yellow, red and orange ribbons that were made of pulled sugar (sugar that is boiled and then pulled like taffy into glistening strips while it is very hot). The captain was resplendent in his black uniform heavily encrusted with gold braid. The dinner guests gasped as the first course was brought to his table on a silver tray. It was a spectacular glittering sturgeon, carved out of ice, towering over a large tin of shiny black Beluga caviar.

The meal began with the caviar and iced vodka, followed by a *petite marmite,* a rich beef consommé, with finely cut strips of carrots and turnips, cabbage balls, and small cubes of beef and chicken. The fish course was turbot, stuffed with lobster mousse and swimming in a golden lobster sauce. Around it were little pastry baskets filled with the sauce and bits of lobster and truffles. The fish itself was admirably white, firm and moist, and the sauce was delicately flavored with lobster. Next we had a rich, juicy fillet of beef garnished with artichoke bottoms, asparagus and potato strips, served with a *périgueux* (truffle) sauce. After that came a tender hearts of lettuce salad with a light vinaigrette dressing. A tray of eight different cheeses was served, including a Camembert, a Brie, Munster, Port-Salut and a Chavignol, and finally came our dessert, a *melon glacé surprise*. It was a pale green "melon" made of ice cream and encircled by spun sugar. The outer layer or "rind" of this dessert was green pistachio ice cream, and the inside was a pale orange ice cream, the flavor and color of cantaloupe.

The wines for that memorable meal included a delightful white Burgundy (Beaune/Clos des Mouches 1966) with the fish, a red Burgundy (Chambertin/Clos de Bèze 1964) with the beef, and finally an elegant Laurent Perrier, Cuvée Grand Siècle, champagne. Such a meal works an unforgettable kind of magic. As we left the dining room that night, however, a sad thought occurred to me. In this age of speed a luxury liner such as the *France* could not last forever. What a blessing to have been aboard while the going was great.

Opposite: On the fantail of the *France* Chef Le Huédé and members of his staff who can be spared from their duties gather for a portrait. Behind the chef is Maître d'Hôtel Louis Pellegrin. Purser Yvon Hervé (wearing glasses) is in the center, and Administrative Purser Jacques Delaunay is at right. Of Chef Le Huédé's 180-man team, 17 rank as chefs in their own right.

VIII

Classic Cooking Comes to America

Back in 1962 Pierre Lamalle, an inspector for the *Guide Michelin,* was invited by Life Magazine to come to the United States and cast a critical eye over some of the country's better restaurants. In response to this invitation, Lamalle traveled to New York, Chicago, San Francisco and New Orleans. He liked America's airplanes, automobiles, skyscrapers, superhighways, supermarkets—and even *some* of the food. He found the steak at the Stock Yard Inn in Chicago "tender and vigorous" and was enthusiastic about the bay shrimp, salmon in wine and *crêpes Suzette* at Ernie's restaurant in San Francisco. But the place that made the profoundest impression on Lamalle was the Pavillon restaurant in New York. He found the crabmeat timbale Nantua there "light, tasty, splendid sauce." Of the roast duck with peaches and a *sauce bigarade,* he said: "In my personal opinion it would be impossible to do this better." The strawberry tart was "tender, excellent," and the Pichon-Longueville 1947 "a great wine." He even praised the coffee for its wonderful aroma.

Michelin inspectors are stingy with their praise, but Lamalle concluded that the Pavillon deserved at least two stars and that it would rank with the best restaurants in Paris. "I would not be surprised if it deserved three stars," he said—which was really letting himself go. He also gave the restaurant the highest mark for comfort and service—acclaiming the engraved glassware, silver, linen, crystal ashtrays and fresh flowers on the table, the delicate green murals, the soft but effective lighting and the "Louis XV but some Louis XVI" furniture.

The Pavillon of those days exemplified a crucial point about classic

When Wendy Afton, of the staff of this book, became Mrs. Richard Rieder, she put her culinary experience to good use. She baked a *coulibiac* (layers of salmon, with mushrooms, dill and a fish velouté in a rich brioche loaf) and served it at her wedding reception. Originally a Russian dish, the *coulibiac* was prepared at Monte Carlo by Escoffier for the Ballet Russe.

LOUIS DIAT
(1885-1957)

Diat worked at Ritz hotels in London, Paris and New York. While chef of New York's Ritz Carlton, he created the cold leek and potato soup known as Vichyssoise.

His recipe, which serves 8, follows:
4 leeks, white part
1 medium onion
2 ounces sweet butter
5 medium potatoes
1 quart water or chicken broth
1 tablespoon salt
2 cups milk
2 cups medium cream
1 cup heavy cream

Finely slice the white part of the leeks and the onion, and brown very lightly in sweet butter, then add the potatoes, also sliced finely. Add water or broth and salt. Boil 35 to 40 minutes. Crush and rub through a fine strainer. Return to heat and add 2 cups of milk and 2 cups of medium cream. Season to taste and bring to a boil. Cool and then rub again through a fine strainer. When soup is cold, add the heavy cream. Chill thoroughly before serving. Finely chopped chives may be added.

cooking. Together with impressionist paintings and Bordeaux and Burgundy wines, the cuisine is one of France's finest and most civilizing exports—but only in the right hands. The reason for the Pavillon's excellence was Henri Soulé, one of the greatest maîtres d'hôtel who ever lived, and himself one of France's most impressive exports.

Soulé was born in Saubrigues on the southwestern coast of France and started his culinary career as a bus boy in a hotel in nearby Biarritz. After two years he moved along to Paris, working as a waiter at the Hôtel Mirabeau, Claridge's hotel and the world-famous Café de Paris. When the French government decided to open a restaurant at the New York World's Fair in 1939, Soulé was made the maître d'hôtel. In the fall of that year, when World War II broke out, he went home and joined the army, but was soon returned to his World's Fair job in the United States, on the theory that he could serve his country better with butter than with guns. After the fair closed in 1940, Soulé remained in New York to open the Pavillon, naming it after the restaurant at the fair and absorbing most of that institution's staff.

The secret of Soulé's success lay in his organizational ability. "He was an overwhelming tyrant who made no compromise with quality," a culinary expert who used to frequent the Pavillon recalls. He was, in fact, a perfectionist; he ran things his own way, and anyone who did not like it could go somewhere else. On one occasion an overbearing woman was shown to a table at the Pavillon. She had scarcely taken her seat when she began to complain about her location. Soulé resolutely refused to move her, explaining that all the other tables were reserved.

"But I don't like this table," the lady insisted.

Pursing his lips and fixing her with an icy stare, Soulé said: "Tell me, good woman, did you come here to eat at the Pavillon or did you come to argue with Soulé?" The good woman ate her meal at her assigned place.

The heart of the Pavillon and of any outstanding restaurant has always been the food, and the food at the Pavillon was superb. The *coulibiac,* the mousse of sole and the saddle of veal Orloff were out of this world. The *oeufs à la neige*—an English custard topped with delicate little puffs of meringue—was a marvel.

The Pavillon spawned a school of fine restaurants in New York. Soulé opened La Côte Basque, and members of his staff launched La Caravelle, La Grenouille, Le Veau d'Or and a dozen other restaurants.

Soulé was, of course, a maître d'hôtel, but France has also exported many front-rank chefs to the United States. The most illustrious was Louis Diat, who served as *chef de cuisine* at the old Ritz-Carlton Hotel in New York from its opening in 1910 to its closing 41 years later. Diat created such fine new dishes as breast of guinea hen Jefferson (guinea hen with ham, creamed tomatoes, wild rice fritters and a whiskey sauce) and chicken Gloria Swanson (sautéed chicken cooked in white wine and cream, served with creamed mushrooms, and garnished with rice and truffles). But his most famous invention was a simple soup that has become a classic in America. In the days before air conditioning, the Ritz had a Japanese roof garden, and Diat was constantly on the lookout for dishes that would cool his customers in the sultry July and August weather. He remembered the simple bourgeois hot leek and potato soup his mother had made when he was a boy in Montmarault in Central France and how he and his family had cooled the soup by adding milk to it. And so on the rooftop of the Ritz he prepared this same cold soup and called it *crème vichyssoise,* after the famous spa not far from his hometown.

After Diat died in 1957 at the age of 72, some of France's other leading chefs came to New York. Maurice Chantreau, a winner of the annual Gold Cup of the Académie Culinaire as the best chef in France, became chef at the Four Seasons. André Soltner, who took charge of the kitchens at Lutèce, became in 1968 the first chef outside of France to win the Meilleur Ouvrier de France award, given to the best French craftsman.

This influx of talent does not mean that the millennium is at hand for American gourmets. There are many dreadful restaurants in New York (and the country at large), and even the finest do not really compare favorably with the best restaurants in France. Yet the growing public interest in classic cooking bodes well for the American table, and—no less important—much of this cooking is being done in the home. Since World War II Americans have broadened their culinary horizons and improved their tastes. Cooking schools, television programs such as Julia Child's—and an avalanche of cookbooks, magazines and newspaper food columns—have spread the culinary faith. The decade of the 1960s saw a tremendous quickening of interest in classic cooking and in the numbers of cooks attempting classic dishes.

During that decade I traveled all over the United States by plane, train, automobile and sometimes on foot (there was a time when I had to hitchhike because my car broke down in North Dakota). My travels took me as far as Alaska and Hawaii, and along the way I encountered many fine classic dishes that were prepared in American homes.

In St. Louis, I dined one evening with an old lady who served an altogether exceptional first course, *vol-au-vent à la reine,* poached breast of chicken in a rich cream sauce served in a puff pastry shell. When I remarked on the tender, flaky texture of the pastry, my hostess laughed.

"Do you know," she said, "it cost me a thousand dollars to learn how to make that. I went all the way to a Paris cooking school to learn the technique, but the funny thing is this. My mother made puff pastry when I was a child, and the way they make it in Paris is not one whit better. Lord knows where she learned the trick, but I never cared about cooking while she was alive and she died with her secret."

In America as in France, the best classic cooking combines superior ingredients with tried and true methods. One of the sheer delights of spring on the East Coast of America is the arrival of shad and shad roe, and if fresh sorrel can be coaxed out of the ground at the same season and creamed for the dish the French call *alose à l'oseille (Recipe Index),* it is a liaison fit for the gods. I have had this dish at a table overlooking Long Island Sound. My hostess had grown her own sorrel; the sauce was admirable and so was the accompanying chilled brut champagne.

I have eaten a creditable lobster Thermidor in a country house in Vermont, lobster bisque in Maine and a beautiful mousse of sole in California *(Recipe Index).* In at least two private homes I have ended a meal with first-rate caramelized balls of cream puffs filled with pastry cream taken from a cone-shaped crisp cake called a *croquembouche*. I have seen American men—one a San Francisco dentist—display the greatest aplomb while turning crêpes in an excellent suzette sauce *(Recipe Index)*. And I have been to a picnic where one of the guests brought along a platter of *riz à l'impératrice (Recipe Index)*, a dessert that is surely the nicest thing that can happen to rice and candied fruits.

One of the most impressive meals of all took place in a modest but handsome apartment with a terrace overlooking a park in Mamaroneck, New York. It was the suburban home of a young couple, both of whom are New York advertising executives. Now when most people in similar circumstances finally arrive home by way of the faltering, antiquated trains of the Penn Central Railroad's New Haven division, they often settle for a quickly grilled steak, something reheated from the weekend, or even a TV dinner. Not this pair. If they have hamburgers, they serve hamburgers *au poivre flambés au cognac*. If they have veal, it is served with fines herbes, and in summer when they prepare a salad it is made from the fresh tomatoes grown on their own terrace.

On this particular evening the dinner began with a splendid, full-bodied clear *consommé Célestine* with freshly made, shredded crêpes. Then it proceeded to a ravishing dish of sole *Marguery (Recipe Index)*, the fish bathed in a rich wine sauce and garnished with shrimp and mussels. After that came boned quail stuffed with foie gras and roasted (the breast meat remaining pink and moist) with a thin sauce to which small green grapes were eventually added. There was a light salad with cheese and a *soufflé Rothschild (Recipe Index)*.

It was midsummer and warm and on the terrace fresh thyme and rosemary were growing. And over a cognac the host, a francophile like the rest of us around that table, lit up a Gauloise. For one haunting moment I felt as if I were in the south of France.

On the opposite coast of America lives Huntley Soyster—a package and label designer in San Francisco—whose favorite pastime is cooking. With his wife, three children and a hunting dog, Soyster occupies a remodeled 45-year-old, five-story house that includes four bedrooms, a wine cellar, a dining room, a large living room and a beautifully equipped kitchen. Both the living room and the kitchen command spectacular views of San Francisco Bay.

A tall, slim man in his forties with sandy hair and light blue eyes, who is known to his friends as Bim, Soyster has been cooking all his life. He grew up in Chevy Chase, Maryland, and in Pasadena, and began cooking in his family's kitchen when he was a boy. Today he specializes in Chinese and Latin American dishes, and he also likes to prepare game —pheasant, duck, quail, pigeon and wild boar killed on his ranch in Mendocino County. But his real diversion is classic French cooking and he can prepare just about anything in the repertory.

"I have a very good palate," he says. "It's not something you can learn. You just have it. When I taste a dish, I know what went into it, what the seasonings are." Soyster's wife Cynthia is also a talented cook, but she leaves most of the fancy cooking to her husband. "Cynthia enjoys cook-

HENRI SOULÉ
(1904-1966)

Soulé, renowned operator of the Pavillon restaurant in New York, was a perfectionist who demanded that everything, including the *langoustes* (spiny lobsters) he is eyeing here, be exactly right.

ing," Soyster says, "and she's a damn good cook. But there have been occasions when she has spent a lot of time and trouble on a dish and we sit down to a dinner and a guest tastes it and says, 'Bim, this is the best thing you have ever done.' So she's decided I might as well do the cooking."

Not long ago the Soysters invited some friends in for a classic meal, and Bim did the cooking. The menu was to include a *consommé royale*, *paupiettes de sole Dugléré* (using local petrale sole), *tournedos Henri IV* and strawberries Romanoff *(all Recipe Index)*.

Bim started lining things up several days before the dinner—an excellent practice when preparing an elaborate classic meal. He made a chicken stock (for the consommé) and a fish stock (for the sole) and trimmed some artichokes as garnishes for the *tournedos*. Two days before the dinner he bought some violets and candied the flowers as decorations for the dessert by dipping them in crystallized sugar syrup. The day before his guests were to arrive, he ordered the *tournedos* from his butcher—specifying that each of the slices of beef fillet was to be an inch and a half thick. On the day of the dinner, Cynthia drove to a fish market and picked out the petrale sole.

Early that afternoon, Bim prepared the strawberries and made some whipped cream for the dessert. Then an hour and a half before dinner time, he started a fire in the barbecue pit in the kitchen, explaining that it takes 45 minutes to get the coals going and another half-hour to get a good film of gray ash on the coals. Later he buttered the *tournedos* and placed them on a rack over the coals, cooking them about six minutes on each side. The rods of the rack made dark stripes on the meat, and after two minutes he turned them 90 degrees to form cross markings.

Dinner was to be at 7:30. The Soysters had hired a butler and a kitchen helper for the occasion as they usually do for dinner parties. Drinks were served in the living room, and when dinner was announced the guests took their places in gilt chairs under a chandelier from Finland that cast a soft glow on the table below. The center of the table was decorated with a round bowl of freshly picked spring flowers, tulips, Ranunculus, daffodils, marigolds—all short-stemmed and closely bunched. The table had been set with 100-year-old Dresden china in a floral pattern, and at each place stood three classic crystal wine glasses, a small one for the white wine, a larger one for the red and a tulip glass for champagne. The softly shining silver, Dresden china, white damask cloth and the medley of spring flowers made a beautiful setting.

The first course, the pale golden consommé, was served sparkling clear in Dresden bouillon cups. In the center of each cup was a round piece of *royale* (custard) which had been cut with a truffle cutter. The flavor was delicate and golden, a gentle introduction to a classic dinner.

Next came the *paupiettes* of petrale sole, snow-white and firm, thick and sweet. The fish was covered with a Dugléré sauce, yet its delicate, delightful flavor dominated, and tiny bits of tomato and parsley added color. With it, Bim served an outstanding California wine from his own cellar—Inglenook Johannisberg Riesling 1968, private reserve—with a fresh bouquet and an aftertaste that he accurately described as "withering dry." Both the wine and the fish supported a key point of classic cooking

When Huntley (Bim) Soyster of San Francisco prepared the classic dinner described in this chapter, the main course was *tournedos Henri IV*. The grilled beef fillet slices are topped with artichoke bottoms filled with *sauce béarnaise*. Neatly stacked *pont neuf* potatoes may accompany this dish.

Getting ready for a classic dinner at his home in San Francisco, Huntley Soyster trims artichokes to provide a garnish for his main course, *tournedos Henri IV*. An ardent gastronome, he learned to cook in his youth from a chef for the Pennsylvania Railroad, and now prepares classic French, Latin American and Chinese dishes for his family and friends.

that applies the world over: if you have fine local ingredients, use them.

The main course, served on pure white Haviland china with gold borders, was the classic *tournedos Henri IV*, brought to the table beautifully cooked and rare. Surmounting the *tournedos* was a California specialty —fresh artichoke bottoms, filled with the classic béarnaise sauce. The béarnaise was thick and velvety—exactly the right complement to the artichokes, and the golden puffs of Lorette potatoes *(Recipe Index)* with the artichokes were superb.

With the meat course came a Château Latour 1953. The guests were so captivated by this remarkable Bordeaux that they sniffed it, sipped it, held it up to the light to see its glorious ruby color. It had all the warmth, texture and grandeur of a *grand vin*.

The final course was strawberries Romanoff, with *crème Chantilly* on it and the charming crystallized violets decorating the cream. The Moët et Chandon cuvée Dom Pérignon 1961 champagne, taken with the fruit, was perfection itself. Afterwards in the living room *café filtre* and liqueurs were served. The matchless view of the bay, with the Golden Gate Bridge all lighted up in the distance, made the world seem far better than it had before. Six thousand miles from its origins, the art of classic French cooking had worked its spell.

Filets de Sole Marguery
FILLET OF SOLE WITH MUSSELS, SHRIMP AND WHITE WINE SAUCE

Preheat the oven to 350°. Spread the tablespoon of softened butter over the bottom and sides of a *gratin* dish large enough to hold the sole in one layer. Fold the fillets lengthwise in half, white side out, arrange them side by side in the buttered dish, and set aside.

Scrub the mussels thoroughly under cold running water with a stiff brush or scouring pad. With a small, sharp knife scrape or pull off the black ropelike tufts from the shells. Combine the mussels, *fumet de poisson* and wine in a 3- to 4-quart enameled or stainless-steel saucepan, cover tightly and bring to a boil over high heat. Reduce the heat to low and simmer for about 2 minutes, shaking the pan from time to time until the mussels open. Discard those that remain closed.

With a slotted spoon, transfer the mussels to a plate; remove and discard their shells and pull off and discard the dark filament that surrounds them. Place the mussels in a bowl and cover with foil to keep them warm. Strain the broth through a fine sieve lined with a double thickness of dampened cheesecloth and pour it evenly over the sole. Cover with buttered wax paper, cut to fit snugly inside the dish. Bring to a simmer on top of the stove, then poach the sole in the middle of the oven for about 10 minutes, or until the fish flakes easily when prodded with a fork.

Wash the *crevettes* or shrimp under cold water and pat them completely dry with paper towels. In a heavy 8- to 10-inch skillet, melt the 2 tablespoons of unsalted butter over moderate heat. When the foam begins to subside, drop in the *crevettes* or shrimp and, turning them frequently with a slotted spoon, sauté for 3 to 4 minutes, or until they turn pink and feel firm to the touch. Transfer the *crevettes* or shrimp to the plate with the mussels.

Carefully pour the poaching liquid from the sole through a fine sieve set over a heavy tin-lined copper or enameled-iron saucepan. Ring the sole in the serving dish with a circle of the *crevettes* or shrimp and a circle of mussels. Drape with foil to keep them warm while you prepare the sauce. Preheat the broiler to its highest setting.

SAUCE VIN BLANC (WHITE WINE SAUCE): Bring the poaching liquid to a boil over high heat. Cook briskly until the liquid is reduced to 4 tablespoons. Remove the pan from the heat. With a wire whisk, beat the egg yolks into the pan and continue to beat briskly for 2 or 3 minutes until the yolks begin to thicken. Place the pan over low heat and cook until the yolks almost double in volume. Lift the pan from the heat from time to time, still whisking, to prevent the egg yolks from curdling.

Off the heat, whisking, pour in the 1¼ cups of clarified butter in a slow, thin stream. After about ¼ cup of the butter has been absorbed the sauce will begin to thicken again and you may whisk in the remaining butter more rapidly. Stir in the lemon juice, salt and pepper.

Taste for seasoning. Then pour the sauce evenly over the sole, shrimp and mussels. Slide the baking dish under the broiler for about 30 seconds, or until the top is lightly browned. Serve at once.

To serve 6

1 tablespoon butter, softened, plus 2 tablespoons unsalted butter

6 eight-ounce sole fillets (preferably Dover sole), skinned

24 mussels in their shells

½ cup *fumet de poisson* (page 32)

½ cup dry white wine

1 pound imported *crevettes (see Glossary)*, or substitute 1 pound small shrimp (about 60 or more to the pound), shelled and deveined

SAUCE VIN BLANC

4 large egg yolks

1¼ cups warm clarified butter *(page 34)*

2 teaspoons strained fresh lemon juice

¼ teaspoon salt

⅛ teaspoon freshly ground white pepper

Potage Germiny
CREAM OF SORREL SOUP

Wash the sorrel under cold running water. With a sharp knife, trim away any bruised or blemished spots and cut off and discard the white stems. Stack the leaves together a handful at a time, roll them lengthwise into a tight cylinder and cut it crosswise as fine as possible.

In a heavy 8- to 10-inch skillet set over moderate heat, melt 2 tablespoons of butter without letting it brown. Add the sorrel and, stirring constantly, cook for 3 or 4 minutes until the shreds have wilted slightly. Set the skillet aside off the heat.

In a heavy 3- to 4-quart saucepan, bring the chicken stock to a simmer over moderate heat, regulating the heat so that only the smallest bubbles form at the edges of the pan. Beat the egg yolks and cream together with a wire whisk. Then, whisking constantly and gently, pour the mixture into the stock in a slow thin stream. Reduce the heat and simmer, stirring constantly, until the soup is thick enough to cling lightly to the wires of the whisk. (Do not allow the soup to come anywhere near the boil or it will curdle.) Strain the soup through a fine sieve into another saucepan and stir in the sorrel.

If you plan to serve the soup hot, immediately swirl in 4 tablespoons of chilled butter. Taste for seasoning and pour the soup into a heated tureen or individual soup plates. Sprinkle with the chervil. If you plan to serve the soup cold, do not add the butter enrichment. Pour the soup into a large bowl; let it cool to room temperature, then refrigerate for at least 4 hours, or until thoroughly chilled. Taste for seasoning and sprinkle with chervil just before serving. The soup may need more salt.

To serve 4 to 6

1 pound fresh sorrel
2 to 6 tablespoons unsalted butter
4 cups *fond blanc de volaille (page 31)*, or substitute 4 cups thoroughly degreased, canned chicken stock
6 egg yolks
1 cup heavy cream
Salt
1 teaspoon finely chopped fresh chervil

Filets de sole à la florentine
FILLET OF SOLE WITH SPINACH AND MORNAY SAUCE

In an enameled or stainless-steel 5- to 6-quart pot, bring 3 quarts of water and 1 teaspoon of salt to a boil over high heat. Drop in the spinach, return the water to a boil and cook briskly, uncovered, for 4 to 5 minutes. Drain the spinach in a large sieve or colander and run cold water over it to set the color. A handful at a time, squeeze the spinach vigorously to remove all the excess liquid. Chop the leaves and set aside.

Preheat the oven to 325°. With a pastry brush, spread 2 tablespoons of the softened butter evenly over the bottom and sides of an 8-by-12-inch baking dish. Scatter the shallots in the bottom of the dish. Season the fillets lightly with salt and pepper, and fold them crosswise in half, white side out. Lay the fillets side by side in the baking dish. Pour the *fumet de poisson* and wine down the sides of the pan. Cover the fish with a sheet of buttered wax paper cut to fit flush against the sides of the baking dish. Bring to a simmer over moderate heat, then place the dish in the middle of the oven. Poach the fillets for 10 to 12 minutes, or until they are tender enough to flake easily when prodded gently with a fork. Do not overcook.

Meanwhile, in a heavy 10- to 12-inch skillet, heat the remaining 6 tablespoons of softened butter over moderate heat until it browns lightly.

To serve 6

Salt
2 pounds fresh spinach, trimmed and thoroughly washed
8 tablespoons butter, softened
A pinch of nutmeg, preferably freshly grated
2 tablespoons finely chopped shallots
Six 6-ounce sole fillets, lightly pounded with the side of a cleaver to a uniform thickness of about ¼ inch
Freshly ground white pepper
¼ cup *fumet de poisson (page 32)*
¼ cup dry white wine

Strawberries Romanoff, served by Bim Soyster in this chapter, are a blend of strawberries, *crème Chantilly,* curaçao and candied violets.

193

Add the spinach and nutmeg and, stirring constantly, sauté for 1 or 2 minutes until almost all of the liquid in the pan has evaporated. With a fork, transfer the spinach to an ovenproof serving platter or large *gratin* dish and spread it out evenly. Carefully lift the poached fillets out of the baking dish and arrange them attractively in one layer on top of the spinach. Drape loosely with foil to keep the fish and spinach warm while you make the sauce.

SAUCE MORNAY (MORNAY SAUCE): Heat the broiler to its highest setting. Working quickly, strain the liquid remaining in the baking dish through a fine sieve into a heavy 1- to 2-quart saucepan, pressing down hard on the shallots with the back of a spoon to extract all the juices before discarding. Boil the liquid briskly until it is reduced to about ½ cup. Reduce the heat to moderate and, with a wire whisk, stir in the béchamel and cream. Simmer for 5 minutes, or until the sauce is smooth, whisking all the while. Remove the pan from the heat. Whisk in 1 egg yolk. Then stir in 6 tablespoons of the grated cheese. Taste for seasoning.

Spoon the sauce evenly over the fillets, masking them completely, and sprinkle the top with the remaining 2 tablespoons of cheese. Slide the dish under the broiler for 30 seconds or so, until the topping is lightly browned. Serve at once.

SAUCE MORNAY

1 cup *sauce béchamel (page 35)*
½ cup heavy cream
1 egg yolk
¼ cup grated imported Parmesan combined with ¼ cup freshly grated imported Gruyère cheese

Côtes de veau à la crème aux morilles
SAUTÉED VEAL CHOPS IN CREAM SAUCE WITH MOREL MUSHROOMS

Place the morels in a deep bowl and pour in enough warm water to cover them by at least 2 inches. Soak the morels for about 30 minutes, then wash them 3 or 4 times in warm water, squeezing them gently each time to rid them of any sand. If any of the caps are more than 1 inch in diameter, cut them in half. Set the morels aside.

Preheat the oven to the lowest setting. Season the veal chops on both sides with salt and a few grindings of pepper. Then dip the chops in flour one at a time to coat them evenly, and briskly shake off the excess. In a heavy 12-inch skillet, warm the clarified butter over high heat until a drop of water flicked into it splutters and evaporates instantly. Sauté the chops in the hot butter for 8 to 10 minutes on each side, turning them with tongs or a spatula and regulating the heat so that they color richly and evenly without burning. Transfer the chops to an ovenproof platter and keep them warm in the oven while you prepare the sauce.

Pour off any excess fat from the skillet, then drop in the shallots and, stirring constantly, cook for 2 or 3 minutes. Add the morels and stir for 2 minutes. Carefully pour the cognac into the skillet. It may burst into flame spontaneously; if not, ignite it with a match. Sliding the skillet back and forth gently, cook until the flames die. Then stir in the cream and the *glace de viande*. Pour in the velouté and continue stirring for 2 or 3 minutes until the sauce becomes smooth, thickens and comes to a boil. Add the lemon juice and taste for seasoning. With a bulb baster, transfer any liquid that has accumulated around the chops to the sauce, stirring it once or twice. Then pour the sauce over the chops, masking them completely, and serve at once. *Côtes de veau à la crème aux morilles* is usually accompanied by steamed white rice or wild rice.

To serve 6

2 ounces dried morels *(see Glossary)*
6 lean loin veal chops, cut about 1½ inches thick and trimmed of excess fat
Salt
Freshly ground black pepper
¾ cup flour
5 tablespoons clarified butter *(page 34)*
2 tablespoons finely chopped shallots
3 tablespoons cognac
1⅓ cups heavy cream
1 teaspoon *glace de viande (page 34)*
½ cup *sauce velouté (page 36)* made with *fond blanc de veau* or *fond blanc de volaille*
½ teaspoon strained fresh lemon juice

Tournedos Henri IV
TOURNEDOS WITH BÉARNAISE SAUCE, ARTICHOKE BOTTOMS AND POTATOES

To serve 6

SAUCE BÉARNAISE: Combine the vinegar, shallots, fresh tarragon stems or dried tarragon, peppercorns and parsley sprigs in a 1- to 1½-quart enameled cast-iron or copper saucepan and bring to a boil over high heat. Cook briskly until the liquid is reduced to about 2 tablespoons. Remove the pan from the heat, and let it cool for a minute or two.

With a wire whisk, quickly beat the egg yolks into the saucepan and continue to beat briskly for 2 or 3 minutes until the yolks thicken. Return the saucepan to low heat and, whisking constantly, cook long enough for the yolks to thicken further and double in volume. Lift the saucepan from the heat from time to time, still whisking, to prevent the egg yolks from becoming too hot and curdling.

Remove the pan from the heat again. Still whisking, immediately pour in the 1¼ cups of warm butter in a slow, thin stream. After about ¼ cup of the butter has been absorbed, the sauce will begin to thicken and you may whisk in the remaining butter more rapidly. The sauce should have the consistency of a light mayonnaise.

Strain the sauce through a fine sieve into a second pan, pressing down hard on the shallots and herbs with the back of a spoon to extract all their juices before discarding them. Taste the béarnaise and season it with salt and the cayenne. Add the tarragon leaves and chopped parsley and use at once or set aside in a warm place until ready to use. The sauce should not wait for more than an hour. Béarnaise is always served lukewarm so it should not be kept hot or reheated.

TOURNEDOS: Light a layer of coals in a charcoal broiler and let them burn until a white ash appears on the surface.

Pat the *tournedos* completely dry with paper towels. Season them with salt and black pepper and brush them on both sides with 4 tablespoons of melted clarified butter. Grill the *tournedos* over charcoal for 2 or 3 minutes, then turn them at right angles so that the grill will form a criss-cross pattern on the surface of the meat. Turn the *tournedos* over and repeat this process on the other side, grilling them until the *tournedos* are cooked to the state of doneness you prefer. Ideally they should be rare.

Place the *tournedos* in a ring on a heated platter, and set an artichoke bottom on top of each one. Fill the artichoke bottoms with as much béarnaise sauce as they will hold. Set a bouquet of watercress in the center of the ring. Arrange the potatoes of your choice attractively on the platter and serve at once.

NOTE: In the event that you do not have a charcoal broiler, sauté the *tournedos* in a heavy skillet with 4 tablespoons of clarified butter, following the directions for *tournedos Rossini (page 109)*. It is not traditional in the French cuisine to use the broiler of a range as a substitute for a charcoal grill.

If the artichoke bottoms have been prepared hours ahead, warm them just before serving. Wash them off and pat them dry with paper towels. In a heavy 8- to 10-inch skillet, heat 4 tablespoons of clarified butter over moderate heat for 10 seconds. Reduce the heat to low and add the artichoke bottoms, concave side down. Then cover the skillet tightly and cook for about 5 minutes until the artichokes are heated through.

SAUCE BÉARNAISE
⅔ cup red wine vinegar

3 tablespoons finely chopped shallots

1 tablespoon finely cut fresh tarragon stems, or substitute 1½ teaspoons crumbled dried tarragon

12 white peppercorns, bruised with the side of a cleaver or heavy knife

8 fresh parsley sprigs

4 large egg yolks

1¼ cups warm clarified butter *(page 34)*

1 teaspoon salt

A pinch of ground red pepper (cayenne)

1 tablespoon finely cut fresh tarragon leaves

1 tablespoon finely chopped fresh parsley

TOURNEDOS
6 six-ounce *tournedos,* each about 1½ inches thick

Salt

Freshly ground black pepper

4 tablespoons melted clarified butter *(page 34)*

6 artichoke bottoms cooked *à blanc (see selle d'agneau Armenonville, page 41)*

A bunch of fresh watercress, washed and trimmed

Pommes château (see filet de boeuf Richelieu, page 138), pommes pont neuf or *pommes Lorette (Recipe Booklet)*

4 tablespoons clarified butter *(page 34)*

To make one 9-inch tart

POIRES

4 cups cold water

2 cups sugar

A 2-inch piece of vanilla bean, split
in half lengthwise

2 one-by-two-inch strips of lemon
peel

2 tablespoons strained fresh lemon
juice

3 large firm ripe pears, preferably
Bosc pears

FRANGIPANE

½ cup whole blanched almonds

2 cups milk

A 2-inch piece of vanilla bean, split
in half lengthwise

2 eggs

2 egg yolks

¾ cup sugar

1 cup flour

6 tablespoons unsalted butter, cut
into ½-inch bits

½ cup dry or stale macaroons
(about 6 macaroons), pulverized
in a blender or with a rolling pin

½ cup imported kirsch

1½ cup apricot jam

¼ cup imported kirsch

A 9-inch *pâte brisée* pastry shell
(*Recipe Booklet*) baked in a
fluted quiche pan

3 tablespoons finely chopped fresh
blanched pistachios

1 dry or stale macaroon, finely
crushed with a rolling pin

Poires Bourdaloue
PEAR AND FRANGIPANE TART

POIRES (PEARS): In a 3-quart enameled casserole, bring the water, 2 cups of sugar, vanilla bean, lemon peel and lemon juice to a boil over high heat, stirring until the sugar dissolves. Remove from the heat.

One at a time, peel the pears, cut them in half lengthwise and remove the stems and cores, dropping each pear into the syrup as you proceed. Shape one of the halves into a peachlike round by cutting off the stem end. The syrup should cover the pears completely; if necessary add a little water. Bring to a simmer over moderate heat, reduce to low, and poach partially covered for 10 to 15 minutes, or until the pears show only slight resistance when pierced deeply with the point of a small knife. Remove the pan from the heat and let the pears cool in the syrup. With a slotted spoon arrange the pears, cored side down, on a wire rack to drain.

To toast the blanched almonds preheat the oven to 350°. Spread the nuts in a shallow roasting pan and toast them in the middle of the oven for about 5 minutes, or until golden brown, turning them occasionally. Pulverize the nuts in an electric blender or with a nut grinder or a mortar and pestle.

In a heavy 2- to 3-quart enameled-iron or copper saucepan, heat the milk and the vanilla bean over moderate heat until small bubbles appear around the edge of the pan. Remove the pan from the heat and cover.

With a wire whisk or a rotary or electric beater, beat the eggs and egg yolks together in a large bowl for a minute or two. Slowly add the sugar and continue to beat until the eggs are thick enough to fall in a ribbon when the beater is lifted from the bowl. Add the flour ¼ cup at a time. When all the flour is absorbed, remove the vanilla bean from the milk and add the hot milk to the bowl in a thin stream, beating all the while. Immediately strain the mixture back into the saucepan.

Stirring deeply into the sides and bottom of the pan with a whisk or a wooden spoon, simmer over moderate heat for 3 to 5 minutes until the mixture thickens into a smooth heavy cream. Do not let the cream boil at any point but simmer it long enough to remove any taste of raw flour.

Pour the mixture into a bowl and stir in the 6 tablespoons of butter bits. Stir in the pulverized almonds and macaroons and the ½ cup of kirsch and let the frangipane cool to room temperature, stirring it every now and then to prevent a skin from forming on top. Then refrigerate it for 3 or 4 hours until thoroughly chilled.

Just before assembling the tart, rub the apricot jam through a fine sieve into a small saucepan with the back of a spoon. Add ¼ cup of kirsch and, stirring constantly, heat the mixture until it clears.

To assemble the tart, spread a thin layer of the apricot glaze in the bottom of the pastry shell with a pastry brush. Spoon in the frangipane cream, spreading and smoothing it out with a spatula. Set the pear round in the center of the cream and around it place the pear halves, arranging them in such a way that their stem ends face the central pear round and radiate from it like the spokes of a wheel. Press the pears gently into the cream. Brush the glaze over the pears and cream. Mix the pistachios and the crushed macaroon and sprinkle them over the pears. Refrigerate again. Remove the tart from the refrigerator about 15 minutes before serving.

Sucre filé
SPUN SUGAR

Before making the syrup, prepare a place in your kitchen to spin it. Place two wooden spoons at least 12 inches long parallel to one another and 18 to 24 inches apart on top of wax paper, with the bowls of the spoons weighted down on a counter or table and the handles projecting from the edge of the surface by 8 or more inches. (If you have no long wooden spoons, use long metal skewers instead.) Cover all the nearby floor and counter space with wax paper or newspapers to catch any drippings of syrup when you spin the sugar.

In a heavy 1- to 1½-quart saucepan, bring the sugar and water to a boil over moderate heat, stirring until the sugar dissolves. Cook briskly, uncovered and undisturbed, until the syrup reaches a temperature of 290° on a candy thermometer, or a few drops spooned into ice water immediately separate into flexible, but not brittle, threads. The syrup should remain absolutely clear. Remove the pan from the heat immediately.

Working quickly, grasp two table forks in one hand so the tines form a fairly straight row. Dip the tines of the fork into the hot syrup and let the excess drip off into the pan. Then, using a figure-eight motion, swirl the syrup over the protruding handles of the spoons. The syrup will quickly harden into glossy threads and cling to the handles. Let the threads accumulate on the handles to the desired thickness, and then sweep them up with both hands and lay them on a plate. Repeat the entire procedure until you have spun all of the syrup into threads. Spun sugar is used as nests for desserts or to veil them.

NOTE: To produce even longer strands of spun sugar, place the spoon handles farther apart—or instead of spoons use thin 3-foot-long wooden poles. Rather than using two forks to spin the sugar, you may make a shaker by cutting the loops from a sauce whisk, leaving a cluster of straight wires 3 or 4 inches in length. Many professional confectioners prefer to use a shaker made of wood studded with nails *(page 93)*.

1 cup sugar
½ cup water
A pinch of cream of tartar

Fraises Romanoff
FRESH STRAWBERRIES IN ORANGE-FLAVORED LIQUEUR WITH CHANTILLY CREAM

Pick over the berries carefully, discarding any that are bruised. Wash the berries quickly under cold water, pat them gently dry with paper towels and remove their stems and hulls. Place the berries in a deep bowl and pour the liqueur and orange juice over them. Cover the bowl with foil or plastic wrap and refrigerate the berries for at least 3 hours, turning them over gently from time to time.

Just before serving, whip the cream in a large chilled bowl with a wire whisk or a rotary or electric beater. When it begins to thicken add the confectioners' sugar and vanilla and continue to beat until the cream forms unwavering peaks on the beater when it is lifted from the bowl.

Transfer the strawberries and all their juices to a serving bowl. Then, using a pastry bag with a decorative tip, pipe the cream over the berries in as fanciful a manner as you like, or ladle the cream over the berries and create decorative swirls and peaks on its surface with a spatula. Garnish the top with crystallized violets and serve at once.

To serve 4 to 6

1 quart ripe strawberries
½ cup Grand Marnier, Curaçao, or Cointreau
½ cup strained fresh orange juice
1 cup heavy cream, chilled
2 tablespoons confectioners' sugar, sifted
½ teaspoon vanilla extract
Crystallized violets *(see Glossary)*

Glossary

MENU TERMS

A French menu provides many valuable clues to the nature and origin of the dishes it lists. The following glossary includes some of the key terms that commonly occur in the titles of classic French dishes.

ALLEMANDE (German): A rich sauce made with veal velouté, cream, egg yolks, lemon juice and nutmeg. Given this name for its blond color.

ARGENTEUIL: With asparagus. The name comes from the commune of Argenteuil in northern France which is famous for its asparagus.

ARLEQUIN (harlequin): Refers to a multicolored dish. Originally the term applied to miscellaneous pieces of food left over in restaurants and sold to the poor. The motley effect was reminiscent of the varicolored costume of a harlequin.

BÉARNAISE: After Béarn, a region of the Pyrenees in southwestern France. A rich sauce made with butter and egg yolks flavored with a reduction of wine vinegar, shallots and tarragon to which chopped parsley and more tarragon are added.

BELLE VUE (beautiful view): An elaborately displayed dish, such as lobster *en belle vue parisienne.*

BERCY: After a suburb and market of Paris. A savory sauce with a meat glaze or fish stock and fish velouté, chopped shallots, white wine, lemon juice, butter and parsley.

BEURRE MAÎTRE D'HÔTEL: Butter mixed with chopped parsley, lemon juice, salt and pepper. Served mostly on grilled meats and fish.

BEURRE NOISETTE (hazelnut butter): Butter that is heated until it is light hazelnut brown and served immediately.

BIGARADE: A bitter orange from Seville. *Sauce bigarade,* a brown sauce flavored with these oranges and caramel, is served with duck.

BORDELAISE, À LA (in the style of the city of Bordeaux): Usually includes Bordeaux wine. *Sauce bordelaise* is made with chopped shallots, pepper, thyme, bay leaf, red wine and a brown glaze. When served with meat dishes it is often garnished with pieces of poached beef marrow and parsley.

BOUQUETIÈRE (a flower girl): A colorful garnish of peas, green beans, cauliflower with hollandaise, château potatoes and artichoke bottoms filled with carrot and turnip pieces.

COQUILLE SAINT-JACQUES (French word for a scallop): The shell is a symbol of St. James the Apostle.

CRÉCY: With carrots. The town of Crécy in northern France is known for its carrots.

CRÈME CHANTILLY: Sweetened whipped cream usually flavored with vanilla or a liqueur. After a city and region in northern France that produces fine cream.

CRESSONNIÈRE (from *cresson,* French for watercress): A dish garnished or prepared with watercress.

DAUPHINE, À LA: Usually refers to deep-fried potato balls made of a mixture of mashed potatoes with puff paste. Named after the wife of the dauphin, eldest son of the king of France and ruler of the Dauphiné region, which is known for its potato and *gratin* dishes.

DAUPHINOISE, À LA: Usually refers to a preparation of sliced potatoes baked with milk, eggs, nutmeg, salt, pepper and cheese.

DEMI-DEUIL (half-mourning): Refers to poached chicken or braised sweetbreads served with *suprême* sauce and garnished with black truffles.

DIANE: Game dishes garnished with crescent-shaped croutons named after the Roman goddess of the moon and the hunt. *Sauce Diane,* a pepper sauce with cream, diced hard-cooked egg whites and truffles is named after Diane de Poitiers, mistress of Henri II.

DIEPPOISE, À LA (in the style of Dieppe, a coastal town in northern France): Seafood with shrimp, mussels and mushroom caps in white wine sauce.

DU BARRY: With cauliflower. After Marie Jeanne Bécu, the Comtesse du Barry, mistress to Louis XV.

DUCHESSE: An elegant garnish or preparation of mashed potatoes mixed with egg yolks, usually piped with a pastry tube.

DUGLÉRÉ: The famous Parisian chef Adolphe Dugléré. The fish sauce invented by him contains shallots, tomatoes, white wine, fish stock, butter and parsley.

DUXELLES: A mixture of finely chopped mushrooms sautéed with chopped shallots. After the Marquis d'Uxelles, a 17th Century French nobleman whose chef was the famous La Varenne.

ESPAGNOLE (Spanish): *Sauce espagnole,* a basic brown sauce, is made with a brown roux, brown stock, onions, carrots, celery, tomatoes, thyme, bay leaf and parsley. Many recipes also include some ham or bacon and mushroom trimmings. *Sauce espagnole* is the traditional base for many other brown sauces. Today it is often replaced by *fond lié.*

FINANCIÈRE, À LA (banker's style): Rich in expensive ingredients. A garnish for poultry and sweetbreads of chicken or veal dumplings, truffles, cocks' combs, mushrooms and olives. Also, *sauce financière,* Madeira sauce flavored with truffles.

FLORENTINE, À LA (florentine style): With spinach. A spinach garnish for eggs, fish and sweetbreads usually topped with Mornay sauce. Italian cooks from the time of Catherine de' Medici are believed to have introduced spinach to France.

GRAND VENEUR (master of the hunt): A pepper sauce *(sauce poivrade)* with game glaze and red currant jelly and sometimes with cream.

HENRI IV: A garnish of artichoke bottoms with béarnaise sauce and potatoes for *noisettes* and *tournedos.* Also, a chicken consommé with vegetables, pieces of chicken and chervil. After Henry IV, King of France born in the Béarn region in 1553.

IMPÉRATRICE, À L': Dishes named after Eugénie, Empress of France and consort of Napoleon III. The best known is *riz à l'impératrice* (empress rice) so called because of the Empress' special fondness for rice.

JARDINIÈRE, À LA (gardener's style): A garnish for large entrées, consisting of diced carrots, turnips and green beans, plus white kidney beans, peas and cauliflower with hollandaise.

JULIENNE: Vegetables cut in thin matchlike strips. Attributed to Jean Julien, a chef of the 18th Century.

LYONNAISE, À LA (in the style of Lyon, a city in east central France, the heart of an onion-growing region): With onions. Refers to a garnish for red meat consisting of braised onions, potatoes sautéed with onions and Lyonnaise sauce. This sauce is made with onions, white wine and meat glaze.

MONTREUIL: Usually with peaches. After a suburb of Paris famous for its peaches. Sometimes refers to a garnish for *noisettes* and *tournedos* made of artichoke bottoms filled with peas and carrot balls. Also, fillet of sole with white wine sauce and potatoes topped with shrimp sauce.

MORNAY: After De Plessis Mornay, a 16th Century French Huguenot leader. A sauce of béchamel with cream and grated cheese and sometimes egg yolks.

MOUSSELINE: With whipped cream. *Sauce mousseline* is hollandaise with whipped cream.

NANTUA (a town in northeastern France): With crayfish. *Sauce Nantua:* Béchamel with cream and crayfish butter, served with eggs, fish and shellfish.

NIÇOISE, À LA: With tomatoes and, usually, garlic. After Nice, on the French Riviera.

NORMANDE, À LA (in the style of the province of Normandy in northwestern France): Fish garnished with mussels, oysters, shrimp, crayfish, strips of fillet of sole or smelts, mushrooms and truffles. Meat, poultry and game dishes with a sauce of apple cider, cream and Calvados brandy. *Sauce normande:* Fish velouté with mushroom and truffle juice enriched with egg yolks, cream and butter.

PARMENTIER: With potatoes. After the food expert Antoine-Auguste Parmentier, who introduced the potato to France in 1786.

PÉRIGOURDINE, PÉRIGUEUX: With truffles. Périgord is a region in southwest France whose capital formerly was Périgueux. Black truffles from this area are the most famous in the world. *Sauce périgueux:* Sauce of meat glaze, truffle juice, and diced truffles. Sometimes includes Madeira and *fond lié. Sauce périgourdine:* Same as *sauce périgueux,* with truffle rounds instead of diced truffles.

POIVRADE: With pepper. A sauce served with game, made with peppercorns, mirepoix, white wine, vinegar and game stock.

PRINTANIÈRE (springlike): A consommé with carrots, turnips, peas, beans and sometimes asparagus spears. Also, a garnish of diced spring vegetables and small sautéed potato balls. Also a combination of glazed onions, turnips and carrots, peas, green beans and asparagus served in a casserole with meat.

QUENELLES: Dumplings of minced fish, meat or fowl, bound with eggs (or eggs and a mixture of flour and butter), then poached and served in a sauce. Small *quenelles* are used to garnish main dishes.

RACHEL: A garnish of artichoke bottoms and beef marrow served with *tournedos* and *noisettes* and accompanied by *sauce bordelaise*. Possibly named after Elisa Rachel Félix, a 19th Century French actress.

REINE, À LA (in queenly style): With chicken.

ROSSINI: A garnish of foie gras and truffles. Named after Gioacchino Rossini, Italian operatic composer, a gourmet who was particularly fond of foie gras. Usually accompanied by a sauce made of meat juices deglazed with Madeira and *fond lié.*

ROUENNAIS: After Rouen, a city in the north of France, famous for its ducks. *Sauce rouennaise* is a *sauce bordelaise* with purée of raw duck livers, ground hot red pepper and lemon juice.

SOUBISE: A purée of cooked onions and rice with béchamel, nutmeg, salt and pepper. Named after Charles de Rohan, Prince de Soubise, a Marshal of France in the 18th Century.

SAINT-GERMAIN: With fresh green peas. A suburb of Paris.

SAINT-HUBERT: A game dish. After St. Hubert, patron saint of hunters. The meat is usually sautéed, and served with mushrooms and *sauce poivrade.*

SUPRÊME (the best): A sauce made of chicken velouté enriched with cream. *Suprême de volaille* is breast of chicken.

VERT-PRÉ (green field): A garnish of green vegetables. Also, a garnish for grilled meats of straw potatoes, watercress and maître d'hôtel butter.

VICHY: A garnish of sliced carrots cooked in Vichy (mineral) water, molded in a timbale and sprinkled with parsley. After a noted spa in central France.

VIN BLANC (white wine): A sauce for fish, made of fish stock, white wine, butter, egg yolks and sometimes velouté.

SPECIAL INGREDIENTS

BEURRE MANIÉ: A mixture of flour and butter rubbed to a paste and used as a quick thickening agent for sauces.

CREVETTES: Tiny shrimp used in France for hors d'oeuvre and garnitures. There are two principal kinds: 1) *Crevette rose* (pink shrimp), whose head is armed with a long, hard, notched point. In cooking, the shrimp becomes pink and the flesh very firm. 2) *Crevette grise* (gray shrimp) is smaller and has a shorter point on the head. It becomes pinkish-gray in cooking. The flesh is soft and not so highly valued as that of the pink shrimp.

CRYSTALLIZED VIOLETS: Violets dipped into sugar syrup cooked just to the point of crystallization, and then dried. Used as dessert decoration. Available in gourmet food shops, usually in 2½-ounce packages.

EAU DE VIE (water of life): Refers to clear, colorless brandy made from fermented fruits or the stems, pits and skins of apples, cherries or grapes. Some common types of *eau de vie* and the fruits from which they are derived are: *fraise,* strawberry; *framboise,* raspberry; *quetsche,* purple plum; *mirabelle,* yellow plum; *poire William's,* William's pear.

FOIE GRAS (fat liver): In cooking it applies to the liver of a goose or duck fattened by forced feeding. Duck foie gras tends to fall apart more easily and thus is less desirable for cooking. The best quality goose foie gras comes from Alsace and southwest France, and is characterized by its creamy-white color tinged with pink and by its firm texture.

Limited quantities of fresh foie gras are available on special order from gourmet shops during the Christmas season, which is when it is produced in France. Canned foie gras is available at these shops year-round in the following variety of qualities and sizes. *Foie gras naturel en bloc:* Best quality, pure goose foie gras. Available only in large oval cans ranging from 7 to 28 ounces. *Bloc de foie gras:* A mixture of best quality and lesser quality foie gras. Usually encased in a thin layer of lard, sometimes contains truffles, in which case it is called *bloc de foie gras truffé:* Available in long trapezoid-shaped cans ranging from 5 to 15 ounces. *Purée de foie gras:* Third ranking in quality; by French law it must contain 75 per cent foie gras and is not to be confused with *purée de foie d'oie:* Purée of goose liver, for which French law stipulates a goose liver content of not less than 50 per cent. Both come in a large variety of can shapes and sizes. A still lower quality is *mousse de foie gras,* which combines pork and eggs with the goose liver.

MARRONS (chestnuts): Unavailable domestically in recent years; the entire supply is imported, principally from France, but also from Italy. Fresh chestnuts are available in the fall at gourmet stores or in Italian markets. Canned chestnuts are available year-round in a variety of forms. *Marrons entiers naturels:* Unflavored nuts packed in water. These come in 10-ounce and 20½-ounce cans, and are prepared in various ways to accompany main dishes. *Purée de marrons nature:* Puréed unsweetened chestnuts. These come in 15-ounce cans. *Crème de marrons:* Sweetened purée of chestnuts. Used in desserts. Available in 17-ounce cans. *Marrons glacés:* Preserved chestnuts glazed with sugar. Eaten as sweets and used for desserts. Available in 7-, 14- and 28-ounce cans. *Marrons en sirop* (whole chestnuts, preserved in vanilla syrup): Available in 7- and 14-ounce cans. *Marrons débris:* Chestnut pieces in vanilla syrup. Available in 7-ounce cans.

MIREPOIX: A mixture of finely chopped vegetables cooked in butter, used to enhance the flavor of a sauce or as a base for braised meats. A *mirepoix* usually contains onions, carrots, celery and a bay leaf and sometimes also includes ham or lean bacon.

PARCHMENT PAPER: Grease-and-moisture-resistant paper used to line pans, wrap foods, or form cones used as pastry tubes. Available in 15-by-15-by-12-inch sheets in packages of 100 sheets at department and baking supply stores. French meat or fish dishes cooked and served in parchment paper are called *en papillote.*

MORELS: delicately flavored mushrooms with elongated caps and a spongelike surface. Found wild in the United States in early spring. Imported from Europe in 6-ounce cans or dried in packages of varying sizes.

NOISETTE: A small round 2- or 3-ounce slice of lamb or mutton, cut from the fillet, rib or leg. The term sometimes refers to a slice of veal or beef fillet.

SALTPETER (potassium nitrate or niter): A crystalline white salt used to enhance pink color of meat. Available at drugstores.

SAUCISSON À L'AIL: Very coarsely ground pork sausage with garlic and other seasonings. Sold in 1- to 1½-pound pieces. The best substitute is *cotechino* sausage.

SPICE PARISIENNE: A ready-made ground spice mixture, also known as *quatre épices.* Formulas vary but it is usually composed of white pepper, cloves, ginger and nutmeg. Not generally sold in the U.S., but an acceptable version may be made by combining 6 tablespoons of white pepper, 4 teaspoons of nutmeg, 3½ teaspoons of ginger and 1½ teaspoons of cloves. Ground allspice—which tastes like a blend of spices—is sometimes substituted for Spice Parisienne; use the same amount.

TRUFFLES: Fresh truffles, imported from France, are sometimes available in the fall and winter on special order from gourmet food shops. These shops also supply truffles the year round packed in water in tins and jars of varying size and quality. The best grade is *peeled:* large, round, dark brown truffles with no holes. Within this category are *extra peeled* and *peeled first choice* qualities. Generally a 7- to 8-ounce can or jar will contain a single truffle approximately the size of the container. The second quality is *brushed:* not quite as perfect, round or dark as the *peeled.* Within this category you also find *extra brushed, brushed first choice* and *brushed fancy* qualities. *Truffle pieces* and *truffle peelings* are also available separately and are of much poorer quality; *truffle purée* is sold in tubes and cans and used on toast.

TRUFFLE JUICE: The water in which truffles are packed acquires a distinctive taste and is used to flavor sauces. As it is consumed, it is usually replaced by dry imported Madeira which in turn takes on the truffle flavor. Once removed from the container, truffles must be kept indefinitely in the refrigerator in tightly lidded jars. The truffles must be covered with liquid.

VANILLA BEAN: Podlike seed of the vanilla tree, generally 5 to 8 inches long, preferred by chefs to the vanilla extract derived from the bean. The bean may be used twice. After the first use, rinse the bean, let it dry completely and then store tightly wrapped.

Recipe Index: English

NOTE: An R preceding a page refers to the Recipe Booklet. Size, weight and material are specified for pans in the recipes because they affect cooking results. A pan should be just large enough to hold its contents comfortably. Heavy pans heat slowly and cook food at a constant rate. Aluminum and cast iron conduct heat well but may discolor foods containing egg yolks, wine, vinegar or lemon. Enamelware is a fairly poor conductor of heat. Many recipes therefore recommend tin-lined copper or enameled cast iron, which do not have these faults.

Recipe Index: French

Stocks and Sauces

Soups

Fish

Fowl and Eggs

Meats

Vegetables

Desserts and Pastry

Mail-Order Sources

The following stores, grouped by region, accept mail orders for many ingredients and utensils necessary for preparing dishes in the classic French tradition. Those stores marked with an asterisk stock gourmet food items, those marked with a dagger carry fine cooking utensils. Because policies, prices, items stocked and managements change, it would be best to check with the store nearest you to determine how best to buy the items you are interested in.

East

Cardullo's Gourmet Shop *
6 Brattle St.
Cambridge, Mass. 02138

Malben Cheese Company *
158 Massachusetts Ave.
Boston, Mass. 02115

The Pot Shop †
Boston Post Rd.
Sudbury, Mass. 02113

Bloomingdale's Inc. *
Lexington at 59th St.
New York, N.Y. 10022

Charles and Company *
340 Madison Ave.
New York, N.Y. 10017

Maison Glass *
52 East 58th St.
New York, N.Y. 10022

Bazaar de la Cuisine †
160 East 55th St.
New York, N.Y. 10022

Bazar Français †
666 Avenue of the Americas
New York, N.Y. 10010

Midwest

Stop and Shop *
16 West Washington St.
Chicago, Ill. 60602

Marshall Field and Company †
111 North State St.
Chicago, Ill. 60602

Market Basket Food *
3205 W. McNichols
Detroit, Mich. 48227

Kitchen Glamor Inc. †
15300 Fenkell
Detroit, Mich. 48227

Heidi's Around the World Food
  Shop *
1149 S. Brentwood
St. Louis, Mo. 63117

Famous Barr Stores * †
601 Olive St.
St. Louis, Mo. 63101

West

Jurgensen's * †
353 North Rodeo Dr.
Beverly Hills, Calif. 90010

Skillets †
1044 Westwood Blvd.
Los Angeles, Calif. 90024

Normandy Lane, City of Paris *
Union Square
San Francisco, Calif. 94108

Simon Bros. *
2849 California St.
San Francisco, Calif. 94115

Williams-Sonoma †
576 Sutter St.
San Francisco, Calif. 94102

Neiman-Marcus Co. * †
Commerce and Ervay Streets
Dallas, Texas 75201

Antone's Import Company *
P.O. Box 3352
Houston, Texas 77001

Foley's Gourmet Shop †
1110 Main St.
Houston, Texas 77001

South

Davison †
180 Peachtree St.
Atlanta, Ga. 30303

Rich's †
45 Broad St.
Atlanta, Ga. 30303

La Cuisine Classique * †
631 Royal
New Orleans, La. 70130

Credits and Acknowledgments

The sources for the illustrations in this book are shown below. Credits for the pictures from left to right are separated by commas, from top to bottom by dashes. Cover and all other photographs in this book are by Mark Kauffman except: 4—The New York Times Studio, Sebastian Milito—Howard Sochurek for LIFE, Walter Daran—Richard Henry, Carl Fischer, Sebastian Milito. 24—Map by Mary Sherman. 46 —Drawing by Albert Sherman. 47—Culvert Pictures. 52-55—Denis Cameron. 57—Bibliothèque Nationale. 59—H. Roger Viollet. 74, 75 —Musée de l'Art Culinaire, Villeneuve-Loubet. 76, 77—From *Le Maître-d' hôtel français* by Antonin Carême published by Bethune et Plon, Paris, 1842. 80—Musée de l'Art Culinaire, Villeneuve-Loubet. 100—From *The Album of The Ritz Hotel*. 101—The Bettmann Archive. 102—Culver Pictures. 103—Radio Times Hulton Picture Library. 121, 123, 125—Musée de l'Art Culinaire, Villeneuve-Loubet. 128 —Bibliothèque Nationale. 149—Robert Doisneau from Rapho Guillumette. 182—Sebastian Milito. 184—The New York Times Studio. 186—Albert Penn for LIFE. 190— Ted Streshinsky.

For their assistance in the production of this book the editors wish to thank the following: *in France,* Pierre Andrieu; Prince and Princesse Armand d'Aremberg; Jean Arnaboldi; Bernard Bassot, Compagnie générale transatlantique; Paul Bocuse, Restaurant Paul Bocuse; Philippe de Boissieu; Henri Cabanel, Syndicat des producteurs de truffes du Périgord; Roger Coupron, Comité interprofessionnel de la conchyculture; M. and Mme Jean Cruse; Robert J. Courtine; Maison Dehillerin et Cie; Jean Delmas, Directeur général Château Haut-Brion; Alexandre Dumaine; Docteur Jean-Bernard Escoffier; Guide Michelin; M. and Mme de Houdetot; René Lasserre, Restaurant Lasserre; Jacques de Lavenère-Lussan, Directeur de la coopérative laitière d' Isigny; Albert Le Petit, Compagnie générale transatlantique; Pierre Mengelatte, Président de l'Académie culinaire de France; Roger Miéral, Président de l'Association du poulet de Bresse; Raymond Oliver, Restaurant Le Grand Vefour; Melkoum Petrossian; Marie-Louise Point, Restaurant Pyramide; Joseph Rameaux, Conservateur du musée de l'Art Culinaire; Charles Ritz, Hôtel Ritz; Waverley Root; Jean de Roualle; Georges Simon, Compagnie générale transatlantique; Marzio Snozzi, Directeur générale de G. H. Mumm et Cie; Claude Terrail, Restaurant La Tour d'Argent; Roger Topolinski, Restaurant Laperouse; Louis Vaudable, Restaurant Maxim's; Roger Verniot, École Hôtelière Jean Drouant; Jean Zembrusky, Hôtel Ritz; *in Ithaca, New York,* Dr. Paul Buck, School of Hotel Administration, Cornell University; *in New York City,* Abelard-Schuman Ltd.; LaCaravelle Restaurant; Albert Cumin, Howard Johnson's Inc.; French Government Tourist Office; Eleanor Lowenstein Goldwater, The Corner Book Shop; Julian Levenson and Julius Wile of Julius Wile, Sons and Co.; Grace Millar; Gino Robusti, Quo Vadis Restaurant; Peter Rossi, Compagnie générale transatlantique; Guy Sironneau, Café St. Denis; Lillian Stuckey, The Spice Association; *in Rye, New York,* Frederic Strauss, Frederic Imports; *in Washington, D.C.,* Teresa Wohl, The National Gallery of Art. *In New York City,* the following shops contributed to the production of this book: Bazaar de la Cuisine; Bazar Français; Bon Marché; Brancusi of New York City Inc.; Buccellati Silver Ltd.; Ceralene Inc.; Ginori Fifth Avenue; Hammacher-Schlemmer; I. Freeman and Son; Iron Gate; Jean's Silversmiths Inc.; Patchin Place Emporium; Plummer McCutcheon; D. Porthault Inc.; Tiffany and Company; David Weiss Importers Inc.
  Sources consulted in the production of this book include: *The Horizon Cookbook,* published by American Heritage Publishing Co. Inc.; *Fine Bouche,* Pierre Andrieu; *The Delectable Past,* Esther B. Aresty; *The Satyricon of Petronius,* trans. by William Arrowsmith; "Curnonsky," by Samuel Chamberlain, *Atlantic Monthly,* June, 1958; *L'art du cuisinier,* Antoine Beauvilliers; *Hering's Dictionary of Classical and Modern Cookery,* trans. by Walter Bickel; *Les Délices de la campagne,* Nicolas de Bonnefons; *Paris à table,* Eugène Briffault; *The Physiology of Taste,*

Jean Anthelme Brillat-Savarin; *L'Art de la cuisine française au XIXème siècle, Le Pâtissier royal parisien au XIXème siècle, Le Pâtissier pittoresque, Le Maître d' hôtel français,* and *Le Cuisinier parisien,* Antonin Carême; *Sauces: The Foundation of French Cuisine,* Wieland Dominicus Chong; *Kitchen and Table,* Colin Clair, quoted on page 51, by permission of Abelard-Schuman Ltd.; *Haute cuisine,* Jean Conil; *Gaietés et curiosités gastronomiques,* Curnonsky and Gaston Derys; *Traditional Recipes of the Provinces of France,* Curnonsky; *Les Classiques de la table,* Marquis de Cussy; *Traité de pâtisserie moderne,* Emile Darenne and Emile Duval; *Table Traits,* Dr. Doran; *Artistic Cookery* and *Grand livre des pâtissiers et des confiseurs,* Urbain Dubois; *La Cuisine classique,* Urbain Dubois and Emil Bernard; *Dictionnaire de cuisine,* Alexandre Dumas; *La Fleur de la cuisine française,* Editions de la Sirène; *The Pleasures of the Table,* George Ellwanger; *Les Grandes heures de la cuisine française,* Cécile Eluard-Valette; *Le Carnet d'epicure, The Escoffier Cook Book, Les Fleurs en cire, Le Guide culinaire, A Guide to Modern Cookery* (trans. by William Heinemann) and *Le Livre des menus,* by A. Escoffier; *The Cooking of Provincial France,* M. F. K. Fisher and the Editors of TIME-LIFE BOOKS; *Apicius,* trans. by Barbara Flower and Elizabeth Rosenbaum; *La Vie privée d'autrefois,* Alfred Louis A. Franklin; *Cook's and Diner's Dictionary,* Funk and Wagnalls; *Gancel's Encyclopedia of Modern Cooking,* J. Gancel; *La Cuisine de tous les mois,* Philéas Gilbert; *The Art of French Cooking,* Golden Press; *Histoire de l'alimentation et de la gastronomie depuis la préhistoire jusqu'à nos jours,* Dr. Alfred Gottschalk; *Le Livre de cuisine, Le Livre de pâtisserie* and *The Royal Cookery Book,* by Jules Gouffé; *Le Répertoire de la cuisine,* Théophile Gringoire and Louis Saulnier; *Illustrated History of French Cuisine,* Christian Guy; *La Belle France,* Paul Hamlyn; *The Art of Dining,* Abraham Hayward; *Escoffier,* Eugène Herbodeau and Paul Thalamas; "Escoffier," by Bernard Frizell, *Horizon,* May, 1961; *The Savoy,* Stanley Jackson; *A Book About the Table,* John C. Jeaffreson; *Host and Guest, A Book About Dinners,* A. V. Kirwan; *The Modern Cook,* Vincent La Chapelle; *France in the Eighteenth Century* and *France in the Middle Ages,* Paul Lacroix; *Histoire de la vie privée des Français,* Le Grand d'Aussy; *L'Art de bien traiter,* L.S.R.; *Le Vray cuisinier françois,* François de La Varenne; *La Cuisine et la table modernes,* Librarie Larousse; *Nobody Ever Tells You These Things,* Helen McCully; *Food and Drink through the Ages,* Maggs Bros. Ltd.; *Les Dons de Comus,* Marin; *Le Cuisinier royal et bourgeois,* Massialot; *Les Soupers de la cour,* Menon; *Tableau de Paris,* Louis Sebastien Mercier; *La Grande cuisine illustrée, Larousse gastronomique* and *Le Grand livre de la cuisine,* by Prosper Montagné; *La France,* Lady Sydney Owenson Morgan; *La Vie de Vatel,* Moura and Louvet; "Sugar architecture of the great chef Carême," Beaumont Newhall, *Vogue,* March, 1962; *Éloges de la cuisine française,* Eduard Nignon; "Les Premiers fêtes de Versailles," *La Revue de Paris,* Pierre de Nolhac; *Classic Sauces and Their Preparation* and *Gastronomy of France* (trans. by Claude Durrell) by Raymond Oliver; *Modern French Culinary Art,* Henri-Paul Pellaprat; *L'Almanach des gourmands* and *Manuel des amphitryons,* by Grimod de la Reynière; *César Ritz, Host to the World,* Marie Louise Ritz; *Daily Life in France under Napoleon,* Jean Robiquet; *La Cuisine,* Madame Saint-Ange; *The Epicure's Companion,* Ann Seranne and John Tebbel; *Lettres de Mme de Sévigné,* Marie de Rabutin-Chantal Sévigné; *Food,* André Simon; *Elegant Wits and Grand Horizontals,* Cornelia Otis Skinner; *Classical Recipes of the World,* Henry Smith; *Je suis restaurateur,* Claude Terrail; *Le Viandier,* Guillaume Tirel; *Chez Maxim's,* Countess of Toulouse-Lautrec; *Maxim's,* M. and Mme Vaudable; *Bibliographie gastronomique,* Georges Vicaire; *Histoire et géographie gourmandes de Paris,* R. Heron de Villefosse; *The Ritz of Paris,* Stephen Watts; *Wines and Spirits,* Alec Waugh and the Editors of TIME-LIFE BOOKS; *Blue Trout and Black Truffles,* Joseph Wechsberg.